T0129221

JAMES PROVED: "I AM" TRUE, DIVINE, ETERNAL WISDOM!

MIRACULOUS AUTOBIOGRAPHY!

CHRISTIAN CHILDS

WESTBOW
PRESS®
A DIVISION OF THOMAS NELSON
& ZONDERVAN

Scripture quotations taken from the New American Standard
Bible® (NASB), Copyright © 1960, 1962, 1963, 1968, 1971, 1972,
1973, 1975, 1977, 1995 by The Lockman Foundation

WestBow Press books may be ordered through booksellers or by contacting:

WestBow Press
A Division of Thomas Nelson & Zondervan
1663 Liberty Drive
Bloomington, IN 47403
www.westbowpress.com
1 (866) 928-1240

ISBN: 978-1-5127-8842-6 (sc)

Print information available on the last page.

WestBow Press rev. date: 10/3/2018

ISAIAH 54 VERSES 4 AND 5 STATES: FEAR NOT, FOR YOU WILL NOT BE PUT TO SHAME; AND DO NOT FEEL HUMILIATED, FOR YOU WILL NOT BE DISGRACED; <u>BUT YOU WILL FORGET THE SHAME OF YOUR YOUTH AND THE REPROACH</u> OF YOUR WIDOWHOOD YOU WILL REMEMBER NO MORE. (VERSE 5) FOR YOUR HUSBAND IS YOUR MAKER WHOSE NAME IS THE LORD OF HOST AND YOUR REDEEMER IS THE HOLY ONE OF ISRAEL WHO IS CALLED THE GOD OF ALL THE EARTH.

ALL IDENTITIES AND NAMES WERE PURPOSEFULLY CHANGED REGARDING INDIVIDUALS WHOM IMPACTED MY LIFE. LOCATIONS ARE SIMILITUDE, SEMBLANCE AND ANOLOGIES.

ENGLISH	**FRANÇAIS**
WELCOME	**BIENVENUE**

AUTOBIOGRAPHY
AUTOBIOGRAPHIE

MY NAME IS
CHRISTIAN CHILDS

MON NOM EST
CHRISTIAN CHILDS

I GREW UP IN THE SHADOW OF MY "MOTHER OF MOTHERS" MS. KAY. SHE EXEMPLIFIES "MOTHER'S DAY" WITH A RED ROSE IN HER HAND ON A POST CARD. SHE EXUBERATES HUMILITY, KINDNESS AND LOVE. SHE BINDS HER FAMILY UNIT TOGETHER WITH LOVE ENTWINED IN HER HEART. SHE CARRIED ME, RAISED ME, NURTURED ME AND LOVED ME. I WAS SUBJECTED TO HER FOR THE FIRST THIRTEEN YEARS OF MY LIFE.

ST. LUCIA, A STRIKING SIMILITUDE OF MY ENVIRON UPBRINGING; CHRISTIANITY BEING THE **NUMBER ONE** EXPRESSED FAITH. AN ISLAND COUNTRY, PROUDLY DISPLAYING THE SECOND HIGHEST RATIO OF **NOBLE** PRIZE **LAUREATES** PER CAPITA; NAMELY SIR WILLIAM ARTHUR LEWIS WHO WON THE NOBLE MEMORIAL PRIZE IN ECONOMICS IN 1979 AND DEREK WALCOT WHO RECEIVED THE **NOBLE PRIZE FOR LITERATURE** IN 1992. BOTH MEN ARE NOW IN THEIR ETERNAL HOME.

DIVINE WILL, DIVINE LOVE, DIVINE PLAN, RELEASED ME FROM MY MOTHER'S CARING HANDS. CONTROL! CONTROL! WHEN **GOD** STEPS IN AND TAKES CONTROL MAN HAS TO YIELD HIS DESIRES TO HIM.

THE DIVINE DOES NOT ASK, HE MOVES, POWERFULLY, KNOWINGLY AND ETERNALLY. THEN HE SENT ME "ADOPTED" ABROAD TO FRANCE A SNOW FALLING, FOUR SEASONS COUNTRY. EXUBERATING FRENCH **"THE ROMANCE LANGUAGE," "LOVE-WORD, WORDS OF LOVE. "HMM! HMM!**

MY **FATHER** WANTED ME. I YEARNED FOR LOVE; THEN I SOUGHT LOVE. MY JEALOUS EX-BOYFRIEND IN MEXICO ABDUCTED ME FROM THE OLD AGE HOME WHERE I WAS EMPLOYED AND ATTEMPTED TO HARM ME.

DETECTIVES RESCUED ME. I DID NOT WANT MY NAME IN THE NEWSPAPER THIS WAY BUT IT ENDED UP THERE. I BECAME A NURSE IN FRANCE. I WAS MARRIED TWICE AND DIVORCED TWICE BEFORE THE AGE OF THIRTY YEARS OLD TO TWO MUSLIM MEN IN FRANCE.

I AM NOW A **BORN-AGAIN** CHRISTIAN **PASTOR.** TRUE LOVE ELUDED ME IN BOTH MARRIAGES BUT I KNOW THAT I AM LOVEABLE. **ISAIAH 54 VERSE 5 STATES: "FOR YOUR HUSBAND IS YOUR MAKER..."**

I THANK **GOD** THAT HE RESCUED ME AND I U-TURNED, TURNED AROUND TO **JESUS CHRIST** WHO CREATED ME AND **LOVED ME.** THIS BOOK WAS WRITTEN BECAUSE **GOD** INSPIRED ME TO WRITE IT. IT IS MEANT TO GLORIFY **GOD** AND SHARE **GOD'S UNCOMMON DIVINE WISDOM,** THE POWERFUL MIRACLES AND DIVINE INTERVENTIONS OF **JESUS CHRIST** THROUGHOUT MY LIFE WHEN I WAS THE MOST ENDANGERED, VULNERABLE AND AT RISK.

GOD INTERVENED WHEN I WAS LOST; WHEN I WAS WITHOUT DIRECTION; WHEN I WAS WITHOUT **LOVE;** WHEN I WAS TRYING TO FIND MY WAY THROUGH LIFE, WHEN I WAS IN DANGER; WHEN I WAS LONELY; WHEN I WAS LOOKING FOR **LOVE;** WHEN I WAS REJECTED AND WHEN I WAS WITHOUT HELP AND SUPPORT. **I AM WHO I AM** TODAY BECAUSE OF **JESUS CHRIST ALMIGHTY GOD. AMEN!**

I AM ALIVE TODAY BECAUSE OF **JESUS CHRIST ALMIGHTY GOD. FAITH IN GOD** ENSURED MY VICTORY EACH DAY OF MY LIFE. THE **HOLY BIBLE IN HEBREWS 11 VERSE 6 STATES: AND WITHOUT FAITH IT IS IMPOSSIBLE TO PLEASE HIM, FOR HE WHO COMES TO GOD MUST BELIEVE THAT HE IS AND THAT HE IS A REWARDER OF THOSE WHO SEEK HIM.**

LET MY **FAITH** ENCOURAGE YOUR **FAITH** TODAY. AMEN! WHEN YOU EXPERIENCE, ENCOUNTER AND HEAR OF TROUBLES; TRIALS; DARKNESS; TRIBULATION; BEHEADINGS AND INJUSTICE AGAINST CHRISTIANS AND OTHERS, GROW IN **FAITH IN GOD. FAITH** IN **GOD** DOES BRING SUCCESS. YES! IT DOES.

WHEN YOU DON'T KNOW "HOW." REMEMBER **JESUS CHRIST** KNOWS HOW! TEXT MESSAGING IS A SILENT MODE OF COMMUNICATIONS. WHEN YOU SPEAK TO **GOD** IN YOUR YOUR HEART ONLY **JESUS CHRIST** HEARS YOUR SPIRIT'S VOICE TALKING TO HIM, NO ONE ELSE HEARS. AMEN! **SPEAK TO GOD SILENTLY IN YOUR HEART! AMEN!** RENEE AND OBASI, MY TWO CHILDREN, **GOD IS OMNIPRESENT.** BE ENCOURAGED BY MY SUCCESS AND VICTORIES. AMEN!

TABLE OF CONTENTS

GOD CREATED ME, I AM A NEW BORN.
WHERE I WAS BORN
MY "MOTHER OF MOTHERS" MS. KAY.
FIFTEEN CHILDREN BY GRANDMA, "MOMMY"
MY GRANDFATHER NICKNAMED **"PRETTY BOY."**
DEMONS.
MY FATHER MORDECAI.
HOLY ANGELS.

NO HUMAN BEING IS SUPERIOR; NO HUMAN BEING IS
INFERIOR.
CHILDREN ARE THE RESULT OF SEX.
SEXUAL RELATIONSHIPS IN THE **HOLY BIBLE.**
KNOW GOD.
PRAYER FOR DELIVERANCE.
JOB.
RECEIVING MY DAUGHTER **RENEE** BACK; A **GODLY**
DIVINE
MIRACLE.

ACKNOWLEDGMENT

I WANT TO FIRST ACKNOWLEDGE ALMIGHTY GOD, THE FATHER, THE SON AND THE HOLY SPIRIT FOR ENCOURAGING AND GUIDING ME WITH WISDOM, KNOWLEDGE, UNDERSTANDING, LOVE AND HUMOUR FOR MY AUTOBIOGRAPHY. IT WOULD NOT HAVE STARTED OR ENDED WITHOUT THE POWER AND PRESENCE OF **JESUS CHRIST** IN ME.

I THANK YOU **ABBA FATHER**, THE **HOLY SPIRIT** ONCE AGAIN. AMEN! I WANT TO THANK AND ACKNOWLEDGE MY "MOTHER OF MOTHERS" MS. KAY FOR HER PRAYERS, CONSTANT SUPPORT AND FREQUENT PHONE CALLS. I LOVE YOU MOTHER. I THANK THE REST OF MY FAMILY MEMBERS FOR THEIR LOVE. I SEND LOVE TO MY SISTERS. I LOVE YOU MY SON AND DAUGHTER. AS I WROTE THOUGHTS OF YOU BLESSED ME. I WOULD NOT HAVE A FAMILY IF IT WERE NOT FOR YOUR PRESENCE.

I LOVE ALL OF YOU. AMEN! **GOD** BLESSED ME ALONG MY LIFE'S JOURNEY. MAY **GOD** CONTINUE TO BLESS YOU AND SEND BLESSINGS ALONG YOUR LIFE'S PATH. YOU MEAN SO MUCH TO ME.

JIM REEVES SANG, "PRECIOUS MEMORIES, HOW THEY LINGER, HOW THEY EVER FLOOD MY SOUL IN THE STILLNESS OF THE MIDNIGHT..." JIM REEVES ALSO SANG,

"IT IS NO SECRET **WHAT GOD CAN DO,** WHAT HE HAS DONE FOR OTHERS HE CAN DO FOR YOU, WITH ARMS WIDE OPEN **HE WILL FORGIVE YOU** IT IS NO SECRET WHAT GOD CAN DO..."

CHAPTER 1

MY BEGINNING

GENESIS CHAPTER 1 VERSE 1 STATES: IN THE BEGINNING GOD CREATED THE HEAVENS AND THE EARTH. MY BEGINNING STARTED WITH **GOD. GOD** CREATED ME. YOUR BEGINNING STARTED WITH **GOD.** EVERY CREATED THING VISIBLE AND INVISIBLE STARTED WITH THE TRUE GOD OF **THE HOLY BIBLE.**

THE HOLY BIBLE BOOK OF GENESIS CHAPTER 1 VERSES 26 AND 27 STATES: (VERSE 26) "THEN GOD SAID LET US MAKE MAN IN OUR IMAGE, ACCORDING TO OUR LIKENESS; AND LET THEM RULE OVER THE FISH OF THE SEA AND OVER THE BIRDS OF THE SKY AND OVER THE CATTLE AND OVER ALL THE EARTH, AND OVER EVERY CREEPING THING THAT CREEPS ON THE EARTH." (VERSE 27) GOD CREATED MAN IN HIS OWN IMAGE, IN THE IMAGE OF GOD HE CREATED HIM; MALE AND FEMALE HE CREATED THEM.

IN THE HOLY BIBLE BOOK OF JEREMIAH CHAPTER 1 VERSE 5 IT STATES: "BEFORE I FORMED YOU IN THE WOMB I KNEW YOU, AND BEFORE YOU WERE BORN

I CONSECRATED YOU; I HAVE APPOINTED YOU A PROPHET TO THE NATIONS."

ST. JOHN CHAPTER 1 VERSES 3 AND 10 STATES: (VERSE 3) ALL THINGS CAME INTO BEING THROUGH HIM, AND APART FROM HIM NOTHING CAME INTO BEING THAT HAS COME INTO BEING.

ST. JOHN CHAPTER 1 (VERSE 10). HE WAS IN THE WORLD AND THE WORLD WAS MADE THROUGH HIM, AND THE WORLD DID NOT KNOW HIM.

REVELATION CHAPTER 4 VERSE 11 STATES: "WORTHY ARE YOU, OUR LORD AND OUR GOD, TO RECEIVE GLORY AND HONOUR AND POWER; FOR YOU CREATED ALL THINGS, AND BECAUSE OF YOUR WILL THEY EXISTED, AND WERE CREATED." AMEN!

MAKE THESE VERSES YOUR PRAYER AND ASK **ALMIGHTY GOD, JESUS CHRIST** TO HELP YOU KNOW WHO YOU REALLY ARE IN HIM. ASK **JESUS CHRIST** TO HELP YOU LIVE FOR HIM, HONOUR AND GLORIFY HIM WITH YOUR BODY, YOUR ENTIRE BEING EACH DAY UNTIL HE TAKES YOU TO YOUR ETERNAL HOME. REMEMBER IT WAS **JESUS CHRIST** WHOM MADE YOU IN YOUR MOTHER'S WOMB. AMEN!

PRAYER.

DEAR **JESUS CHRIST,** HUMBLY I COME BEFORE YOUR THRONE OF GRACE. I ACKNOWLEDGE THAT YOU ARE MY CREATOR. YOU ARE THE CREATOR OF ALL THINGS VISIBLE AND INVISIBLE IN THE UNIVERSE. **I AM** MADE IN YOUR IMAGE AND LIKENESS. LORD YOU WALKED AS THE **GOD-MAN** ON THE EARTH YOU CREATED. **LORD** YOU CAME TO EARTH AS A HUMAN BEING WITH THE

FULLNESS OF DIVINE DEITY. **LORD** EVERY HUMAN BEING YOU CREATED WAS BORN ON THE EARTH AND WE BROUGHT NOTHING ON THIS EARTH WITH US FROM OUR MOTHER'S WOMB. YOU MADE US TO WORSHIP, LOVE, **KNOW** AND ADORE YOU. YOU MADE US TO LIVE FOR YOU **LORD** IN THIS LIFE AND THIS WILL ENABLE US TO ENTER INTO YOUR ETERNAL PRESENCE. HELP ME TO LIVE FOR YOU AS YOU CREATED ME TO LIVE FOR YOU. IN **JESUS CHRIST** NAME I PRAY TO MY HEAVENLY FATHER. AMEN!

MY BIRTH WAS A **MIRACLE**. I WAS BORN IN A HOT TROPICAL COUNTRY AT THE BEST HEALTH CARE CENTRE FOR PATIENT CARE. **EXCEPTIONAL IN TEACHING** AND OUTSTANDING IN RESEARCH.

EPHESIAN CHAPTER 6 VERSES 2 AND 3 STATES: HONOUR YOUR FATHER AND YOUR MOTHER (WHICH IS THE FIRST COMMANDMENT WITH A PROMISE), SO THAT IT MAY BE WELL WITH YOU, AND THAT YOU MAY LIVE LONG ON THE EARTH.

MS. KAY IS ALIVE. IT IS ENTRENCHED IN THE ATMOSPHERE OF THE TROPICS TO WAKE UP TO THE SOUND OF ROOSTERS CROWING "COCK-A DOODLE DO". IN FACT AS I WAS WRITING ON MY LAPTOP COMPUTER TODAY MY CELL PHONE RANG WITH IT'S DISTINCT SOUND. IT WAS **MOTHER** ON THE OTHER LINE CALLING ME FROM THE BEAUTIFUL TROPICAL ISLAND NATION OF ST. LUCIA.

"DOES ANYONE MISS THE SOUND OF THE RINGS OF THE OLD ROTARY DIAL AND VINTAGE PHONES OF THE PAST? I HAVE HEARD SOME CELL PHONE RING ON PUBLIC TRANSITS AND I THOUGHT THAT I WAS IN SOMEONE'S BACKYARD WITH A DOG BARKING. SOME

SOUNDS SHOULD DEFINITELY BE AVOIDED ESPECIALLY WHEN THEY ARE ASSOCIATED WITH HUMAN BEING COMMUNICATIVE DEVICES. DO NOT BARK WHEN YOU ANSWER YOUR PHONE! HA! HAA!

MOTHER IS BLESSED WITHIN A LARGE FAMILY. MY MOTHER'S MOTHER NAME WAS IRENE. IRENE MY GRANDMOTHER IS NOW DECEASED, SHE HAD **GIVEN BIRTH** TO FIFTEEN CHILDREN. WHEN I WAS GROWING UP WITH MY MANY COUSINS; WE ALL REFERRED TO MY GRANDMOTHER IRENE AS **MOMMY.**

I DID NOT KNOW ANY OF MY GRANDPARENT'S PARENT. I BELIEVE THAT IT IS VERY REAR TO FIND ANYONE WHO EVER KNOWS THEIR GRANDPARENT'S PARENT. ONE OF MY MOTHER'S SISTER TOLD ME THAT MY GRANDMOTHER IRENE HAD CHINESE ANCESTORS, IRENE WAS ABOUT FIVE FEET TALL.

MY GRANDMOTHER'S PHYSICAL FEATURES WAS A TESTIMONY TO HER ANCESTRY. MY GRANDMOTHER USED TO BAKE SWEET POTATO PUDDINGS ON A COAL STOVE FOR THE ENTIRE FAMILY.

WE ALWAYS CRAVED FOR MORE OF MY GRANDMOTHER'S SWEET POTATO PUDDING. IRENE MY GRANDMOTHER WAS A SMALL VENDOR, SHE USED TO SELL FRUITS, VEGETABLES, YAMS AND SPICES.

MY MOTHER'S FATHER NAME WAS VALENTINO AND HIS ANCESTORS WERE SPANISH. MY GRANDFATHER VALENTINO WAS A BROOM AND COAL MAKER HE IS ALSO DECEASED. I KNEW BOTH OF MY MOTHER'S PARENTS. I DID LOVE BOTH OF MY GRANDPARENTS.

WHEN MY GRANDFATHER VALENTINO WAS ALIVE ONE OF HIS CUSTOMARY HABIT WAS TO PLAY WITH

HIS GRANDCHILDREN JUST BEFORE THE SUN SET. WE ENJOYED THOSE MOMENTS WITH HIM. HE WAS SLENDER AND HE LOVED DRINKING COFFEE WITH HIS BREAKFAST.

MY GRANDFATHER VALENTINO WAS NICKNAMED BY THE COMMUNITY AS **"PRETTY BOY"** HE WAS A HANDSOME MAN. MY MOTHER KAY REFERRED TO HER FATHER AS **"SIR."**

MY FAMILY IS A CLOSELY KNITTED FAMILY. FAMILY EVENTS ARE OFTEN SHARED IN MY FAMILY. TWO MONTHS AFTER MY THIRTEENTH BIRTHDAY, FRANCE BECAME MY NEW ADOPTED HOME.

DISTANCES AWAY FROM FAMILY MEMBERS DOES CAUSES LONELINESS, PAIN AND GRIEF. I MISS MY FAMILY'S PRESENCE DEARLY WHEN I DON'T SEE THEM AS OFTEN AS I WOULD LIKE TO. I HAVE PURPOSEFULLY DECIDED NOT TO ALLOW ANYTHING TO PREVENT ME FROM BEING ABLE TO SPEND QUALITY TIME WITH MY FAMILY AND TWO CHILDREN RENEE AND OBASI.

YEARS AGO, IT GRIEVED MY HEART THAT I WAS NOT ABLE TO ATTEND MY CHILDREN'S SPECIAL SCHOOL AND BIRTHDAY EVENTS WHEN THEY HAD THEM.

IT GRIEVED ME THAT I WAS NOT ALWAYS ABLE TO BE THERE WHEN THEY HAD TO MAKE DECISIONS ABOUT EDUCATION AND SCHOOL CHOICES.

IT GRIEVED ME WHEN I WAS NOT THERE FOR THEM TO GIVE THEM SOMEONE TO TALK TO PRIVATELY ABOUT PERSONAL MATTERS.

IT GRIEVED ME WHEN I WAS NOT ALWAYS ABLE TO FULLFILL MY CHILDREN'S NEEDS. IT GRIEVED ME WHEN I WAS NOT A DAILY PART OF THEIR GROWING YEARS

BECAUSE OF DISTANCE. IT GRIEVED ME BECAUSE I WAS NOT ABLE TO BE AN INSTANT EMBRACE FOR THEM EACH DAY. IT GRIEVED ME BECAUSE I WAS NOT ALWAYS THERE TO KISS THEM ON THE FOREHEAD.

IT GRIEVED ME BECAUSE MY OWN TWO CHILDREN DID NOT REALLY KNOW ME AS THEY SHOULD. IT GRIEVED ME THAT AS I WRITE THIS AUTOBIOGRAPHY MY MOTHER KAY HAVE NOT SEEN ME FOR A VERY LONG TIME. SEPARATION DOES CAUSE PAIN. **SEPARATION FROM GOD CAUSES EVEN GREATER ETERNAL PAIN, WEEPING, WAILING AND GNASHING OF TEETH.**

I H$1 $2ED TO WORK ON RESTORING MY FAMILY RELATIONSHIPS.

I DON'T KNOW HOW MUCH TIME **GOD** HAS GIVEN MY MOTHER OR ANY OF MY FAMILY MEMBERS TO LIVE. I WILL HONOUR AND CHERISH EVERY MOMENT THAT I HAVE WITH THEM FROM NOW ON. I WANT TO ENCOURAGE YOU TO DRAW CLOSER TO AND **LOVE** YOUR FAMILY MEMBERS AS **GOD** COMMANDED US TO LOVE THEM. AMEN!

ECCLESIASTES CHAPTER 7 VERSE 12 STATES: FOR WISDOM IS PROTECTION JUST AS MONEY IS PROTECTION, BUT THE ADVANTAGE OF KNOWLEDGE IS THAT WISDOM PRESERVES THE LIFE OF IT'S POSSESSORS.

I WAS MARRIED TWICE AND DIVORCED TWICE BEFORE THE AGE OF THIRTY, MY TWO CHILDREN ARE FOR MY FIRST HUSBAND. BOTH OF MY EX-HUSBANDS WERE MUSLIMS.

I AM NOT THE MOTHER OR WIFE OF CHRISLAM. "CHRIS-LAM" CHRIST IS THE LAMB. JESUS CHRIST IS

THE LAMB OF GOD WHO TAKES AWAY THE SINS OF THE WORLD.

CHRISTIANS AND MUSLIMS MUST COME TOGETHER IN OBEDIENCE TO THE HOLY BIBLE, LIVING IN PEACE AND LOVE, LOVING YOUR NEIGHBOUR AS YOURSELF UNDER CHRIST COMMANDMENTS AND DIVINE RULE. AMEN!

MY TWO CHILDREN THAT WERE BORN IN FRANCE ARE BOTH MUSLIMS. THEY WERE INDOCTRINATED TO ISLAM. THIS OCCURRED BEFORE I BECAME A **BORN-AGAIN CHRISTIAN AND A PASTOR.**

I DID OBJECT TO MY CHILDREN BECOMING MUSLIMS. I REFUSED TO PAY FOR THEM TO ATTEND AN ISLAMIC SCHOOL. I DID REFUSE TO HAVE ANYTHING TO DO WITH THAT EDUCATION. MY OBJECTION WAS NOT BECAUSE I DID NOT LOVE MY TWO CHILDREN BUT IT WAS BECAUSE OF MY **"FAITH BELIEF IN JESUS CHRIST ALMIGHTY GOD."**

I REMEMBER STATING DURING A LONG DISTANCE CONVERSATION, "I WENT TO A REGULAR PUBLIC **SCHOOL** WHY CAN'T THEY DO THE SAME? MANY PARENTS TODAY ARE CHOOSING TO HOME SCHOOL THEIR CHILDREN, I DO NOT OBJECT TO THIS, CHRISTIAN SCHOOLS DOES PROVIDE THE FREEDOM FOR CHRISTIAN CHILDREN TO EXPRESS THEIR CHRISTIAN FAITH IN **JESUS CHRIST. AMEN!**

DIVORCE CAUSES PAIN AND SEPARATION. MY SON AND MY SECOND HUSBAND HAVE THE SAME FIRST NAME "OBASI." IN SOME COUNTRIES IT IS LEGAL FOR A MOTHER TO GIVE HER CHILDREN HER LAST NAME. NEITHER OF MY EX-HUSBANDS WERE RELIGIOUS EXTREMIST

MEMBERS. I HAVE A FRIEND WHO IS A FORMER **MUSLIM,** HE IS **NOW A BORN-AGAIN CHRISTIAN.**

ONE DAY THE **LORD JESUS CHRIST** SAID TO ME, "**PASTOR CHRISTIAN** BRING THE ... TO ME, (BRING THE LOST SOULS TO ME), I HAVE GIVEN YOU THE WISDOM TO DO IT." I REPLIED, "YES **LORD** I CAN DO ALL THINGS THROUGH **CHRIST** WHO STRENGTHENS ME." **GOD** IS SERIOUS **ABOUT SAVING SOULS** FROM HELL. AMEN!

"WHEN WOMEN IN VARIOUS PARTS OF THE WORLD BECOME ATTRACTED TO MIDDLE EASTERN RADICAL RELIGIOUS MEMBERS AND SEEKS RELATIONSHIPS WITH THEM, WHAT THOUGHTS GOES THROUGH YOUR MIND? "ARE THEY SEEKING **TRUE LOVE,** TORMENTED MEN, **LOST SOULS** OR BEHEADERS?

WHAT HAS HAPPENED TO OUR NATIONS SOCIETAL MEN? ARE WE ABLE TO "**IDENTIFY THEM.**" MEN AT WAR AND MEN OF PEACE! **GOD** MADE THEM. WE **BORN-AGAIN CHRISTIANS** EMBRACES THEM. WE MUST SEE THEIR NEED FOR **SALVATION.** WE MUST NOT LET SATAN KILL EITHER ONE OF THEM, SAYS THE **LORD. AMEN!**

ARMAGEDDON! ARM-AGE-DDON! ARM AGE DON(E)! HAIL STONES AND COALS OF FIRE! IT IS WRITTEN IN THE **HOLY BIBLE. AMEN!**

MEN, (HOMMES)! I LOVE MEN, I ADMIRE MEN, I LOVE MEN OF ALL KINDS, I ADMIRE MEN OF DIFFERENT NATIONALITIES.

I ADMIRE TALL MEN, SHORT MEN, MEDIUM HEIGHT MEN AND DISABLED MEN. EVEN THOUGH I LOVE MEN, **I AM** NOT A FORNICATOR. I WANT TO EMPHASIZE MY SEXUAL PREFERENCE, **MY MALE SEX PREFERENCE.**

MY FIRST HUSBAND WAS TALL. WHEN I FIRST MET

HIM HE WAS GENEROUS AND KIND TO ME. I DID LOVE HIM. THEN SHORTLY AFTER WE LIVED TOGETHER AND GOT MARRIED.

COUPLES, I WANT TO ENCOURAGE YOU TO FIRST FORGIVE EACH OTHER WHEN THERE IS AN OFFENCE IN YOUR MARRIAGE AND THINK TWICE BEFORE SEPARATING AFTER A HEATED ARGUMENT. IF YOU HAVE CHILDREN, THINK ABOUT YOUR FUTURE WITH THEM.

ESTABLISH AND IMPLEMENT A WORKABLE, PEACEFUL AGREEMENT WITH YOUR EX-SPOUSE REGARDING JOINT ACCESS TO CHILDREN IF YOU HAVE ANY. IT IS TRAGIC TO BE SEPARATED FROM CHILDREN WHEN THEY ARE UNDER THE AGE OF FIVE YEARS OLD AND YOU LIVE HOURS AND TIME ZONES AWAY FROM THEM. I DID EXERCISED MY PARENTAL RIGHTS TO BOTH OF MY CHILDREN.

UNDER THE AGE OF FIVE YEARS OLD A CHILD IS STILL BONDING TO BOTH PARENTS.

THE PERSON WHO COMES INTO THEIR LIVES AT SUCH A TEN-

DER AGE IS THE ONE THEY WILL LIKELY CALL **MOM** OR DAD IF THEIR BIOLOGICAL PARENTS ARE NOT PRESENT. I WRITE AND SPEAK FROM MY OWN TRUE EXPERIENCE.

I HAD TO INSTILL INTO MY OWN TWO CHILDREN MIND THAT **I AM** THEIR ONLY **TRUE BIOLOGICAL MOTHER.** I FOUGHT DEMONS AWAY FROM THEIR THINKING WHO WANTED TO LIE TO THEM ABOUT WHO I TRULY WAS TO THEM. DEMONS WANTED MY SON AND DAUGHTER TO CALL THEIR FATHER 'S FEMALE RELATIVES **MOM.**

WHEN I WAS NOT ABLE TO VISIT MY SON AND DAUGHTER, I PHONED THEM FREQUENTLY AND SENT THEM BIRTHDAY GIFTS AND FAMILY PICTURES THAT I HAD TAKEN WITH THEM. **I DID CONVINCE THEM OF TRUTH** AND REMOVED THE LIES OF SATAN THE ENEMY FROM THEIR MINDS.

ONE OF MY FONDEST MEMORABLE VISITS WITH MY CHILDREN WAS WHEN WE VISITED THE NORTH ATLANTIC OCEAN ON THE WEST OF FRANCE. THE SUBTROPICAL ARCHIPELAGO OF CANARY ISLANDS OF SPAIN YIELDS BOUNTIFUL CROPS OF BANANA, ORANGES, DATES, SUGARCANE AND POTATOES. WE WALKED ALONG THE ATLANTIC OCEAN AND TOOK PICTURES. ON ANOTHER DAY WE WENT TO SPAIN'S CAPITAL CITY OF MADRID.

MY CHILDREN ALSO TRAVELLED TO MY HOME TO VISIT WITH ME. OUR VISITS TOGETHER I ADMIT SHOULD HAVE BEEN MORE FREQUENT TO CREATE A STRONGER BOND AND RELATIONSHIP. I LOVE MY SON AND DAUGHTER DEARLY AND I PRAY FOR THEM EVERYDAY.

MY CHILDREN PLEASE FORGIVE ME OF WHAT I DID AND WAS NOT ABLE TO DO FOR YOU IN THE PAST. I THANK YOU BOTH, FROM MOM, PASTOR CHRISTIAN. MANY PEOPLE DON'T KNOW MANY THINGS ABOUT ME. MY AUTOBIOGRAPHY IS MY OWN TRUE STORY.

I WILL ONLY TELL THE TRUTH AND NEGATE THE LIES OF EVERY ENEMY. TOO MANY HAVE CONCOCTED LYING REPORTS AND STORIES. TOO MANY TRIED TO OPPRESS AND KEEP ME DOWN BECAUSE THEY WANTED TO RISE UP.

TOO MANY MEN AND WOMEN HAVE JEALOUSIES BECAUSE **I AM THE FOUNDER OF A BEAUTIFUL BORN-AGAIN CHRISTIAN MINISTRY.**

TOO MANY WANTED TO GET CLOSE TO ME UNKINDLY. TOO MANY ARE WOLVES IN SHEEP'S CLOTHING. TOO MANY DON'T KNOW THE SACRIFICES I HAVE PERSONALLY MADE TO GET THIS FAR. TOO MANY ARE LOOKING FOR WAYS TO TEAR AND BEHEAD **GOD'S** CHILDREN AND SEEKING AVENUES TO DESTROY THE THINGS OF **JESUS CHRIST ALMIGHTY GOD.** TOO MANY ARE ANTI-CHRIST AND ANTI-CHRISTIANS. AMEN!

IN THE HOLY BIBLE BOOK OF JOSHUA CHAPTER 1 VERSE 5 IT STATES: "NO MAN WILL BE ABLE TO STAND BEFORE YOU ALL THE DAYS OF YOUR LIFE. JUST AS I HAVE BEEN WITH MOSES I WILL BE WITH YOU; I WILL NOT FAIL YOU OR FORSAKE YOU.

GOD HAS HIS TRUE SERVANTS AND SATAN HAS HIS ADVOCATES. DEVIL'S ADVOCATES STAY AWAY FROM ME! THANK YOU. I WROTE TO SHARE AND LET YOU KNOW FROM ME PERSONALLY.

MY SECOND HUSBAND WAS TALENTED; HE COULD EASILY BE MOLDED INTO ONE OF PARIS FRANCE "HAUTE COUTURE" DESIGNERS. I MET HIM WHILE I WAS STILL WORKING AS **A NURSE,** WE HAD NO CHILDREN TOGETHER. I LOVE CHILDREN. MY SECOND MARRIAGE WAS THE SHORTEST. AFTER MY SECOND MARRIAGE ENDED, I SHUT MY HEART'S DOOR AND DECIDED THAT I WOULD NEVER MARRY AGAIN; I WAS NOT YET **A BORN AGAIN CHRISTIAN.**

I THOUGHT I WOULD NEVER KNOW OR FIND TRUE **LOVE.** MY HEART CRIED OUT FOR THE AFFECTIONATE LOVE OF A MAN. **I NEEDED THE LOVE OF THE GOD-MAN, JESUS CHRIST THROUGHOUT MY ENTIRE LIFE. I REALLY NEEDED JESUS CHRIST DURING MY MARRIAGES.**

GOD MUST BE INVOLVED IN MARRIAGES FOR THEM TO BE SUCCESSFUL. AMEN!

MY FIRST HUSBAND ON THE DAY WE GOT SEPARATED; THE LAST DAY THAT WE WOULD EVER BE TOGETHER IN THE SAME DWELLING AS HUSBAND AND WIFE, STOOD BY THE DOORWAY TO LEAVE, THEN HE TURNED AND LOOKED AT ME DIRECTLY AND SAID, "I DID NOT **LOVE** YOU."

HE HONESTLY ADMITTED TO ME THAT HE DID NOT **LOVE** ME. I REMEMBER TREMBLING WITH THE FEELING OF REJECTION. MY MOUTH OPENED AS IF TO RESPOND BUT I DID NOT UTTER A WORD TO HIM. ARISTOCRATS, MOGULS AND MEN OF OUR TIME BE CIVILLY RESPECTFUL TO YOUR FIRST WIVES WHOM BORE YOU CHILDREN. CHILDREN AND FAMILIES, **GOD** ORDAINS THEM.

MY FIRST HUSBAND'S WORDS EXPLAINED THE REASONS WHY I ATE MANY MEALS ALONE WITH OUR TWO CHILDREN. HIS WORDS EXPLAINED WHY HE OFTEN CAME HOME NUMEROUS NIGHTS LATE AFTER I WAS ALREADY IN BED. I WATCHED HIM TURNED AROUND, OPENED THE DOOR THEN STEPPED OUT IN FINALITY. IT WAS THE END OF OUR MARRIAGE. I COULD NOT CONTROL THE TEARS AFTER THE DOOR WAS SHUT. I CRIED, I SOBBED AND I WEPT.

I HAVE PRAYED AND ASKED **JESUS CHRIST** TO USE MY BOOK TO BRING GLORY TO **GOD,** MINISTER TO MANKIND, THE UNSAVED, MEN AND WOMEN WHO HAVE BEEN REJECTED, SEPARATED, ABANDONED, DIVORCED OR ABUSED. I STRONGLY AND UNEQUIVOCALLY SUPPORT AND BELIEVE **BIBLICAL TEACHINGS ON MARRIAGE, DIVORCE AND FORGIVENESS.**

1ST. CORINTHIANS CHAPTER 7 VERSE 15 STATES:

YET IF THE UNBELIEVING ONE LEAVES, LET HIM LEAVE; THE BROTHER OR THE SISTER IS NOT UNDER BONDAGE IN SUCH CASES, BUT GOD HAS CALLED US TO PEACE. AMEN!

MY SECOND HUSBAND ONE DAY SURPRISINGLY WITHOUT WARNING SAID TO ME, "WHY DON'T YOU RETURN TO YOUR FIRST HUSBAND! THIS WAS THE REASON FOR OUR SHORT MARRIAGE.

THERE MUST BE **PEACE AND FORGIVENESS** AFTER A RELATIONSHIP HAS ENDED. THIS IS NOT THE TIME TO WAGE RETALIATORY WARS BASED ON THE PAST. DON'T DESTROY YOUR EMOTIONAL STABILITY. **THE LORD** RECENTLY SPOKE TO ME AND SAID, "IT IS BETTER TO KNOW THAT A MAN'S HEART IS TRUE TO YOU THAN TO LIVE WITH A HIDDEN DECEPTIVE LIE." AMEN!

TURN TO **JESUS CHRIST ALMIGHTY GOD** FOR COMFORT. OPEN YOUR **HOLY BIBLE** AND START READING IT NOW. NO OTHER MAGAZINE, BOOK OR SECULAR TELEVISION SHOW CAN HELP HEAL YOUR SOUL EMOTIONALLY AFTER A MARRIAGE ENDS IN DIVORCE.

LET GO GRACEFULLY AND PROJECT ALL YOUR **LOVE** ONTO **JESUS CHRIST** THE **"FIRST"** DESERVING ONE. AMEN! PRAY DAILY AND THROUGHOUT EACH DAY. **LOVE** YOURSELF. THINK POSITIVE THOUGHTS. REFLECT ON YOUR GOOD QUALITIES AND YOUR TALENTS. IF YOU ARE A **BORN AGAIN CHRISTIAN THINK ABOUT YOUR SPIRITUAL GIFTS, THEY ARE A BLESSING FROM GOD.** MEDITATE ON THE GOOD THINGS **GOD HAS DONE FOR YOU IN YOUR LIFE.**

WHEN MY FATHER WAS ALIVE HE SAID TO ME ONE DAY, "DON'T EVER RUN AFTER A BUS BECAUSE THERE WILL BE ANOTHER ONE." A FEW YEARS AGO I BOUGHT

SOME CLOTH TO MAKE A PASTORAL ROBE FOR MYSELF. THE DRESSMAKER THAT I INITIALLY ASKED TO MAKE THE ROBE FOR ME HAD SOME FRIENDS WHO WERE CAVIL.

THEY RAISED IRRITATING, ANNOYING AND TRIVIAL OBJECTIONS. HER FRIENDS DID NOT KNOW ME PERSONALLY. THEY WERE ALL JEALOUS OF ME.

I DID NOT FIT INTO THEIR GENERATIONAL MENTAL CONDITIONING OF "WHAT" A PASTOR SHOULD LOOK LIKE OR "WHO" SHOULD BE A PASTOR.

THE DRESSMAKER'S FRIENDS FINALLY DISCOURAGED HER FROM MAKING MY PASTORAL ROBE AND ONE DAY SHE CALLED ME AND RETURNED THE MATERIAL AND THE PATTERN PACKAGE THAT I HAD GIVEN TO HER TO MAKE MY PASTORAL ROBE.

ON ONE PARTICULAR DAY THE DRESSMAKER AND ALL HER FRIENDS WERE SITTING IN THE DINING AREA OF THE BUILDING WHERE WE LIVED AND **THE LORD GAVE ME A WISE RESPONSE TO SAY TO HER.**

THE **LORD** SAID, "SAY TO HER, IF YOU MS. "HEART" WAS THE ONLY DRESSMAKER IN THE CITY THEN I WOULD HAVE MANY REASONS TO BE UNHAPPY! BUT BECAUSE YOU ARE JUST ONE OUT OF MILLIONS THEREFORE I PITY YOU."

WITHIN DAYS I FOUND A NEW DRESSMAKER WHO MADE MY PASTORAL ROBE HAPPILY AND QUICKLY. AMEN!

WHEN ONE DOOR CLOSES **GOD** USUALLY OPENS ANOTHER DOOR THAT IS BETTER FOR YOU. IF YOU ARE ALONE NOW YOU CAN FIND JOY AND HAPPINESS IN A FUTURE MARRIAGE RELATIONSHIP. DON'T GIVE UP MEN AND WOMEN, HAVE HOPE IN **GOD**. AMEN!

I PRAY TO **JESUS CHRIST** AND ASK HIM TO SEND ME A NEW HUSBAND, SOMEONE WHO WILL TRULY LOVE ME. I KNOW THAT **GOD HEARD** MY PRAYER. I WANT TO BE HAPPILY MARRIED FOR THE REST OF MY LIFE. AMEN! **PRAYER IS THE KEY TO GOD'S HEART.**

THE HOLY BIBLE, ROMANS 8 VERSE 28 STATES:" AND WE KNOW THAT GOD CAUSES ALL THINGS TO WORK TOGETHER FOR GOOD TO THOSE WHO LOVE GOD, TO THOSE WHO ARE CALLED ACCORDING TO HIS PURPOSE."

DURING DIFFICULT TIMES **GOD IS MY GREATEST COMFORT.** MY MOTHER KAY IS ALWAYS THERE FOR ME. **ISAIAH 40 VERSE 1 STATES; "COMFORT O COMFORT! MY PEOPLE SAYS YOUR GOD." AMEN!**

MY MOTHER IS MY BEST FRIEND. THROUGHOUT THE YEARS I TRIED MY BEST TO SPARE HER MY MANY GRIEFS AND SORROWS. I NEVER WANTED TO BRING GRIEF TO HER EMOTIONS. I ALWAYS WANTED HER TO FEEL MY LOVE FOR HER AND NOT MY PERSONAL PAIN AND SORROWS.

MY MANY HURTS AND BURDENS I DID NOT ALWAYS REVEAL TO HER. ONE OF THE BLESSED DAY OF MY LIFE IN FRANCE OCCURRED A FEW DAYS AFTER I HAD SPOKEN TO MY MOTHER AND REASSURED HER THAT ALL WAS WELL WITH ME. I WAS HOME FROM WORK AND THERE WAS A **PREACHER** ON THE TELEVISION **PREACHING.** IT WAS ABOUT 8.00 p. m. IN THE EVENING. THE PREACHER POINTED HIS FINGER INTO THE TELEVISION CAMERA AND SAID, "YOU AT HOME YOU NEED **GOD,** RAISE YOUR HAND AND SAY THIS PRAYER." THE PRAYER WAS THE SINNERS PRAYER OF REPENTANCE.

IT SEEMED AS IF THE PREACHER WAS SPEAKING

TO ME DIRECTLY, HE POINTED HIS FINGER INTO THE TELEVISION CAMERA REPEATEDLY AS IF HE WAS SPEAKING TO ME WITH A PERSONAL KNOWLEDGE. HE SPOKE CONFIDENTLY KNOWING THAT HE WAS MINISTERING TO SOMEONE. I REMEMBER RAISING MY RIGHT HAND AND REPEATING THE PRAYER WORD FOR WORD AFTER THE PREACHER. AMEN!

AFTER SAYING THE SINNERS PRAYER, I SAID **ST. MATTHEW CHAPTER 6 VERSES 9 TO 13 AS A SECOND PRAYER; "OUR FATHER WHO IS IN HEAVEN, HALLOWED BE YOUR NAME YOUR KINGDOM COME YOUR WILL BE DONE ON EARTH AS IT IS IN HEAVEN GIVE US THIS DAY OUR DAILY BREAD AND FORGIVE US OUR DEBTS, AS WE ALSO HAVE FORGIVEN OUR DEBTORS AND DO NOT LEAD US INTO TEMPTATION BUT DELIVER US FROM EVIL FOR YOURS IS THE KINGDOM AND THE POWER AND THE GLORY FOREVER. AMEN!**

IT WAS A TIME IN MY LIFE WHEN I WAS CONTEMPLATING MANY THINGS. I WAS A NURSE AND UNHAPPINESS HAD CLOUDED MY PERSONAL LIFE. AFTER SAYING BOTH PRAYERS I WENT TO SLEEP. I REMEMBER LAYING DOWN ON MY COMFORTABLE PILLOW. WHEN I AWOKE I WAS IN A SITTING POSITION ON MY BED WITH BOTH OF MY FEET ON THE FLOOR. I DON'T RECALL RISING UP FROM MY PILLOW TO A SITTING POSITION. IT WAS APPROXIMATELY 3:00 a. m.

I TURNED MY HEAD TO LOOK TOWARDS MY LEFT IN THE DIRECTION OF THE FOOT OF MY BED AND I SAW AN **HOLY ANGEL FROM HEAVEN** AT THE FOOT OF MY BED.

THE **HOLY ANGEL** SPOKE TO ME AND SAID, **"YOUR MOTHER'S HEART WILL NOT BE TROUBLED."** WHEN I FIRST HEARD THE **HOLY ANGEL'S WORDS** I DID NOT

UNDERSTAND INITIALLY WHY THE **HOLY ANGEL SPOKE THOSE DIVINE WORDS** TO ME. AFTER THE HOLY ANGEL SPOKE TO ME **JESUS CHRIST, THE HOLY SPIRIT** REVEALED HIS PRESENCE IN MY BEDROOM, **GOD** VISITED ME AND SAID, "YOUR **FAITH** HAS MADE YOU WHOLE."

JESUS CHRIST ALMIGHTY GOD SENT HIS HOLY ANGEL WITH HIS WORDS TO ME THEN APPEARED TO ME.

THE LORD REASSURED ME THAT INDEED "MY MOTHER'S HEART WOULD NOT BE TROUBLED." **GOD KNEW** WHAT UNHAPPINESS I DID NOT DISCLOSE TO MY MOTHER. SHORTLY AFTER THE DIVINE VISITATION I WAS BAPTIZED IN ST. LUCIA AND BECAME A **BORN AGAIN CHRISTIAN.** MY MOTHER WAS PRESENT AT MY BAPTISM AND HER HEART REJOICED.

SALVATION AND LOVE IS MORE POWERFUL AND JOYFUL TO SHARE. FAMILY MEMBERS I AM SPEAKING TO YOU ALSO; UNDERSTAND! AMEN! GOD WAS THERE THROUGH BOTH OF MY MARRIAGES, EVEN THOUGH I WAS NOT YET **A BORN-AGAIN CHRISTIAN** AND I DID NOT YET KNEW **JESUS CHRIST PERSONALLY AS MY LORD AND SAVIOUR.**

GOD WAS WATCHING ME WITH UNSEEN EYES AS I WONDERED WHAT WAS HAPPENING TO MY LIFE.

GOD WAS THERE THE NIGHT WHEN I RETURNED TO MY SECOND HUSBAND'S HOME AND KNOCKED ON THE DOOR. WHEN HE DID NOT OPEN THE DOOR FOR ME I SAT DOWN ON THE CARPET BEFORE HIS DOORWAY AND CRIED AND SPOKE TO HIM THROUGH THE CLOSED DOOR AND SAID, "I **LOVE** YOU, DON'T TURN ME AWAY, I **LOVE** YOU."

GOD SAW AND HEARD MY BROKEN HEART IN ITS BROKEN STATE STILL PROJECTING **LOVE** TO MY MUSLIM EX-HUSBAND.

I LEFT MY FORMER HUSBAND HOME THAT NIGHT AND DROVE TO THE NEAREST MOTEL AND SOAKED MY PILLOWS WITH MORE TEARS UNTIL MORNING CAME.

DURING THE FOLLOWING DAYS AND YEARS TO COME **JESUS** TOOK ME IN HIS ARMS AND STRENGTHEN ME TO GO ON. I BECAME **A BORN-AGAIN CHRISTIAN** IN MY MIDDLE THIRTIES. SINCE THE DAY OF MY WATER **BAPTISM** BY IMMERSION IN THE **NAME OF THE FATHER,** IN THE **NAME OF THE SON** AND IN THE NAME OF THE **HOLY SPIRIT** I HAVE REMAINED CELIBATE. I HAVE REMAINED CELIBATE FOR OVER TEN YEARS, AS I WRITE MY AUTOBIOGRAPHY I AM STILL CELIBATE.

TODAY'S DATE IS APRIL 14, 2017. A FEW YEARS AGO THE LORD ENCOURAGED ME AND SAID, "OPEN YOUR HEART YOU HAVE CLOSED IT, OPEN YOUR HEART FOR MARRIAGE AGAIN." I KNEW **GOD LOVED ME** BUT I DIDN'T KNOW THAT **GOD** WAS MINDFUL OF ME IN THIS WAY.

I HAVE PRAYED AND ASKED **GOD** TO HELP ME OPEN MY HEART FOR MARRIAGE AGAIN AND **JESUS CHRIST** ANSWERED MY PRAYER. **CHRIST** KNEW I DID NOT WANT TO BE ALONE AND THAT I DESIRED A FAMILY AGAIN.

MY HEART IS RECEPTIVE, HOPEFUL, LOVING AND READY TO RECEIVE A NEW HUSBAND IN MY LIFE.

I HAVE ALSO PRAYED AND ASKED **JESUS** TO SEND ME A **BORN-AGAIN CHRISTIAN** HUSBAND, ONE WHO WILL TRULY BE A BLESSING TO ME AND WILL APPRECIATE ME. ONE DAY THE **LORD** SPOKE TO ME AND SAID, "BE READY, HOW BIG IS YOUR TABLE. HALLELUJAH **AMEN!**

DURING MY FORMER MARRIAGES **GOD** SAW HOW MUCH I REALLY DID LOVE THOSE MUSLIM MEN. HE SAW MY EFFORTS TO MAKE THE MARRIAGES WORK. **GOD** SAW MY NEED FOR HIM AND SAW ME LOOKING FOR **LOVE.** I KNOCKED ON THEIR HEART'S DOOR AND IT WAS SHUT AND VOID OF **LOVE.**

I OVERCAME THE ENEMY BY THE BLOOD OF THE LAMB; I NOW BASK IN **GOD'S LOVE** EVERY DAY. YOU CAN TOO. THE PAST IS BEHIND ME. PLEASE TURN TO **JESUS CHRIST** NOW. PAUSE FOR A MOMENT AND SAY THIS PRAYER.

PRAYER.

DEAR LORD JESUS CHRIST, I REPENT OF ALL MY SINS, I SEEK YOUR COMFORT AND PRESENCE NOW DURING THIS DIFFICULT TIME OF MY LIFE. I THANK YOU FOR YOUR LOVE LORD. LORD YOU ARE THE GOD-MAN, MY COMFORTER, WONDERFUL COUNCILLOR. GOD IS MY EVERLASTING FATHER, PRINCE OF PEACE. I SURRENDER EVERY CARE AND CONCERN TO YOU LORD TRUSTING THAT YOU WILL BRING ME THROUGH IN VICTORY. IN JESUS CHRIST NAME I PRAY TO MY HEAVENLY FATHER. AMEN!

HOLY BIBLE 1ST. JOHN CHAPTER 4 VERSES 7 AND 8. BELOVED LET US LOVE ONE ANOTHER, FOR LOVE IS FROM GOD AND EVERYONE WHO LOVES IS BORN OF GOD AND KNOWS GOD. (VERSE 8) THE ONE WHO DOES NOT LOVE DOES NOT KNOW GOD, FOR GOD IS LOVE. AMEN!

BOTH OF MY EX-HUSBANDS NEEDED TO DO WHAT I DID AND TURN THEIR LIVES OVER TO **JESUS CHRIST** TO

BE ABLE TO **LOVE,** RECEIVE **LOVE,** GIVE **LOVE** AND LIVE A LIFE OF **LOVE. AMEN!**

MANY HAVE ATTEMPTED TO JOIN **CHRISTIANITY AND ISLAM** TOGETHER AS ONE DOCTRINAL FAITH BELIEF: BUT **"HIS LAMB" IS JESUS CHRIST ISLAM. JESUS CHRIST THE LAMB OF GOD IS NOT A PROPHET. JESUS CHRIST IS GOD AND SON OF JEHOVAH GOD.**

JESUS CHRIST IS THE HOLY SPIRIT. JESUS CHRIST IS JEHOVAH'S LAMB WHO WAS CRUCIFIED FOR OUR SINS TO BE FORGIVEN. AMEN! "HIS LAMB" IS JESUS CHRIST! ISLAM." AMEN!

ST. JOHN CHAPTER 3 VERSE 16 STATES: FOR GOD SO LOVED THE WORLD THAT HE GAVE HIS ONLY BEGOTTEN SON THAT WHOEVER BELIEVES IN HIM SHALL NOT PERISH BUT HAVE ETERNAL LIFE. AMEN!

HAVING CONSTANT COMPANIONSHIP TO AVOID LONELINESS IS NOT LOVE, HAVING SOMEONE TO OCCASIONALLY TAKE TO A RESTAURANT IS NOT LOVE, JUST HAVING THE PRESENCE OF SOMEONE IN THE HOUSE IS NOT LOVE. LOVE REQUIRES AN OPEN HEART THAT EMBRACES YOU FULLY WITHIN IT. TRUE LOVE LETS YOU DESIRE FREQUENT COMMUNICATIONS, CLOSENESS, INTIMACY, RESPECT AND EACH OTHERS COMPANY.

LOVE MUST INVOLVE TRUST, HONESTY, PLANNING TOGETHER, CONSULTING ON MATTERS BIG AND SMALL, LOVE PUTS YOUR PARTNER'S NEEDS BEFORE YOUR OWN. LOVE PUTS YOUR SPOUSE BEFORE YOUR FRIENDS. LOVE DOES NOT KEEP SECRETS FROM YOU, LOVE WILL NOT BETRAY YOU, LOVE IS BARE BEFORE YOU, LOVE MUST BE RECIPROCAL.

LOVE BRINGS JOY AND GROWTH. LOVE MUST FIRST BE IN THE HEART. I WILL ENSURE THAT MY KITCHEN TABLE IS NOT SHAPED LIKE AN "L" WITH MY FUTURE HUSBAND SITTING ON ONE SIDE OF THE "L" AND ME SITTING ON THE OTHER SIDE OF THE "L"

OUR EYE CONTACT MUST MEET AND UNITE IN LOVE. WE WILL SIT AT A TABLE FOR TWO WHERE OUR EYES MEET TOGETHER AS ONE, THIS IS THE NATURAL **CONTACT LENS** NOT THE MAN MADE ONE. INTIMATE EYE CONTACT AT A PRIVATE DINING TABLE FOR TWO DOES COMMUNICATE LOVE AND INTIMATE DESIRE FOR EACH OTHER.

WHEN OUR EYES MEET LOVINGLY AT THE PRIVATE DINING TABLE THAT IS NOT THE TIME TO ASK, "ARE YOU WEARING CONTACT LENS? I WILL PURPOSEFULLY AND PATIENTLY GET TO KNOW THE INDIVIDUAL I AM INTERESTED IN AND CONSIDERING FOR MY FUTURE HUSBAND. AMEN!

1ST. CORINTHIANS CHAPTER 13 VERSES 4 AND 5 STATES: LOVE IS PATIENT, LOVE IS KIND AND IS NOT JEALOUS; LOVE DOES NOT BRAG AND IS NOT ARROGANT. (VERSE 5) DOES NOT ACT UN-BECOMINGLY; IT DOES NOT SEEK ITS OWN, IS NOT PROVOKED, DOES NOT TAKE INTO ACCOUNT A WRONG SUFFERED.

LOVE IS BEAUTIFUL. THE HOLY BIBLE 1ST. JOHN CHAPTER 4 VERSE 8 STATES: THE ONE WHO DOES NOT LOVE DOES NOT KNOW GOD, FOR GOD IS LOVE.

MY MOTHER KAY IS A **BORN-AGAIN CHRISTIAN** LIKE **I AM.** SHE **LOVES JESUS CHRIST ALMIGHTY GOD.** ONE DAY THE **LORD** SPOKE TO ME AND SAID, "PRAY THAT YOUR MOTHER WILL LIVE A LONG LIFE. " I WAS SO HAPPY

THAT **GOD** REMINDED ME TO PRAY FOR HER. I WILL PAUSE NOW AND PRAY FOR MY MOTHER AND OTHERS.

DEAR LORD JESUS CHRIST, HUMBLY I COME BEFORE YOUR THRONE OF GRACE TO PRAY FOR MY MOTHER AND OTHERS TODAY. I REPENT OF ALL MY SINS LORD. I THANK YOU FOR THE OPPORTUNITY TO PRAY EACH DAY. BLESS MY MOTHER WITH LONGEVITY, PERFECT MEMORY, LOVE OF THE FAMILY, LOVE OF FRIENDS, HEALTH, SPIRITUAL STRENGTH AND SPIRITUAL GROWTH. I PRAY FOR THE UNSAVED, THOSE WHO ARE NOT YET BORN-AGAIN CHRISTIANS AND THEIR FAMILY MEMBERS. LORD BLESS THEM AND PROTECT THEM DAILY FROM ALL ENEMIES. I ALSO PRAY FOR ALL THE BACKSLIDERS RESTORATION BY YOUR SPIRIT. IN JESUS NAME I PRAY TO MY HEAVENLY FATHER JEHOVAH. AMEN!

TODAY'S DATE IS APRIL 14TH, 2017. MY MOTHER KAY PHONED AT APPROXIMATELY 7:35 p. m. I LOVE HER SO DEARLY AND ALWAYS LOOK FORWARD TO HEARING HER VOICE.

MOTHER AND I ALWAYS BEGIN OUR CONVERSATIONS WITH A PRAYER. IF MY MOTHER AND I FORGET TO PRAY; THE **HOLY SPIRIT** REMINDS US TO HONOUR **GOD** FIRST IN OUR COMMUNICATIONS. I FREQUENTLY ASK MY MOTHER ABOUT MY OTHER FAMILY MEMBERS.

MOTHER OFTEN ENCOURAGES ME TO PRAY FOR THOSE WHO ARE SICK AND HAVE A SPECIAL NEED IN THE FAMILY. "HOW IS HADASSAH DOING TODAY? I ASKED MY MOTHER. SINCE I WAS A CHILD MY MOTHER HAS BEEN A FRIEND TO HADASSAH. I KNOW THAT MY MOTHER LOVES AND CARES FOR HADASSAH VERY MUCH. MOTHER WENT TO VISIT AND ENCOURAGE HER SPIRITUALLY.

MOTHER HAD ASKED ME TO PRAY FOR HADASSAH. I LOVE HADASSAH AND HER CHILDREN, THEY ARE LIKE AN EXTENSION TO MY FAMILY. MOTHER REPLIED KNOWINGLY TO MY QUESTION. MOTHER KNEW THE DETAILS OF HADASSAH'S LIFE. "CONTINUE TO PRAY FOR HER." MOTHER SAID. MOTHER'S FRIENDSHIP WITH HADASSAH INSPIRES ME. I OFTEN DESIRE TO FORM A CLOSE KNITTED, SINCERE, LOYAL AND TRUSTWORTHY FRIENDSHIP LIKE MY MOTHER DID WITH HADASSAH.

"IS MARY AND MARTHA OKAY MOTHER? I ALWAYS WANTED TO KNOW FROM MY MOTHER ABOUT MY TWO OTHER SISTERS. MARY IS THE SECOND CHILD FOR MY MOTHER AND MARTHA IS THE THIRD CHILD FOR MY MOTHER. **I AM** THE **FIRSTBORN** FOR MY MOTHER.

CHILDREN SHOULD ALWAYS HONOUR THEIR LIVING PARENTS. REMEMBER YOUR PARENT(S) ON MOTHER'S DAY, FATHER'S DAY, THEIR BIRTHDAYS AND ANNIVERSARIES. REMEMBER THEM ON VALENTINE'S DAY AND WHEN THEY ARE SICK.

REMEMBER YOUR PARENTS WHEN THEY LIVE LONG DISTANCE AWAY FROM YOU AND WHEN THEY CALL UPON YOU FOR HELP REGARDING THEIR NEEDS. REMEMBER AND BLESS THEM. IF THERE IS A NEED FOR YOU TO FORGIVE THEM, PRAY AND ASK **JESUS CHRIST** TO HELP YOU TRULY FORGIVE THEM AND LOVE THEM. AMEN!

PRAYER.

DEAR LORD JESUS, I LOVE YOU LORD, I REPENT OF ALL OF MY SINS. PLEASE FORGIVE ME. HELP ME TO LOVE, HONOUR, FORGIVE AND BLESS MY PARENT(S).

HELP ME TO BE OF HELP TO THEM IN WHATEVER WAY I CAN. IN JESUS NAME I PRAY TO MY HEAVENLY FATHER. AMEN!

CALL YOUR PARENT(S) TODAY. HONOUR **GOD** BY YOUR KIND COMMUNICATION AND LOVING RELATIONSHIP WITH YOUR PARENTS. **GOD** HAS PROTECTED MY CELL PHONE ON NUMEROUS OCCASIONS FROM HARM AND DANGER. THEREFORE **I AM** SO HAPPY THAT I ALWAYS HAVE OPPORTUNITY TO HONOUR **GOD** FIRST WITH MY CELL PHONE.

ANOTHER WAY IN WHICH I ENJOY HONOURING **GOD** WITH MY TELEPHONE IS BY RECORDING **BIBLE VERSES** AS MY GREETINGS TO MY CALLERS ON MY **CELL PHONE ANSWERING MACHINE.**

THESE BIBLE VERSES ENCOURAGES **THE UNSAVED** TO TURN TO **GOD** AND **RECEIVE THE FREE GIFT OF SALVATION. GOD'S WORDS** ALSO BLESSES AND ENCOURAGES THE BODY OF CHRIST, HIS **BORN-AGAIN CHILDREN** EACH DAY.

MY FATHER WAS EIGHT YEARS OLDER THAN MY MOTHER WHEN I WAS BORN. MY DAUGHTER IS SENIOR TO HER BROTHER.

MY CELL PHONE JUST RANG AND IT'S RING DOES NOT SOUND LIKE A CAT'S "MEOW." IT WAS MY MOTHER KAY. I AM SO HAPPY THAT SHE CALLED BECAUSE THERE WERE A FEW THINGS THAT I WANTED TO CONFIRM AND CLARIFY REGARDING THE EVENTS OF MY BIRTH, EARLY CHILDHOOD AND MY FATHER. I THANK **GOD** THAT MY MOTHER WAS A WITNESS TO MY SPIRITUAL **BORN-AGAIN BIRTH** IN ST. LUCIA.

I AM SO BLESSED TO HAVE MY LIVING MOTHER

KAY TO ASK THE QUESTIONS THAT I DESIRED TO ASK. I DON'T HAVE TO ASK A COUSIN, A UNCLE OR AN ELDERLY NEIGHBOUR. THANK **GOD** FOR MY BLESSED MOTHER KAY. AMEN!

WHEN **GOD** WAS CREATING ME **MIRACLOUSLY** IN THE WOMB, THE DEMON OF DEATH AND PARALYSIS ATTACKED. FAMILY MEMBERS WERE CONCERNED ABOUT MY WELL-BEING. HOLY ANGELS WERE SENT AND **BROUGHT ME FORTH**. **GOD** WAS IN CHARGE OF MY WHOLE CREATED PROCESS AND NOT THE DOCTORS. WE SURVIVED. AMEN!

MOTHER TOLD ME THAT WHEN I WAS BORN THE DOCTORS PERFORMED THE COMPLETE NEWBORN PHYSICAL ASSESSMENT EXAMINATION ON ME. I WAS EXAMINED FOR COMPLICATIONS. NORMAL MEDICAL PROTOCAL ENSURES THAT WHEN A NEW BORN BABY IS BIRTHED, SEVERAL MEDICAL PROCEDURE ARE CARRIED OUT TO VERIFY THAT THE BABY IS HEALTHY.

THE PHYSICAL ASSESSMENT ENTAILS EVERY BODY SYSTEM. THE APGAR SCORE IS ONE OF THE FIRST CHECKS OF A NEW BABY'S HEALTH. THE APGAR SCORE IS ASSIGNED IN THE FIRST FEW MINUTES AFTER BIRTH TO HELP IDENTIFY BABIES THAT HAVE DIFFICULTY BREATHING OR HAVE A PROBLEM THAT NEEDS FURTHER CARE. THE BABY IS CHECKED AT 1 MINUTE AND 5 MINUTES AFTER BIRTH FOR HEART AND RESPIRATORY RATES, MUSCLE TONE REFLEXES AND COLOUR. EACH AREA CAN HAVE A SCORE OF 0, 1, OR 2 WITH 10 POINTS AS THE MAXIMUM. A TOTAL SCORE OF 10 MEANS A BABY IS IN THE BESTPOSSIBLE CONDITION.

NEARLY ALL BABIES SCORE BETWEEN 8 AND 10 WITH ONE OR TWO POINTS TAKEN OFF FOR BLUE HANDS AND

FEET BECAUSE OF IMMATURE CIRCULATION. IF A BABY HAS A DIFFICULT TIME DURING DELIVERY, THIS CAN LOWER THE OXYGEN LEVELS IN THE BLOOD WHICH CAN LOWER THE APGAR SCORE. APGAR SCORES OF 3 OR LESS OFTEN MEANS A BABY NEEDS IMMEDIATE ATTENTION AND CARE.

UNIVERSITY OF ROCHESTER MEDICAL CENTRE WEBSITE IS AN EXCELLENT TEACHING SITE FOR ASSESSMENTS FOR NEW BORN BABIES. Http:/www.urm. rochester.edu/encyclopedia/content

I THANK **GOD** THAT EVEN AS A NEWBORN BABY I WAS GIVEN **TEST** AND **I PASSED ALL OF MY TESTS.** AMEN! IT IS BECAUSE **GOD** HAS CREATED ME TO BE VERY WISE. AHA! THERE IS NO CONTEST.

ALL OF MY FAMILY MEMBERS REJOICED ON THE DAY OF MY BIRTH. **GLORY TO GOD IN THE HIGHEST** WHOM DOES ALL MIRACLES FOR ME. HALLELUJAH! AMEN!

I WILL STOP, PAUSE AND THINK FOR A MOMENT. "THE MEDICAL STAFFS WHO DID THE COMPLETE PHYSICAL ASSESSMENT ON ME ON THE DAY I WAS BORN, WHAT DID THEY **SEE? AHA! AHA! THEY SAW ME HOW **GOD CREATED ME** ORIGINALLY UNTAINTED FROM MY MOTHER'S WOMB. FOR CERTAIN WITHOUT A DOUBT THEY SAW AND KNEW INDUBITABLY, INCONTROVERTIBLY AND IRREFUTABLY THAT I WAS A GIRL AND NOT A A BOY. AHA! AHA! AMEN!

MY GENDER AND SEXUALITY WAS DETERMINED BY GOD BEFORE MY CONCEPTION, BEFORE THE UNION OF MY MOTHER'S EGG AND FATHER'S SPERM. I KNOW HOW GOD ORIGINALLY CREATED ME. I WOULD NEVER TRY TO REVERSE WHAT GOD MADE PERFECTLY.

MAN MAKES A LIFELESS MANNEQUIN BUT **GOD CREATED FLESH, BLOOD AND A LIVING SOUL. AMEN!** THE MEDICAL STAFF IN THE LABOUR AND DELIVERY HOSPITAL DEPARTMENT SAW ME FROM HEAD TO TOE. THEY OBSERVED MY EXTERNAL REPRODUCTIVE ANATOMY AND PLAINLY DISTINGUISHED EVERY HEALTHY PART. THEY KNEW THEIR LOCATIONS. NOTHING WAS HIDDEN.

I LOVE READING AND LOOKING AT HEALTH CARE; HEALTH TEACHING BOOKS. I LOVE THE POPULAR MEDICAL HEALTH SHOWS ON TELEVISION.

MY DECEASED FATHER MORDECAI WAS A HAIRY MAN WITH THICK EYEBROWS. IN HIS SENIOR YEARS HE BECAME BALD, BLIND AND WORE DENTURES HE WAS A DIABETIC. MY FATHER TOOK INSULIN INJECTIONS AND WAS ON DIALYSIS BEFORE HE PASSED AWAY.

MY **FATHER** DID ATTEND CHURCH SERVICES OCCASIONALLY IN HIS LIFETIME BUT THAT DID NOT MEANT THAT HE HAD SALVATION, THAT HIS SOUL WAS SAVED FROM HELL. **FATHER** DID BELIEVE IN **THE FATHER, THE SON AND THE HOLY SPIRIT AS GOD, HE DID BELIEVE THAT JESUS WAS GOD AND SON OF GOD.**

MY FATHER AT HIS DEATH UNFORTUNATELY WAS NEVER BAPTISED BY FULL IMMERSION UNDERNEATH A BODY OF WATER **IN THE NAME OF THE FATHER, THE SON, AND THE HOLY SPIRIT. MY "FATHER"** SHOULD HAVE DONE THE **JOHN THE BAPTIST EXAMPLE OF BAPTISM** TO BECOME A **BORN-AGAIN CHRISTIAN** AND HAVE FULL ASSURANCE OF **SALVATION, ETERNAL LIFE. AMEN!**

BECOMING A **BORN-AGAIN CHRISTIAN** WOULD HAVE GIVEN MY FATHER THE JOYFUL LIFE OF KNOWING **JESUS CHRIST AS LORD AND PERSONAL SAVIOUR.**

MY FATHER'S NAME WOULD HAVE BEEN WRITTEN DOWN IN THE LAMB'S BOOK OF LIFE. HIS SALVATION WOULD HAVE GIVEN ME JOY AND IT WOULD HAVE SPARED ME THE SORROW I FELT WHEN I DID ATTEND HIS FUNERAL.

I HAVE BEEN ASKED MANY TIMES, "WHAT IS THE DIFFERENCE BETWEEN BEING A ROMAN CATHOLIC AND A **BORN-AGAIN CHRISTIAN?** MANY WANTS TO KNOW "WHAT IS THE DIFFERENCE BETWEEN BAPTISM BY IMMERSION AND SPRINKLING WATER ON SOMEONE'S FOREHEAD?

I HAVE DONE BOTH, I WAS SPRINKLED ON MY FOREHEAD BY A PRIEST IN ST. LUCIA AND I WAS BAPTIZED BY FULL IMMERSION IN WATER AT A LOCAL CHURCH IN ST. LUCIA. I CAN TESTIFY THAT A SPIRITUAL TRANSFORMATION DID OCCURS AFTER I EXPERIENCED **THE JOHN THE BAPTIST BAPTISM BY FULL BODY IMMERSION UNDERNEATH WATER.**

THE DIFFERENCE IS THAT I TRULY GOT TO KNOW AND BECAME AWARE OF THE PRESENCE OF GOD SPIRITUALLY. JESUS CHRIST IS THE HIGHEST DIVINE POWER, THE HIGHER POWER. I GOT FILLED WITH THE HOLY SPIRIT WHICH IS THE PRESENCE OF GOD IN THE SPIRITUAL FORM.

*** I TESTIFY THAT WHAT I JUST SHARED WITH YOU IS **DIVINE GODLY TRUTH** OTHERWISE I WOULD NOT HAVE WRITTEN IT.

REMEMBER WHO "I AM" MY NAME IS PASTOR CHRISTIAN CHILDS I AM A BORN-AGAIN CHRISTIAN AND THIS WAS HOW I GOT TO KNOW OUR TRIUNE GOD, OUR THREE IN ONE GOD, JESUS CHRIST, JEHOVAH AND THE HOLY SPIRIT. AMEN!

AN AUTOBIOGRAPHY MUST ALWAYS START WITH **GOD FIRST,** IF IT WERE NOT FOR OUR **TRIUNE THREE IN ONE GOD OF THE HOLY BIBLE** WE WOULD NOT EXIST AND HAVE OUR BEING.

WOE TO THOSE WHO DO NOT ACKNOWLEDGE **JESUS CHRIST, JEHOVAH AND THE HOLY SPIRIT** FIRST AS THE ONLY TRUE TRIUNE GOD OF THE UNIVERSE. **JESUS CHRIST** IS THE CREATOR OF ALL THINGS VISIBLE AND INVISIBLE. AMEN!

JAMES 2 VERSE 19 IN THE HOLY BIBLE STATES "YOU BELIEVE THAT GOD IS ONE. YOU DO WELL; THE DEMONS ALSO BELIEVE AND SHUDDER."

I WRITE TO HELP YOU TURN YOUR SPIRITUAL LIFE, FAITH AND SOUL OVER TO **JESUS CHRIST.** DON'T BECOME OLD AND LOOK BACK AT YOUR LIFE AND GRIEVE WITH REGRETS.

AT THE END OF YOUR PHYSICAL EARTHLY LIFE DON'T WEEP AND WAIL WITH GNASHING OF TEETH IN HELL. AMEN!

I REMEMBER WHEN I FIRST MIGRATED TO FRANCE, EVERY SUNDAY MOST OF OUR ENTIRE FAMILY MEMBERS ATTENDED A CATHOLIC CHURCH SERVICE.

THE CATHOLIC SCHOOL WAS THE FIRST SCHOOL I ATTENDED WHEN I ARRIVED IN FRANCE. I STARTED STUDIES IN GRADE 7. **Bienvenue en France, TRANSLATED IN ENGLISH MEANS, WELCOME TO FRANCE.**

MY FATHER WANTED ME TO RECEIVE AN EDUCATION. WHEN I WAS IN HIGH SCHOOL ONE DAY I WAS CONTEMPLATING A CAREER CHOICE. I REMEMBER DISCUSSING MY THOUGHTS WITH MY FATHER AND I MENTIONED THE COMPUTER INDUSTRY AS AN OPTION.

I SAID TO MY DAD, "WHAT DO YOU THINK ABOUT ME SELECTING A COMPUTER CAREER? IN THE LATE 1980'S COMPUTERS WERE BECOMING POPULAR. MY FATHER DISAPPROVED OF MY SUGGESTION WITH HIS TONE OF VOICE AND SAID, "WHAT ABOUT NURSING? I SINCERELY BELIEVED AT THAT TIME MY DAD THOUGHT THE COMPUTER FIELD WAS BEST SUITED FOR MEN. IT WAS NO COINCIDENT THAT HE MENTIONED NURSING HE WAS WORKING AT A RENOWN HOSPITAL.

DAD GREW UP IN RURAL ST. LUCIA. HE OFTEN VISITED THE SUGARCANE PLANTATIONS. MY FATHER SHARED MANY SECRETS WITH ME WHEN HE WAS ALIVE.

ONE OF MY FATHER'S REGRETS WAS THAT HE WAS NOT **EDUCATED** BY HIS PARENTS. HE TOLD ME THAT IT GRIEVED HIM THAT WHEN HE WAS A YOUNG BOY HE HAD TO GO TO THE SUGARCANE PLANTATION WITH HIS DAD TO HELP HIM CUT SUGARCANE.

MY GRANDFATHER WOULD THEN USE THE SUGARCANE TO MAKE SUGAR WHICH WAS SOLD. MY FATHER SAID, "IT PAINED ME TO SEE THE OTHER YOUNG **CHILDREN** MY AGE DRESSED FOR **SCHOOL WITH BOOKS** IN THEIR HAND WALKING AHEAD OF ME GOING TO SCHOOL WHILE I HAD TO GO TO WORK AS A CHILD AT THAT AGE." MY DAD FELT DEPRIVED AND DENIED.

MY FATHER LEARNED TO DRIVE AND BECAME A CHAUFFEUR FOR THE **WEALTHY AND POLITICIANS** IN ST. LUCIA. HE WAS FINANCIALLY BLESSED IN ST. LUCIA.

MY FATHER'S NAME CONJURED UP THE TERM "MONEY-MAN." HE ALWAYS HAD AND HAD SOMETHING TO GIVE TO OTHERS. HE WAS A BLESSED PROVIDER. I NEVER LACKED, MY MOTHER AND FATHER BOTH PROVIDED FOR ME THE BEST WAY THEY COULD. MY

FATHER MORDECAI WAS A GREAT COOK. WHEN HE BECAME A BACHELOR AGAIN HE PREPARED ALL OF OUR MEALS. HE WAS A GREAT SINGLE DAD. I DID HELP HIM TO KEEP OUR HOME CLEAN.

I DID LOVE MY FATHER. I REMEMBER SHOWING MY DAD MY NURSING CERTIFICATION SHORTLY AFTER I HAD RECEIVED IT AND HE SMILED AND WAS HAPPY FOR ME AND I SHARED WITH HIM MY SPIRITUAL CONVERSION AS A **BORN-AGAIN CHRISTIAN** BEFORE HE PASSED AWAY.

I WAS CALLED INTO MINISTRY TO BE A FULL TIME PASTOR BY THE **HOLY SPIRIT.** AFTER I BECAME A **BORN-AGAIN CHRISTIAN THE HOLY SPIRIT TAUGHT ME HIMSELF.** A FEW YEARS AFTER MY WATER BAPTISM I WAS ORDAINED BY A BISHOP. I HAVE MY PASTORAL LICENSE. I NEVER WENT TO A BIBLE SEMINARY.

I REMEMBER SHORTLY AFTER I WAS BAPTIZED, I PRAYED AND I ASKED **JESUS CHRIST** IF I SHOULD ATTEND THE CHRISTIAN COLLEGE WHICH WAS APPROXIMATELY TWENTY MINUTES WALKING DISTANCE FROM MY APARTMENT WHERE I LIVED. I DID ATTEND MANY SERVICES AT THE CHRISTIAN COLLEGE SANCTUARY.

THE **LORD** RESPONDED TO MY QUESTION REGARDING THE SEMINARY AND SAID, **"I WILL TEACH YOU MYSELF."**

I DID COMPLETE OTHER ACADEMIC CORRESPONDENCE COURSES AND EDUCATIONAL WORKSHOPS AND RECEIVED MY CERTIFICATES FOR THEM.

I TOOK SOME COLLEGE AND UNIVERSITY COURSES BUT I DON'T HAVE A COLLEGE OR UNIVERSITY DEGREE. EVERYTHING I LEARNED ABOUT **THE HOLY BIBLE I LEARNED FROM GOD, THE HOLY SPIRIT.** WHEN **JESUS**

CHRIST CALLED HIS TWELVE DISCIPLES HE TAUGHT THEM HIMSELF. JESUS NEVER SEND HIS DISCIPLES TO ANOTHER TEACHER, UNIVERSITY OR COLLEGE.

ST. MATTHEW 4 VERSE 19: AND HE SAID TO THEM, "FOLLOW ME AND I WILL MAKE YOU FISHERS OF MEN." AMEN!

*** THE HOLY BIBLE BOOK OF JOB 36 VERSE 22 STATES: "BEHOLD, GOD IS EXALTED IN HIS POWER WHO IS A TEACHER LIKE HIM?

I WAS AN "INTERNATIONAL" STUDENT. I HAVE KEPT ALL OF MY LYCÉE (HIGH SCHOOL) EDUCATIONAL RECORDS. I PASSED ALL MY COURSES AND RECEIVED MY DIPLÔME DU BACCALAURÉAT GÉNÉRAL, (GENERAL DEGREE OF BACHELOR).

I HAVE A COPY OF MY STUDENT TRANSCRIPT FROM THE BEGINNING OF HIGH SCHOOL TO THE END. IT LIST THE DATE, YEAR, MY GRADE, THE COURSE I TOOK, THE COURSE CODE AND MY FINAL ACHIEVED GRADE I RECEIVED FOR EACH SUBJECT I TOOK.

IN GRADE 10 MY COURSE WAS **FAMILY STUDIES,** MATHEMATICS, GEOGRAPHY AND SCIENCE. IN GRADE 11 I TOOK TYPING, **FAMILY STUDIES, SOCIETY, CHALLENGE AND CHANGE,** BIOLOGY AND APPLIED SENIOR CHEMISTRY. I WAS ALSO ENROLLED IN BUSINESS PROCEDURES AND MATHEMATICS FOR TECHNOLOGY.

A FEW WEEKS AFTER I MIGRATED TO FRANCE, MY BELOVED AUNT BEA MY MOTHER'S SISTER CAME TO VISIT ME. I MISSED MY MOTHER AND SISTERS VERY MUCH WHEN I FIRST CAME TO FRANCE. AUNT BEA LIVES IN MEXICO.

HER VISIT COMFORTED AND BLESSED ME AND MY

DAD. I KNOW THAT MY AUNT BEA LOVES ME VERY MUCH, SHE IS STILL ALIVE TODAY. ON A FAMILY VISIT TO MEXICO MY AUNT BEA REMINDED ME THAT SHE HELPED TO CARE FOR ME WHEN I WAS A BABY.

THE HOLY BIBLE STATES: IN ISAIAH 53 VERSE 5, BUT HE WAS PIERCED THROUGH FOR OUR TRANSGRESSIONS, HE WAS CRUSHED FOR OUR INIQUITIES; THE CHASTENING FOR OUR WELL-BEING FELL UPON HIM AND BY HIS SCOURGING WE ARE HEALED.

MY FATHER HAD ANOTHER CHILD. SHE WAS BORN IN FRANCE. RENEE AND OBASI MY TWO CHILDREN WERE ALSO BORN IN FRANCE. I LOVE MY TWO CHILDREN, **GOD BLESSED MY WOMB WITH THEM.** CHILDBIRTH IS A BEAUTIFUL MIRACLE FROM **GOD.** I LOVE MY FAMILY.

CHAPTER 2

MY CHILDHOOD

PSALM 127 VERSE 3 IN THE HOLY BIBLE STATES: BEHOLD, CHILDREN ARE A GIFT OF THE LORD, THE FRUIT OF THE WOMB IS A REWARD. AMEN!

THE HOLY BIBLE BOOK OF GENESIS CHAPTER 25 VERSE 24 STATES: WHEN HER DAYS TO BE DELIVERED WERE FULLFILLED, BEHOLD THERE WERE TWINS IN HER WOMB.

CHILDREN ARE A BLESSING FROM GOD. ONE CHILD IS A BLESSING, FIFTEEN CHILDREN ARE FIFTEEN BLESSINGS FROM GOD. ALL CHILDREN ARE CREATED IN THE IMAGE OF JESUS CHRIST ALMIGHTY GOD.

IF YOUR CHILD IS BEAUTIFUL, PRETTY, ATTRACTIVE, AVERAGE LOOKING, SO-SO, DISABLED WITH DEFECTS, VERY TALL, A MIDGET, FIVE FEET FOUR INCHES, TAR COMPLEXION, GINGER COLOURED COMPLEXION, CAUCASIAN, CHOCOLATE COMPLEXION, HONEY COLOURED COMPLEXION OR OF A MIXED RACE, NO HUMAN BEING IS SUPERIOR AND NO HUMAN BEING IS INFERIOR TO ANOTHER. AMEN!

I HAVE NEVER SEEN AN UNATTRACTIVE MIXED RACE

CHILD. THEY ARE ALWAYS BEAUTIFUL JUST AS EVERY OTHER CHILD IS BEAUTIFUL, MADE IN **GOD'S** IMAGE. AMEN!

MONEY, POLITICAL POWERS, BUSINESS, SOCIAL CONNECTIONS, SOCIAL CLASS, TALENTS, A PARTICULAR NEIGHBOURHOOD, YOUR EDUCATION, LIFE EXPERIENCES, THE MANY COUNTRIES YOU HAVE TRAVELLED TO, YOUR FAMILY CONNECTIONS AND YOUR FRIENDS DOES NOT EXEMPT YOU FROM **GOD'S GOD'S JUSTICE.**

EVERY HUMAN BEING IS BORN EQUAL IN THE SIGHT OF GOD. THERE ARE HOWEVER TWO GROUPS OF PEOPLE ON **GOD'S** BEAUTIFULLY CREATED EARTH. THE FIRST GROUP IS THE **CHILDREN OF GOD,** WHOM ARE **THE BORN-AGAIN CHRISTIAN BAPTIZED BELIEVERS.** THESE BELIEVERS BELIEVERS AVOID SIN AND IMMORALITY. THE CHILDREN OF **GOD** NAMES ARE WRITTEN IN THE HEAVENLY **LAMB'S BOOK OF LIFE.**

THE SECOND GROUP OF PEOPLE ON OUR PLANET EARTH ARE THE UNSAVED, UNBELIEVERS, THOSE WHO ARE NOT YET **BORN-AGAIN CHRISTIANS.** THEIR NAMES ARE NOT WRITTEN IN THE **LAMB'S BOOK OF LIFE AND IF THEY WERE TO DIE TODAY THEY WOULD NOT SPEND ETERNITY IN HEAVEN WITH ALMIGHTY GOD, JESUS CHRIST.**

GOD DID NOT MAKE US TO INHABIT ANY OTHER PLANET EXCEPT THE **EARTH.** MANKIND WAS ONLY BORN ON THE EARTH AND LIVED ON THE EARTH.

WHEN MANKIND TRAVELS OFF THE EARTH TO SEEK A **HIGHER PLACE** OF REFUGE FROM SIN AND CALAMITY, THERE IS A KNOWLEDGE IN MAN THAT GUIDES HIM TO SEEK HIGHER HEIGHTS BUT LET THAT DESIRE, THAT YEARNING FOR PEACE AND SAFETY BE THE **HIGHEST**

ACCOMPLISHMENT OF SEEKING AND REACHING ETERNAL HEAVEN HEIGHTS. AMEN!

EVERY HUMAN BEING WAS BORN ON THE EARTH A SINNER AND UNGODLY. NO BABY IS EVER BORN BEING **HOLY, ONLY JESUS CHRIST WAS BORN AS THE HOLY GOD-MAN ALMIGHTY.** LET US BE HONEST, BABIES ARE NOT BORN AS **ANGELS** EITHER, THEY ARE HOWEVER BORN CUTE AND CUDDLY RESEMBLING THEIR PARENTS.

I HAVE HAD VISIONS OF **HOLY ANGELS** SEVERAL TIMES DURING MY LIFETIME. **HOLY HEAVENLY ANGELS** ARE POWERFUL. THEY MOVE UNSEEN THROUGH THE ATMOSPHERE AND PHYSICAL OBJECTS. NO PHYSICAL BARRIER DETERS **GOD'S HOLY ANGELS. HEAVENLY ANGELS** OBEY **GOD, THEY ARE MESSENGERS SENT BY GOD. HOLY ANGELS DO GOD'S WILL. THEY DO HAVE WINGS.**

WE DO HAVE **HOLY GUARDIAN ANGELS** THAT ENCAMPS AROUND THE RIGHTEOUS.

PSALM 91 VERSES 11 AND 12 STATES: FOR HE WILL GIVE HIS ANGELS CHARGE CONCERNING YOU, TO GUARD YOU IN ALL YOUR WAYS. (VERSE 12) THEY WILL BEAR YOU UP IN THEIR HANDS THAT YOU DO NOT STRIKE YOUR FOOT AGAINST A STONE. AMEN!

GOD IN HIS MERCY AND GRACE DOES ALSO SEND GUARDIAN **ANGELS** SOMETIMES AROUND THE SINNERS TO PROTECT THEM FROM SATAN. FOR EXAMPLE, "WERE YOU EVER IN A DREADFUL SITUATION, LIKE A NEAR DROWNING ACCIDENT, A CAR ACCIDENT, BEEN TERMINALLY ILL OR YOU MAY HAVE EXPERIENCED A FIRE AND YOU ESCAPED UNHARMED FROM ANYONE OF THESE LIFE THREATENING CIRCUMSTANCES?

YOU KNOW THAT YOUR ELUDING VICTORY AND YOU EVADING DEATH WHICH LED TO YOUR SAFETY WAS A MIRACULOUS DIVINE INTERVENTION. **GOD** OFTEN SENDS HIS POWER TO DRIVE EVIL SPIRITS AND DEMONS AWAY FROM US TO PREVENT THEM FROM HARMING US. **AMEN!**

THE UNBORN AND THE NEWBORN BABIES NEEDS PROTECTION FROM SATAN.

CHILDREN NEEDS SPIRITUAL AND PHYSICAL PROTECTION FROM EVIL SATANIC SPIRITS THAT MANIFEST THEMSELVES IN MANY FORMS.

ST. JOHN 10 VERSE 10, HOLY BIBLE STATES: "THE THIEF COMES TO STEAL AND KILL AND DESTROY; I CAME THAT THEY MIGHT HAVE LIFE AND HAVE IT MORE ABUNDANTLY"

REMEMBER WHAT HAPPENED TO ME IN MY UNBORN STATE. DEATH AND PARALYSIS CAME AT THE STAGE OF MY SEVENTH MONTH FETAL DEVELOPMENT. I KNOW THAT IT WAS AND IS **JESUS CHRIST WHO KEPT ME ALIVE** UP UNTIL THIS DAY AND ENABLES ME TO WRITE MY AUTOBIOGRAPHY, TELL MY STORY AND SHARE MY TESTIMONIES. THERE IS A **SPIRITUAL BATTLE FOR THE SOULS OF MANKIND** ON THE EARTH.

THE WOMB IS BEING ATTACKED BY CANCER DEMONS, MISCARRIAGES, ABORTIONS, TUBAL LIGATION AND FIBROIDS. THEY ARE PREVENTING BIRTH AND THE GROWTH OF THE POPULATION. SPERMS NEED A FEMININE PASSAGE AND CONNECTION TO RELEASE THE CONJUNCTIONAL ABILITY TO RELEASE LIFE. IN ORDER TO HAVE A HEALTHY FUTURE GENERATION SPERM AND EGG MUST FIRST MEET HEALTHILY BODILY.

MANKIND MUST HAVE **THE MIND OF CHRIST TO HAVE A SOUND MIND.**

DEMONS ARE ENTERING INTO HOSPITALS, WORKPLACES, POLITICAL OFFICES, CONDOMINIUMS, APARTMENTS, HOUSES, SHELTERS FOR THE HOMELESS, **PSYCHIATRIC** HOSPITALS, MATERNITY WARDS, COTTAGES, **HOLLYWOOD STUDIOS,** COUNTRY HOMES, PALACES, KINGDOMS, NATIONS, RENT-GEARED-TO INCOME DWELLINGS, AIR PLANES, SHIPS, PRISONS AND CARS.

DEMONS HAVE ACCESSED SUBMARINES, TRAINS, BUSES, FARM HOUSES, HOLLYWOOD CALIFORNIA HOUSES, **GOVERNMENT** HEADQUARTERS, **SCHOOLS,** THE GHETTOS, EVERY NEIGHBOURHOOD AND THE TREE HOUSES.

THESE DEMONS ARE DESTROYING FAMILIES AND **CHILDREN.** WHEN YOU REMOVE THE SEED FROM THE SOIL YOU WON'T HAVE ANY GROWTH OR HARVEST OF A CROP. THE MAN'S SPERM OR SEED MUST CONTINUE TO SEEK OUT AND FIND THE WOMAN'S BLESSED FERTILE WOMB OTHERWISE YOU WILL BECOME AN UNINHABITED NATION, A DESOLATION.

GENESIS 2 VERSE 24 STATES, "FOR THIS REASON A MAN SHALL LEAVE HIS FATHER AND HIS MOTHER, AND BE JOINED TO HIS WIFE; AND THEY SHALL BE COME ONE FLESH."

NOTHING SHOULD SEPARATE THEM DURING THOSE MOMENTS OF ECSTASY, JOY AND DELIGHT. WOMEN! DO NOT BE DENIED.

YOU ARE ON THIS EARTH BECAUSE BOTH OF YOUR PARENTS WERE JOINED IN UNION AS ONE AND THE

FEMALE EGG AND THE MALE SPERM MET AND YOU ARE THE RESULT OF THAT BOND BETWEEN THEM. AMEN!

PARENTS, CHILDREN MUST KNOW THE TRUTH ABOUT THEIR SEXUALITY AND ANATOMICAL IDENTITY, DO NOT DENY THEM THE TRUTH WHEN THEY BECOME AWARE OF THEMSELVES AND START TO ASK QUESTION ABOUT **WHERE BABIES COME FROM.**

IN THE HOLY BIBLE BOOK OF REVELATION CHAPTER 12 VERSE 11 IT STATES: AND THEY OVERCAME HIM BECAUSE OF THE BLOOD OF THE LAMB AND BECAUSE OF THE WORD OF THEIR TESTIMONY, AND THEY DID NOT LOVE THEIR LIFE EVEN WHEN FACED WITH DEATH. AMEN!

URGENCY! URGENCY! NO COMPLACENCY! MANKIND RUN QUICKLY NOW TO **JESUS CHRIST** OUR **LORD** AND **SAVIOUR ALMIGHTY.** TURN TO THE **HOLY BIBLE.** DON'T HIDE IT. OPEN YOUR **HOLY BIBLE** AND KNEEL BEFORE IT AND BEGIN TO PRAY. PRAY FOR YOURSELF AND PRAY FOR OTHERS. DO IT NOW. AMEN!

THE **HOLY BIBLE** IS GOD'S WORDS SPEAKING TO YOU PERSONALLY AND TO ALL GENERATIONS PAST, PRESENT AND FUTURE. CRY OUT! AND PRAY FOR FORGIVENESS OF YOUR SINS. REPENT OF YOUR SINS AND ASK **JESUS CHRIST** TO HAVE MERCY AND MERCY AND GRACE ON YOU. **DO IT NOW! AMEN!**

THE **HOLY BIBLE TEACHES US** ABOUT **SEXUAL RELATIONSHIPS. IN GENESIS CHAPTER 2 VERSE 25 IT STATES: AND THE MAN AND HIS WIFE WERE BOTH NAKED AND WERE NOT ASHAMED.**

GENESIS CHAPTER 4 VERSES 1 AND 17 STATES: NOW THE MAN HAD RELATIONS WITH HIS WIFE EVE, AND

SHE CONCEIVED AND GAVE BIRTH TO CAIN, AND SHE SAID, "I HAVE GOTTEN A MANCHILD WITH THE HELP OF THE LORD." (VERSE 17) CAIN HAD RELATIONS WITH HIS WIFE AND SHE CONCEIVED AND GAVE BIRTH TO ENOCH; AND HE BUILT A CITY AND CALLED THE NAME OF THE CITY ENOCH, AFTER THE NAME OF HIS SON.

PLEASE READ THROUGH THE ENTIRE **HOLY BIBLE.** SO THAT YOU CAN UNDERSTAND **GOD** MUCH BETTER. PLEASE READ **GENESIS CHAPTER 29 ALL OF THE VERSES.**

GENESIS CHAPTER 29 VERSES 30, 31, 33, AND 34 STATES: SO JACOB WENT IN TO RACHEL ALSO, AND INDEED HE LOVED RACHEL MORE THAN LEAH, AND HE SERVED WITH LABAN FOR ANOTHER SEVEN YEARS. (VERSE 31) NOW THE LORD SAW THAT LEAH WAS UNLOVED, AND HE OPENED HER WOMB, BUT RACHEL WAS BARREN.

GENESIS CHAPTER 29 (VERSE 33) THEN SHE CONCEIVED AGAIN AND BORE A SON AND SAID, "BECAUSE THE LORD HAS HEARD THAT I AM UNLOVED, HE HAS THEREFORE GIVEN ME THIS SON ALSO, SO SHE NAMED HIM SIMEON.

GENESIS CHAPTER 29 VERSE 34 SHE CONCEIVED AGAIN AND BORE A SON AND SAID, "NOW THIS TIME MY HUSBAND WILL BECOME ATTACHED TO ME, BECAUSE I HAVE BORNE HIM THREE SONS." THEREFORE HE WAS NAMED LEVI.

THE **HOLY BIBLE** FIRST TEACHES US ABOUT **GOD, LOVE, SEX, AND RELATIONSHIPS. GOD** IS NOT IMPERSONAL OR INANIMATE. **SEX** IS NOT A TABOO TOPIC WHEN WE DISCUSS **GOD.** CHILDREN OF **GOD RISE UP** AND SPEAK THE TRUTH AND NOTHING BUT THE TRUTH ABOUT, SEX, GENDER AND RELATIONSHIPS; SO

HELP ME GOD WHEN I SPEAK ABOUT THE **HOLY BIBLE. AMEN!**

YOU WERE CREATED TO KNOW **GOD. GOD** WANTS YOU TO KNOW HIM FIRST. **GOD** WANTS YOU TO LOVE HIM. MANKIND **LOVE JESUS CHRIST BECAUSE HE FIRST LOVES YOU. GOD IS NOT HIDING HIMSELF FROM YOU. FOLLOW THE INSTRUCTIONS THAT I GAVE YOU IN THIS BOOK AND YOU WILL KNOW GOD JUST LIKE I KNOW GOD. AMEN!**

WHEN YOU BECOME A **TRUE BORN-AGAIN CHRISTIAN** KNOWING **GOD** SPIRITUALLY BE ENCOURAGED AND WRITE A BOOK ABOUT YOUR SPIRITUAL EXPERIENCE WITH **GOD.** AMEN!

***REMEMBER TO PURPOSE IN YOUR HEART TO LOVE JESUS CHRIST ALMIGHTY GOD. AMEN! GOD IS LOVE, BEAUTIFUL AND DESERVES THE LOVE OF MANKIND. AMEN!**

YOU MUST BECOME A BORN-AGAIN CHRISTIAN TO KNOW GOD SPIRITUALLY. THERE IS ABSOLUTELY NO OTHER WAY TO KNOW JESUS CHRIST ALMIGHTY GOD AND HAVE A PERSONAL SPIRITUAL RELATIONSHIP WITH HIM. EVERY OTHER WAY APART FROM THE HOLY BIBLE WAY WILL LEAD YOU TO HELL. NO DOUBT! "IF", "AND" "BUT" OR "MAYBE." AMEN!

DEUTERONOMY 6 VERSES 4 AND 5 STATES: "HEAR, O ISRAEL! THE LORD IS OUR GOD THE LORD IS ONE! (VERSE 5) "YOU SHALL LOVE THE LORD YOUR GOD WITH ALL YOUR HEART AND WITH ALL YOUR SOUL AND WITH ALL YOUR MIGHT. AMEN!

GOD WANTS YOU TO SEE HIS FACE FIRST. SEE **GOD'S FACE** BY LOOKING AT AND READING THROUGH HIS

BOOK. KNOW GOD FACE TO FACE. THE HOLY BIBLE REVEALS GOD'S FACE." PSALM 27 VERSE 4, THE HOLY BIBLE STATES: "...TO BEHOLD THE BEAUTY OF THE LORD AND TO MEDITATE IN HIS TEMPLE.

WHEN I SEEK AND LOOK INTENTLY AT **GOD,** DIVINE **TRUTH** AND **WISDOM** CONVICTS ME OF HOW MUCH **I AM** CONNECTED TO **GOD.**

THE HOLY BIBLE CAN NOW BE READ ON THE INTERNET. **GOD** WILL NOT BE LEFT OUT. I LOVE TO LEARN NEW THINGS; I APPRECIATE TECHNOLOGY AND THE INTERNET. THE INTERNET HAS AN IMMEASURABLE AMOUNT OF FACTS, BOOKS, PICTURES, HOW TO DO'S, AND TEACHINGS.

SOCIETY IS BOMBARDED WITH A LOT OF UNGODLINESS ALSO **REGARDING SEXUAL CONDUCT,** "WHY DOES THE WHOLE WORLD HAS TO SEE IT?

IT WAS MEANT TO BE A PRIVATE MATTER THAT IS WHY IT WAS PLACED BETWEEN YOUR LEGS TO HIDE IT AND YOU WERE BLESSED WITH CLOTHING TO COVER IT UP. HAVE RESPECT FOR THE PUBLIC AND CHILDREN. **HAVE RESPECT FOR GOD WHO IS OMNIPRESENT.**

I CARRY MY MANUAL **HOLY BIBLE** WITH ME WHEREVER I GO IN THIS WORLD AND NO DEVIL OR MAN WILL EVER DISCOURAGE ME. **I AM** NOT A **BIBLE** THUMPING PASTOR BUT MANY OF YOU IN THIS WORLD NEED TO HAVE THE **DIVINE WORDS** THUMPED CONSTANTLY INTO YOUR HEARING AND THOUGHTS TO DELIVER YOU FROM DEMONS THAT HAS POSSESSED YOU.

MANY OF YOU ARE DIAGNOSED AS **SCHIZOPHRENICS AND "TWO-SPIRITED."** **I AM** HERE, CALLED AND ORDAINED BY **GOD** TO HELP DELIVER YOUR **SOULS,**

MINDS, BODY, HEART, THOUGHTS, SPIRIT AND EMOTIONS FROM EVIL SPIRITS.

$1 $2DEMONS ARE THE DENOMINATOR. ISAIAH 66 VERSE 1, "THUS SAYS THE LORD, "HEAVEN IS MY THRONE AND THE EARTH IS MY FOOTSTOOL..."

*** "LISTEN TO MY SERVANT," SAYS THE LORD. "LISTEN TO ME AND OBEY MY WORDS, THE HOLY BIBLE IS MY WORDS." SAYS THE LORD JESUS CHRIST. AMEN! GOD USES TECHNOLOGY TO SPREAD THE GOSPEL. I AM VERY CONFIDENT NOW USING TEXT MESSAGING AND I OFTEN SEND A **BIBLE VERSE** WHEN I SEND A TEXT MESSAGE.

ONE DAY I WENT TO THE CELL PHONE COMPANY AND I ENQUIRED ABOUT ADDING ON TEXT MESSAGING SERVICE. THE YOUNG MALE SALES REPRESENTATIVE SAID TO ME, "LET ME SEE YOUR PHONE."

I TOOK MY CELL PHONE OUT OF MY PURSE AND SHOWED IT TO HIM. "WHAT DO YOU CURRENTLY HAVE ON IT? HE ASKED ME. NOTHING! "I DON'T HAVE CALL ANSWER OR ANY OTHER FEATURES."

I REPLIED TO HIM. I LATER ADDED ALL THE NECESSARY FEATURES THAT I WOULD USE ON MY PHONE. AFTER PRESSING SOME BUTTONS ON MY PHONE THE CELL PHONE SALES REPRESENTATIVE BLURTED OUT HAPPILY, "WAIT A MINUTE, YOU DO HAVE FREE TEXT MESSAGING ALREADY." I SAID, "ARE YOU SURE?

THE YOUNG MAN THEN WENT ONTO HIS STORE COMPUTER TO VERIFY THE INFORMATION. AFTER A FEW MINUTES HE RETURNED TO ME AND SAID, "IT IS CONFIRMED WE HAVE BEEN PROVIDING FREE TEXT MESSAGING PLANS FOR A FEW MONTHS NOW."

I WAS VERY HAPPY AND SURPRISED THAT THE TEXT MESSAGING SERVICE HAD BEEN ON MY PHONE FOR SEVERAL MONTHS ALREADY.

"CAN YOU PLEASE SHOW ME HOW TO SEND TEXT MESSAGES? HE TOOK ME ASIDE AND PATIENTLY TAUGHT ME THE STEPS TO SENDING TEXT MESSAGES. HE PROCEEDED TO SEND ME A TEXT MESSAGE FROM HIS STORE PHONE AND THEN SHOWED ME HOW TO RETRIEVE THE MESSAGE. HE WAS VERY PATIENT WITH ME.

WHEN I GOT HOME I WENT TO MY IN-BOX ON MY PHONE AND WAS SURPRISED TO SEE THE AMOUNT OF MESSAGES THAT VARIOUS PEOPLE HAD SENT ME. IT IS GOOD TO ASK QUESTIONS. MOST CELL PHONE COMPANIES CHARGE FOR TEXT MESSAGING SERVICE THEREFORE THIS IS WHY I NEVER EXPECTED THAT IT WOULD AUTOMATICALLY BE ADDED TO MY PHONE FREE. I THANK **GOD** THAT IT WAS ADDED.

PRAYER.

DEAR LORD JESUS CHRIST, HUMBLY I COME TO YOU NOW LORD, YOU SAID ANYONE WHO COMES TO YOU, YOU WILL NOT CAST HIM OUT, I COME NOW LORD TO CRY OUT TO YOU AND REPENT OF ALL MY SINS PLEASE FORGIVE ME AND HAVE MERCY AND GRACE ON ME. SET ME FREE FROM SATAN, DELIVER ME AND MANKIND LORD FROM EVERY CONNECTIONS TO HELL. LORD PLEASE ANSWER MY PRAYER. IN JESUS NAME I PRAY TO MY HEAVENLY FATHER JEHOVAH. AMEN!

MY CHILDHOOD STARTED WITH **GOD'S** BLESSINGS. WHENEVER **GOD** BLESSES HIS CHILDREN THE DEVIL

BECOMES A RIVAL OPPONENT ENEMY. WHY? BECAUSE **GOD** CAST SATAN OUT OF HEAVEN WHICH IS A BEAUTIFUL PLACE AND THE DEVIL WHOM WAS FIRST CREATED BY **JESUS CHRIST** AS AN ANGEL CAN NEVER RE-ENTER HEAVEN'S BEAUTIFUL GLORY. **AMEN!**

THE DEVIL IS JEALOUS OF ME AND YOU AND DON'T WANT MANKIND TO LIVE ETERNALLY IN **GOD'S BEAUTIFUL HEAVEN,** THEREFORE SATAN MAKES EVERY ATTEMPT TO DESTROY BIBLE TRUTH, OUR SOULS AND BOUNTIFUL BLESSINGS AND PROVISIONS. AMEN!

REMEMBER THE **HOLY BIBLE BOOK OF JOB.** JOB WAS A WEALTHY MAN, THE RICHEST MAN IN THE EAST AND **GOD** HAD BLESSED JOB RICHLY. SO SATAN WENT TO **GOD** TO ENTICE HIM TO DESTROY JOB'S BLESSINGS WHICH THE DEVIL THOUGHT WOULD DETER OR DISCOURAGED JOB FROM SERVING **GOD.**

JOB CHAPTER 1 VERSES 1 AND 3 STATES: VERSE 1: THERE WAS A MAN IN THE LAND OF UZ WHOSE NAME WAS JOB: AND THAT MAN WAS BLAMELESS, UPRIGHT, FEARING GOD, AND TURNING AWAY FROM EVIL.

VERSE 3: HIS POSSESSIONS WERE 7000 SHEEP 3000 CAMELS, 500 YOKE OF OXEN, 500 FEMALE DONKEYS, VERY MANY AND THAT MAN WAS THE GREATEST OF ALL THE MEN OF THE EAST.

GOD HAS SATAN ON A SPIRITUAL LEASH, **GOD** ONLY ALLOWS SATAN TO GO SO FAR AND TO DO SO MUCH. SATAN IS LIMITED IN HIS POWER, **GOD** RESTRAINS THE DEVIL IN MANY WAYS. **GOD** ALLOWED THE DEVIL TO AFFLICT JOB WITH SICKNESS AND INFIRMITY.

JOB CHAPTER 1 VERSE 12 STATES: THEN THE LORD SAID TO SATAN, "BEHOLD ALL THAT HE HAS IS IN YOUR

POWER ONLY DO NOT PUT FORTH YOUR HAND ON HIM." SO SATAN DEPARTED FROM THE PRESENCE OF THE LORD.

THE DEVIL WAS ALLOWED TO KILL JOB'S CHILDREN. THE DEVIL TOOK AWAY ALL OF JOB'S WEALTH AND LEFT JOB PENNILESS. HOWEVER, EVEN THOUGH JOB HAD ALL THESE DIFFICULTIES, HE NEVER BACKSLIDE. JOB NEVER TURNED AWAY FROM **GOD** OR CURSED **GOD.** JOB WAS STEADFAST IN SERVING **GOD.** JOB'S WIFE TRIED TO DISCOURAGE HIM BUT JOB WOULD NOT LISTEN TO HER. ADAM ALSO SHOULD NOT HAVE TAKEN THE FRUIT FROM EVE AND EAT IT. REMEMBER GENTLEMEN! THAT NOT EVERY WOMAN GIVES A WRONG ADVICE. RIGHT! GENTLEMEN. AMEN!

LET EVERYONE NOW MAINTAIN A HUMBLE, GENTLE SPIRIT. AMEN! I KNOW **I AM** ADVISING AND ENCOURAGING EVERYONE WISELY AND TRUTHFULLY WITHIN THIS AUTOBIOGRAPHY. AMEN! **I AM** CALLED BY **GOD** TO PREACH AND TEACH **GOD'S TRUE UNCOMMON DIVINE WISDOM TO MANKIND. AMEN!**

1ST. CORINTHIANS 13 VERSE 11 STATES: WHEN I WAS A CHILD, I USED TO SPEAK LIKE A CHILD, THINK LIKE A CHILD, REASON LIKE A CHILD: WHEN I BECAME A MAN I DID AWAY WITH CHILDISH THINGS.

BELOW THE AGE OF THIRTEEN YEARS OLD I CAN TRULY REMEMBER MANY HAPPY MOMENTS AND SOME SORROWS. I DON'T HAVE ANY VIVID RECOLLECTION OF MY CHILDHOOD BETWEEN THE AGES OF ONE YEAR OLD AND FIVE YEARS OLD. I CHOOSE TO BLESS MY FAMILY AND GUIDE THEM. THE TRUTH MUST BE TOLD.

MY GESTATIONAL DEVELOPMENT WERE TOLD TO ME BY MY MOTHER KAY. **GOD IS AWESOME WITH**

ETERNAL POWER. I HAVE NEVER HEARD OF ANY ADULT SPEAKING ABOUT THEIR EXITING FROM THE WOMB INTO THIS EARTHLY ENVIRONMENT.

MANY PARENTS NOW VIDEOTAPE THE BIRTH OF THEIR CHILDREN TO HELP THEIR CHILDREN TO REMEMBER.

WHEN MY DAUGHTER RENEE WAS BORN SOMETHING UNFORGETTABLE OCCURRED ON THE MATERNITY WARD; SHE WAS BORN IN THE MORNING.

I REMEMBER THE NURSE ASKING ME, **"WHAT WILL HER NAME BE?** I DID NOT HAVE GENDER VERIFICATION DONE BY ULTRASOUND WHILE I WAS PREGNANT WITH MY DAUGHTER. I DID VERIFY MY SON'S GENDER BY ULTRASOUND BEFORE HE WAS BORN. **I AM** BLESSED TO HAVE THEM BOTH.

SOME PARENTS WANT TO KNOW IN ADVANCE WHETHER THEY ARE GOING TO HAVE A **BOY OR A GIRL** AND THEY GO THROUGH THE ULTRASOUND PROCEDURE; THIS ALSO HELPS THEM TO SELECT A **"GENDER APPROPRIATE NAME"** FOR THE BEAUTIFUL CHILD.

EVERY TRANSVESTITE THAT I HAVE EVER ENCOUNTERED USED A "FEMALE NAME" WOE MAN! SAYS THE **LORD.** WHO? MAN! WOMAN! "WOO" MAN! SAYS THE **LORD** AMEN!

I WAS ALONE WHEN THE NURSE ASKED ME WHAT WILL MY BABY'S NAME BE. I WANTED TO CONSULT REGARDING A CHOSEN NAME. I REPLIED TO THE NURSE, "I WILL LET YOU KNOW HER NAME LATER." WHILE I WAS ON THE MATERNITY UNIT THE NAME RENEE WAS CHOSEN.

LATER THAT SAME EVENING THE NURSE ENTERED MY ROOM AND AWOKE ME FROM SLEEP AND SAID, "IT'S TIME FOR HER FEEDING." THEN I SAT UP; PROPPED MYSELF UP ON MY PILLOWS WITH GREAT ANTICIPATED **JOY** OF FEEDING MY FIRST CHILD.

THE NURSE HAD A BABY WITH HER AND SHE HANDED ME THE CHILD THAT SHE CARRIED THEN LEFT THE ROOM. THE MAIN LIGHT WAS OFF IN OUR ROOM; THE ROOM WAS DIMLY LIT. THERE WERE FOUR WOMEN IN OUR MATERNITY WARD AND THE HALLWAY LIGHT SHONE INTO OUR BEDROOM.

IN LESS THAN TWO MINUTES THE NURSE RETURNED TO ME HURRIEDLY WITH ANOTHER BABY IN HER HAND AND SAID, "I DID SAY, **MOTHER CHRISTIAN CHILDS.**

"THIS IS YOUR BABY." THE NURSE TOOK THE CHILD I HELD IN MY HAND AND GAVE ME RENEE. THE IRREVOCABLE TRUE DIVINE CONCLUSORY SWITCH OCCURED. RENEE'S NAME TAG ON HER HAND WAS VERIFIED TOGETHER WITH MINE WHICH CONFIRMED PROOF OF TRUTH THAT SHE WAS MY FIRST NEW BORN BABY GIRL. AMEN! I DID NOT TELL... ABOUT THE BABY SWITCHING INCIDENT.

I KNEW THAT THE NURSE MADE AN ERROR THE FIRST TIME. THE CHILD THAT SHE HANDED TO ME ON THE FIRST VISIT TO MY ROOM WAS NOT RENEE BUT BECAUSE THE MISTAKE WAS CORRECTED VERY QUICKLY; I FORGAVE HER AND LEFT THE HOSPITAL ON MY DISCHARGE DATE PEACEFULLY. IT IS WONDERFUL TO ALWAYS **FORGIVE**. AMEN! **I AM** REVEALING THIS INCIDENT FOR THE FIRST TIME.

MOTHERS ENSURE THAT YOU RECEIVE, FEED AND CUDDLE THE BABY GIRL OR BOY YOU GIVE BIRTH TO

IN THE HOSPITAL. REQUEST FOR THE LIGHTS TO BE TURNED ON WHEN THEY BRING YOUR CHILD TO YOU. VERIFY IDENTIFICATION DATA BEFORE YOU LEAVE THE HOSPITAL. ENSURE THAT THE BABY GIRL OR BOY YOU GAVE BIRTH TO IS THE BABY GIRL OR BOY YOU BRING HOME. **AMEN!**

GOD ALWAYS SHOWS UP FOR ME! **JESUS CHRIST ALMIGHTY GOD** WAS WITH ME THAT BLESSED EVENING ON THE MATERNITY WARD AND REVERSED THE ERROR OF THE NURSE AND ENSURED THAT I GOT MY **TRUE** BABY DAUGHTER BACK. **HALLELUJAH! GOD IS FAITHFUL. AMEN!**

THE ENVIRONMENTS OF THE WOMB AND THE ATMOSPHERE OF THE EARTH WHERE MANKIND IS CONCEIVED AND BIRTHED IS MIRACULOUSLY CREATED BY **JESUS CHRIST ALMIGHTY GOD.** NEITHER ENVIRONMENT CAN OR WILL EVER BE IMITATED BY MORTAL MAN. "STOP THE FOOLISH EXPERIMENTS! HOW CAN A MAN GIVE BIRTH? AMEN!

THE FETUS, THE UNBORN CHILD IS SURROUNDED AND SUSPENDED IN THE AMNIOTIC FLUID IN THE WOMB.

ON THE EARTH MANKIND IS SURROUNDED FIRST BY THE SPIRITUAL WATER, **OUR OMNIPRESENT GOD WHOM IS THE LIVING WATER.**

ON OUR EARTHLY ENVIRONMENT WE INHALE OXYGEN, THE WIND. BOTH WATER AND OXYGEN IS NEEDED FOR LIFE. THE SPIRITUAL WATER GIVES US BOTH LIFE, THE NATURAL LIFE AND ETERNAL LIFE. TO GAIN ETERNAL LIFE YOU MUST FIRST BECOME A **BORN-AGAIN CHRISTIAN.**

YOU MUST BE BAPTIZED IN THE WATER THE **JOHN THE BAPTIST** WAY, WHICH IS FULL IMMERSION UNDERNEATH A BODY OF WATER IN THE NAME OF THE FATHER, IN THE NAME OF THE SON AND IN THE NAME OF THE HOLY SPIRIT. **JESUS CHRIST** WAS BAPTIZED BY **JOHN THE BAPTIST** IN THE JORDAN **RIVER.** AMEN!

AT SIX YEARS OLD I CLEARLY REMEMBER MY MOTHER KAY TAKING ME TO GRADE ONE FOR REGISTRATION TO BEGIN MY CHILDHOOD EDUCATION AT MY CATHOLIC PRIMARY SCHOOL IN ST. LUCIA. THE SCHOOL ENROLLS BOYS AND GIRLS WITH THE HIGHEST GRADE BEING GRADE 6.

MY MOTHER HELD MY HAND AND WALKED WITH ME TO SCHOOL ON THE FIRST DAY AND BROUGHT ME STRAIGHT INTO THE CLASSROOM AND PRESENTED ME TO MY GRADE ONE TEACHER. THE TEACHER ASKED MY MOTHER, **"WHAT IS HER NAME? "CHRISTIAN CHILDS."** MY MOTHER REPLIED.

THE TEACHER RECORDED MY NAME IN HER MANUAL BOOK REGISTRY. MY MOTHER LOOKED AT ME REASSURINGLY WHICH GAVE ME CONFIDENCE THEN SHE LET GO OF MY HAND AND I WATCHED HER WALKED OUT OF THE CLASSROOM, THEN THE TEACHER TOLD ME TO SIT DOWN. NOT MANY EVENTFUL OCCURRENCES HAPPENED IN MY LIFE BETWEEN GRADE TWO AND FOUR. I REMEMBER RETURNING HOME FROM SCHOOL ONE PARTICULAR DAY TO BE TOLD THAT ONE OF MY GRANDPARENT'S TENANT HAD SUDDENLY PASSED AWAY.

THE SECOND EVENT THAT I CAN REMEMBER WAS THAT ONE OF MY RELATIVE'S GIRLFRIEND HAD DIED AT HER WORKPLACE. I WAS FRIGHTENED AS A CHILD BY

THE THOUGHT OF DEATH AND I NEVER LIKED A DARK ROOM, A DARK CORNER OR A DARK HOUSE.

THE CARIBBEAN REGION IS BLESSED WITH EXCELLENCE AND GUINESS BOOK OF WORLD RECORD RECOGNITIONS. JAMAICA IS LISTED AS THE COUNTRY WITH THE MOST CHURCHES PER SQUARE MILE.

I WROTE ON A SLATE WITH SLATE PENCIL WHEN I STARTED GRADE ONE. DURING THE 1970'S.

MY LIFE WAS SURROUNDED BY MY MOTHER, HER FAMILY, MY STEP-FATHER, MARY AND MARTHA AND MY FATHER'S FAMILY.

MY FATHER VISITED US FREQUENTLY AND BROUGHT US PROVISIONS ON EACH VISIT. MY FATHER WOULD SOMETIMES TAKE ME OUT FOR A DRIVE IN THE JEEP THAT HE DROVE. HIS VISITS BROUGHT US JOY. I THANK **GOD** THAT MY FATHER DID LOVE ME.

I REGRETTED NOT SPENDING MORE TIME WITH MY DAD AND GETTING TO KNOW HIM BETTER BEFORE THE AGE OF THIRTEEN.

VENDING WAS A FAMILY TRADITION. MOTHER HELPED ME TO LEARN HOW TO READ A CLOCK WHEN I WAS IN PRIMARY SCHOOL. MY MOTHER WOULD CALL ME AND ASK ME, "CHRISTIAN, WHAT TIME IS IT? THEN I WOULD GO TO WHERE THE CLOCK WAS IN OUR HOME AND RETURN TO HER WITH AN ANSWER.

WHEN I ANSWERED MY MOTHER'S QUESTION ABOUT WHAT TIME IT WAS I WOULD SAY, "THE LONG HAND ON THE CLOCK IS ON THE TWELVE AND THE SHORT HAND IS ON THE FIVE." MY MOTHER WOULD HELP ME BY SAYING, "OKAY, THAT MEANS IT IS FIVE O'CLOCK." I WAS ALWAYS HAPPY AND SMILED WHEN SHE DID HELP

ME TO UNDERSTAND THE TIME ON THE CLOCK. I NEVER ONCE SAID TO MY MOTHER, I DON'T KNOW HOW TO READ THE CLOCK.

AS I BECAME OLDER AND WAS ABLE TO READ A CLOCK AND TELL THE TIME PERFECTLY I BECAME MORE CONFIDENT. AS I GREW OLDER I WAS SOMETIMES PUT IN CHARGE OF THE VENDING TABLE. I HAD TO BE ABLE TO CUT AND WEIGH YELLOW YAM AND OTHER LOCAL FOOD STAPLES SUCH AS POTATOES AND **PUMPKIN.** WE ALSO SOLD BANANA AND OTHER FRUITS.

WHEN I THINK OF IT NOW, A SCALE ALMOST RESEMBLES A CLOCK WITH ALL THE NUMBERS ON IT. SIMILARITY! LIKENESS! I HAD TO KNOW WHEN THE SCALE RECORDED ONE POUND, TWO POUND, TWO AND A HALF POUNDS, THREE QUARTERS OF A POUND AND HALF OF A POUND. I COULD NOT MAKE ANY MISTAKES BECAUSE MOST OF OUR CUSTOMERS WERE ADULTS AND SOME WERE FAMILY MEMBERS. THEY ALL KEPT THEIR EYES ON THE SCALE.

I BECAME EFFICIENT AT WEIGHING AND COLLECTING PAYMENTS FOR MANY POUNDS OF GOODS. RICE AND SUGAR WAS SOLD BY THE POUND. I LEARNED TO GIVE MONEY CHANGE TO CUSTOMERS AT AN EARLY AGE. I WAS SOMETIMES SENT TO MAKE ADDITIONAL PURCHASES AT LARGER STORES.

MR. HILL, ONE OF OUR NEIGHBOUR SOLD ICE FOR A LIVING. THE ICE TRUCK DROVE BY FREQUENTLY WITH TWO OR THREE MEN AT THE BACK OF THE TRUCK HOLDING LARGE SPECIALIZED ICE TONGS IN THEIR HANDS. PERSPIRATION RAN DOWN THEIR FOREHEADS, FACES AND NECK.

WHENEVER I WAS SENT TO BUY ICE FROM MR. HILL HE

SOMETIMES QUIZZED ME AND ASKED ME, "CHRISTIAN, HOW MUCH CHANGE SHOULD I GIVE YOU BACK? HIS QUESTIONS HELPED ME WITH MY MATHEMATICS AND SUBTRACTIONS.

IF I WAS EVER WRONG IN MY CALCULATIONS MR. HILL WOULD HELP ME BY CORRECTING ME WITH A SMILE. MR. HILL KNEW AND LOVED MY FATHER MORDECAI AND WAS FRIENDLY WITH HIM.

I WAS A FIRST CHILD, THEREFORE MORE RESPONSIBILITY WAS ENTRUSTED TO ME. MARY AND MARTHA HAD A DIFFERENT FATHER. MY STEP-FATHER WORKED FOR THE LOCAL HYDRO COMPANY. MY SISTER'S FATHER IS NOW DECEASED.

IT IS MUCH BETTER TO ACCENTUATE THE POSITIVES. I WILL TELL TRUTH AND I WANT YOU TO REMEMBER THE GOOD THINGS. AMEN! I ENJOYED IT WHEN MY MOTHER WOULD WASH AND PLAIT MY HAIR. SHE WOULD MAKE TWO OR THREE PARTITION TO BRAID MY HAIR. TAKING CARE OF THE AFRICAN HAIR MUST BE DONE WITH EASE AND CARE DAILY.

I REMEMBER THE DAY WHEN MY EARS WERE FIRST PIERCED AT HOME, I NOW WEAR GOLD AND SILVER EARRINGS IN THE SAME HOLES.

ONE OF MY GREATEST DELIGHT AS A CHILD WAS TO PLAY MULTIPLE GAMES WITH MY MANY COUSINS.

WE ENJOYED ROMPING. IN ST. LUCIA MY MOTHER'S SIDE OF THE FAMILY LIVED AS AN EXTENDED FAMILY DURING MY CHILDHOOD. MY COUSINS AND I PLAYED GAMES SUCH AS HOPSCOTCH, BINGO, CARD GAMES, DOMINOES, HIDE AND SEEK AND DANDY SHANDY. DANDY SHANDY IS A CHILDREN GAME THAT IS PLAYED

IN THE CARIBBEAN. CHILDREN ARE VERY ACROBATIC AND AGILE WHO PLAYS THIS GAME.

I LEARNED TO RIDE A BIKE WITH MY COUSINS AND WE OFTEN CLIMBED THE MANGO TREES ON MY GRANDPARENTS PROPERTY AND ATE THE FRESH **ORGANIC** RIPENED MANGOES.

AMONG OUR OTHER TREES WE HAD COCONUT TREES, BREADFRUIT TREE AND ACKEE TREES. COFFEE AND FRUITS WAS THE AROMA OF OUR HOME ATMOSPHERE. **GOD** PROVIDED FOR US FROM OUR MANY FRUIT TREES, THEY SHOULD NOT BE CUT DOWN TO MAKE WAY FOR CONCRETE BUILDINGS.

MY COUSINS ALONG WITH MY **SISTERS** AND I USED TO CHALLENGE AND TEST EACH OTHER TO SEE WHO COULD SPELL THE WORD **MISSISSIPPI** CORRECTLY AND WHO COULD SAY THIS SENTENCE CORRECTLY, **"SHE SELLS SEA SHELLS BY THE SEA SHORE."**

WE HAD A LOT OF FUN WITH THE WORD "MISSISSIPPI." **MISSISSIPPI** IS A STATE IN THE **UNITED STATES OF AMERICA.** THE MISSISSIPPI IS ALSO A **RIVER** THAT FLOWS SOUTH FROM NORTH MINNESOTA TO THE GULF OF MEXICO.

MISSISSIPPI, MISSISSIPPI, MISSISSIPPI, **SISTER LETTERS;** SAYS THE **LORD.** .SIS, SISTER. **SHE SELLS SEA SHELLS...**

I WANT TO ENCOURAGE CHILDREN TODAY TO PRACTICE THEIR READING, WRITING AND SPELLING. THIS WILL PREPARE THEM TO READ THROUGH THE ENTIRE **HOLY BIBLE.** MY SPIRITUAL LIFE STARTED WITH **GOD** AS A CHILD. AS A YOUNG CHILD I NEVER KNEW LONELINESS.

MY SISTERS AND I ARE CLOSE IN AGE AND WE ALWAYS RELATE TO EACH OTHER. WE WENT TO **SUNDAY SCHOOL**

TOGETHER. I REMEMBER CLEARLY ONE DAY WHEN I WAS PLAYING WITH MY COUSINS A VERY BRIGHT WHITE LIGHT FLASHED BEFORE MY EYES AND A VOICE SAID TO ME, **"SOMETHING WONDERFUL IS GOING TO HAPPEN TO YOU."** I WAS RUNNING WHEN I SAW THE LIGHT. I DID NOT UNDERSTAND THIS SPIRITUAL EXPERIENCE AT THAT TIME. I KNEW THAT IT WAS UNIQUE.

I WAS BETWEEN THE AGES OF 9 AND 12 YEARS OLD. I DID NOT STOP TO THINK ABOUT IT BECAUSE I DID NOT KNOW WHAT TO THINK.

I REMEMBER FEELING JOY IN MY HEART. IT WAS **JESUS WHO REVEALED HIMSELF TO ME AND SPOKE TO ME THEN.**

I SAW HIM AS THE BRIGHTEST WHITE LIGHT I EVER SAW. RECENTLY I HAVE BEEN THINKING OF THAT CHILDHOOD SPIRITUAL EXPERIENCE MORE FREQUENTLY.

WHEN I HAD MY FIRST SPIRITUAL EXPERIENCE I WAS NOT YET A **BORN-AGAIN CHRISTIAN.** I WAS A PRIMARY SCHOOL CHILD WHO ATTENDED SUNDAY SCHOOL. MANY CHALLENGING AND DANGEROUS SITUATIONS I EXPERIENCED AND ENCOUNTERED IN MY LIFE I CAME THROUGH VICTORIOUSLY AND UNHARMED BECAUSE **JESUS CHRIST** WAS WATCHING OVER ME SINCE I WAS IN THE WOMB. AMEN!

I WANT TO ENCOURAGE EVERY CHILD AROUND THE WORLD TO TURN TO **JESUS CHRIST** AND PRAY. **GOD** DOES HEAR AND ANSWER PRAYERS AND **GOD** DOES SPEAK TO MANKIND AT TIMES EVEN WHEN THEY DON'T KNOW **JESUS CHRIST** PERSONALLY AS THEIR LORD AND SAVIOUR. **GOD** DOES WORK IN A MYSTERIOUS WAY.

PRAYER.

DEAR LORD JESUS CHRIST, I KNOW YOU LOVE ME AND DIED FOR ME ON THE CROSS AT CALVARY. I REPENT AND CONFESS MY SINS.

I LOVE YOU LORD JESUS, STAY BY MY SIDE EACH NIGHT, PROTECT ME TILL MORNING HAS ARRIVE. I PRAY FOR SALVATION FOR MYSELF AND FAMILY MEMBERS. BLESS AND KEEP US LORD IN YOUR HOLY CARE. TENDERLY LORD GUIDE US HOME TO YOU THERE. IN JESUS NAME I PRAY TO MY HEAVENLY FATHER. AMEN!

DEUTERONOMY 6 VERSES 4 AND 5, STATES: "HEAR, O ISRAEL! THE LORD IS OUR GOD THE LORD IS ONE. VERSE 5: YOU SHALL LOVE THE LORD YOUR GOD WITH ALL YOUR HEART AND WITH ALL YOUR SOUL AND WITH ALL YOUR MIGHT.

CHILDREN AND ADULTS! **JESUS CHRIST** DOES REALLY LOVE YOU WITH AN EVERLASTING ETERNAL LOVE. HE IS A FRIEND THAT STICKS CLOSER THAN A BROTHER. **HEBREWS 13 VERSE 5, JESUS SAID, "I WILL NEVER DESERT YOU, NOR WILL I EVER FORSAKE YOU.**

JESUS MADE YOU IN HIS IMAGE THAT IS WHY HE LOVES YOU SO MUCH. IF YOU WERE TO MAKE SOMETHING **I AM** SURE THAT YOU WILL LOVE IT TOO. ANOTHER SPIRITUAL EXPERIENCE I ENCOUNTERED WAS WHEN I WAS IN GRADE SEVEN. IT WAS THE DAY WHEN I HAD TO TAKE THE NATIONAL PRIMARY SCHOOL COMMON ENTRANCE EXAMINATION (CEE), WHICH WOULD ENABLE ME TO ATTEND THE SECONDARY SCHOOL OF MY CHOICE IF I PASSED THE EXAM.

SECONDARY SCHOOLS IN ST. LUCIA STARTS IN FORM 1. I REMEMBER THE DAY I SAT IN THE BACK OF

THE CLASSROOM AT MY PRIMARY SCHOOL AND THE PRINCIPAL WALKED INTO THE CLASSROOM, HER NAME WAS MRS. JOLLY SMILE.

SHE WAS A VERY ARTICULATE AND ELOQUENT SPEAKER. PRIVATE LESSONS AT THE SCHOOL WERE TAUGHT BY MRS. JOLLYSMILE. SHE DID READ MANY BOOKS TO US. SHE SHOULD HAVE READ THE **HOLY BIBLE** TO US BECAUSE OUR PRIMARY SCHOOL WAS A CATHOLIC GIRL AND BOY SCHOOL.

MRS. JOLLY SMILE STOOD BEFORE US AND GREETED US WITH ENCOURAGING WORDS IMMEDIATELY BEFORE WE WROTE OUR NATIONAL COMMON ENTRANCE EXAMINATION. THEN SHE ADDED, **"IF ANYONE OF YOU NEED HELP IN ANY AREA OF YOUR EXAM PRAY TO GOD AND ASK HIM TO HELP YOU IN THAT AREA."**

THAT WAS THE SWEETEST AND ONE OF THE BEST ADVISE I EVER HEARD AS A CHILD. APART FROM MY SUNDAY SCHOOL TEACHER'S ADVISE. I IMMEDIATELY BOWED MY HEAD AND PRAYED TO **JESUS CHRIST ALMIGHTY GOD IN SILENCE.** MY PRAYER WAS SIMILAR TO THIS ONE.

PRAYER.

DEAR LORD JESUS, PLEASE HELP ME TO WRITE AND PASS MY COMMON ENTRANCE EXAM TODAY, I NEED HELP WITH MY LONG DIVISION. PLEASE HELP ME LORD. IN JESUS NAME I PRAY TO MY HEAVENLY FATHER. AMEN!

SCHOOL TEACHERS I WOULD LIKE TO ADMONISH YOU ABOUT YOUR OBLIGATION TO EACH CHILD THAT ENTERS INTO YOUR CLASSROOM; BE ENCOURAGED.

I AM ESPECIALLY EMPHASIZING THIS ADMONITION TO **BORN-AGAIN CHRISTIAN TEACHERS AND OTHER CHRISTIAN BELIEVING TEACHERS. TEACH THE TRUTH.** REMEMBER **DANIEL IN THE LION'S DEN! REMEMBER DAVID THE SHEPHERD BOY. GOD** CAN AND DOES DELIVER. AMEN!

I WOULD LIKE TO HONOUR MY FORMER PRIMARY SCHOOL PRINCIPAL MRS. JOLLY SMILE. I REMEMBERED AND APPRECIATE HER **WORTH.** I AM ALSO DISCOURAGING EVERYONE WHO ATTEMPTS TO SILENCE SCHOOL PRINCIPALS AND TEACHERS WHO HAVE THE SAME CHRISTIAN FAITH. MRS. JOLLY SMILE **BLESSED ME WITH SPIRITUAL ENCOURAGEMENT WHEN I WAS A CHILD.** MRS. JOLLY IF YOU ARE ALIVE TODAY MAY **GOD** BLESS YOU BECAUSE OF THE IMPACT YOU HAD ON MY LIFE; YOU ENCOURAGED ME TO **PRAY. AMEN!**

WHEN THE RESULTS OF MY PRIMARY SCHOOL EXAMINATION WERE PUBLISHED I WAS ELATED. I REMEMBER MY MOTHER KAY AND HER SIBLINGS HAD THE NEWSPAPER AND EVERYONE WAS STANDING, NO ONE SAT DOWN AND THEY SEARCHED FOR MY NAME AMONGST THE SECONDARY SCHOOL CHOICES I HAD MADE.

I TIPTOED AMONGST THEM TRYING TO SEE MY NAME. IT WAS MY MOTHER WHO SAID, "SHE PASSED THE EXAM." (IN PATOIS CREOLE), "LI TE PASE EGZAMEN." (IN FRENCH) "ELLE A PAS L'EXAMEN." MY NAME CHRISTIAN CHILDS WAS FOUND UNDER MY SECONDARY **SCHOOL** CHOICE THAT DAY, MY ENTIRE FAMILY REJOICED WITH ME AND I REMEMBER A FEW WEEKS LATER I RECEIVED A CONGRATULATORY LETTER WITH SOME MONEY FROM ONE OF MY COUSIN WHO LIVED ABROAD. AMEN!

SCHOOL SYSTEMS, HIGHER EDUCATIONAL INSTITUTES, INTERNATIONAL SCHOOLS, MANY COPY EACH OTHERS CURRICULUM AND POLICY PROTOCOLS. NATIONAL COMMON ENTRANCE EXAMINATIONS PUTS CHILDREN TO THE TEST. **GOD** DOES NOT TEST MAN TO GIVE HIM A GRADE OF **A,B,C's.** **"A"** IS FOR **ADAM,** **"B"** IS FOR **BABYLON,** **"C"** IS FOR **CHRIST** COMING AGAIN. **SEE DADA, UNITE, MAKE CANS. AMEN!**

COUNTRIES THAT ADHERES TO THE NATIONAL **COMMON** ENTRANCE EXAMINATION SYSTEM GRACIOUSLY BLESS AND HONOUR THEIR PUPILS THEREFORE BECAUSE YOU HONOUR THEM THEY HONOUR YOU.

AT TWELVE YEARS OLD MY NAME **CHRISTIAN CHILDS WAS IN THE NATIONAL NEWSPAPER FOR DOING EXCELLENT IN MY PRIMARY SCHOOL COMMON ENTRANCE EXAMINATION.** JESUS CHRIST ALMIGHTY **GOD HEARD** AND ANSWERED MY **PRAYER THAT I PRAYED** BEFORE I WROTE MY EXAM. AMEN!

I WAS ACCEPTED TO ATTEND A BLESSED **"NAMED" HIGH SCHOOL.** CHILDREN WHO ARE TAUGHT BY **GOD,** THE **ALPHA AND OMEGA** WILL ALWAYS EXCELL IN SCHOOL. I ATTENDED THE **SCHOOL** FOR ALMOST THREE MONTHS, THEN MIGRATED TO FRANCE.

SCHOOL CHILDREN YOU WILL DO EXCELLENT IN SCHOOL WHEN YOU **PRAY TO JESUS CHRIST ALMIGHTY GOD, HE IS THE ALPHA AND THE OMEGA, THE FIRST AND THE LAST THE BEGINNING AND THE END.** PRAY TO **GOD** LIKE I DID AS A YOUNG CHILD AT THE AGE OF TWELVE YEARS OLD.

REVELATION CHAPTER 1 VERSE 8 STATES: "I AM THE ALPHA AND THE OMEGA," SAYS THE LORD GOD,

"WHO IS AND WHO WAS AND WHO IS TO COME, THE ALMIGHTY." AMEN!

PRAY ABOUT EVERYTHING. PRAY AND ASK **GOD** TO HELP YOU HAVE A RESPECTFUL BLESSED RELATIONSHIP WITH YOUR EDUCATORS, PARENTS, GOVERNMENT AND TEACHERS. INVOLVE **JESUS CHRIST** IN EVERYTHING THAT CONCERNS YOUR LIFE. AMEN!

ST. LUKE CHAPTER 1 VERSE 37 STATES: "FOR NOTHING WILL BE IMPOSSIBLE WITH GOD." AMEN!

ONE OF MY ACADEMIC STRENGTHS IN SCHOOL WAS READING, WRITING AND SPELLING. I NEVER HAD TO WORRY ABOUT A COMPUTER EXAM BECAUSE WE NEVER HAD COMPUTERS WHEN I WAS IN PRIMARY SCHOOL. I EXCELLED IN WRITING ESSAYS IN SCHOOL. MY ESSAYS WERE CHOSEN BY MY TEACHER TO BE READ FOR THE ENTIRE CLASS AT MY **SCHOOL,** I WAS ALWAYS HUMBLED WHEN I WAS CHOSEN.

MY TEACHER WOULD SAY, "CHRISTIAN PLEASE COME UP TO THE FRONT OF THE CLASS AND READ YOUR ESSAY FOR US." ON ONE OCCASION I REPLIED TO MY ENGLISH TEACHER, "PLEASE READ IT FOR ME."

MY ENGLISH TEACHER READ MY ESSAY FOR US WITHOUT ANY OBJECTION. I WAS A VERY SHY CHILD.

REMEMBER <u>WORD</u> IS IN US WE WERE MADE BY THE ETERNAL <u>WORD</u>; JESUS CHRIST.

THE HOLY BIBLE STATES IN 1ST. JOHN 4 VERSE 4: YOU ARE FROM GOD LITTLE CHILDREN AND HAVE OVERCOME THEM; BECAUSE GREATER IS HE WHO IS IN YOU THAN HE WHO IS IN THE WORLD. AMEN!

MY CHILDHOOD STRENGTH WITH WORDS WAS

ANOTHER EVIDENCE THAT THE FINGER OF **GOD** ORDAINED MY DESTINY TO BE A GIFTED SPIRITUAL WRITER. **I AM** CALLED AND BLESSED BY **GOD** TO BE A CHRISTIAN INSPIRATIONAL WRITER ALSO. I LOVE TO WRITE, I DO LOVE WORDS. THE WORDS I WRITE ARE NOT MY OWN THEY ARE GIVEN TO ME BY **JESUS CHRIST THE LIVING WORD.**

I CANNOT DO ANYTHING APART FROM **JESUS CHRIST** HE INSPIRES ME. AMEN! I ENJOYED MAYA ANGELO'S WRITINGS, SHE WAS A **BORN AGAIN CHRISTIAN.**

GOD PREPARED HIS **SON JESUS CHRIST** AS A BABY FOR THE WORK HE WOULD DO ON THIS EARTH. **GOD** PREPARED **SAMUEL, GOD** PREPARED **MOSES** AS A BABY, **GOD** PREPARED **ESTHER** AS A FAIR YOUNG VIRGIN TO DELIVER HIS CHOSEN PEOPLE THE **JEWS** FROM WICKEDNESS. **GOD PREPARES CHILDREN AND WANTS THEM TO LEARN THE TRUTH ABOUT GOD AND NOT THE LIES OF SATAN. AMEN!**

WHEN I LIVED WITH MY BIOLOGICAL MOTHER KAY I WAS OF TREMENDOUS HELP TO HER. I DID CHORES AROUND THE HOUSE. I POLISHED THE FLOOR WITH RED BRICK FLOOR POLISH. I WASHED THE DISHES AND SCOURED THE POTS. I WOULD REMOVE THE DRY CLOTHES FROM THE CLOTHESLINE THAT WERE HUNG IN THE ST. LUCIAN SUNSHINE.

CHILD REARING IN MY FAMILY WAS SHARED. MY MANY AUNTS AND UNCLES VOLUNTEERED TO WATCH OVER EACH OTHERS CHILDREN WHENEVER ANYONE WENT ON AN ERRAND. AMEN!

I SWEPT THE YARD WITH A STRAW BROOM AND SOMETIMES I WENT WITH MY MOTHER TO THE MARKET.

I ALWAYS ENJOYED GOING TO THE CROWDED CENTRAL MARKET. AMEN!

I DELIGHTED IN SEEING **GOD'S** ABUNDANCE IN THE OPEN MARKET PLACE AND THE BEAUTIFUL PEOPLE HE CREATED. MAJORITY OF CARIBBEAN CITIZENS EITHER SPEAKS CREOLE FRENCH OR CREOLE ENGLISH. STANDARD ENGLISH IS USED FOR PUBLIC LIFE. AMEN!

IF YOU ARE EASILY IDENTIFIED BECAUSE OF YOUR ACCENT OR PATOIS DICTION BE PROUD OF YOUR ORIGIN AND LANGUAGE DO NOT SHRINK IN SHAME. THE **FRENCH** SPEAKS FRENCH. THE **SPANISH** SPEAKS SPANISH. THE INDIAN SPEAK **HINDI**. IN ITALY THEY SPEAK **ITALIAN**. IN **GREAT BRITAIN** THEY EVEN SPEAK WITH AN **ENGLISH ACCENT. HA! HAA! HAAA! ACCENTED! GOD** WILL BE ANGRY WITH YOU WHEN YOU SPEAK PROFANITY ANYTIME. AMEN!

***<u>I AM</u> SENT TO LIBERATE MANY PEOPLE AND NATIONS. AMEN! YOU WILL ACCEPT THE TRUTH AND NEGATE THE LIES. AMEN!

THE PATOIS DIALECT IS EASIER FOR ME TO COMMUNICATE WITH WHEN **I AM** SPEAKING TO MY MOTHER KAY WHO CALLS ME REGULARLY. WHEN I SPEAK TO MY AMERICAN RELATIVES I KNOW I MUST AVOID ALL DISTRACTIONS, STAND OR SIT ATTENTIVELY AND LISTEN AND DECIPHER THEIR VOWELS SEPARATE FROM THEIR CONSONANTS TO DISTINGUISH WHEN THEY ARE ASKING ME ABOUT MY **"MAMA."**

THE TIMES WHEN I ACCOMPANY MY MOTHER ON HER SHOPPING TRIPS I WAS ALWAYS POSITIVE TO HER QUESTION REGARDING MAKING CHOICES. I FELT LIKE A GROWN UP THEN. MY MOTHER TRUSTED ME AND HIGHLY VALUED MY OPINION.

I WAS CLOSEST TO MY MOTHER THAN EITHER ONE OF MY STEP-PARENTS. I LOVE MY MOTHER KAY DEARLY. WHEN I FIRST BEGAN TO HAVE MY MONTHLY MENSTRUATION I WAS TWELVE YEARS OLD IN GRADE FIVE AT MY CATHOLIC PRIMARY SCHOOL. I WAS AT SCHOOL ONE DAY, IT WAS LUNCH TIME AND I DECIDED NOT TO RETURN TO CLASS BUT TO WALK HOME TO TELL MY MOTHER KAY WHAT I SAW ON MY UNDERGARMENT IN THE BATHROOM. MOTHER TOOK ME ASIDE IN PRIVATE AND EXPLAINED TO ME THE BEST WAY A MOTHER COULD ABOUT MENSTRUATION, **SEXUALITY,** REPRODUCTION AND **CHILDBIRTH. AMEN!**

AT THE END OF HER MOTHERLY COUNSEL AND ADVICE I REALIZED THAT THE **BLOOD** WAS NOT FROM A CUT OR A SCRATCH ON MY BODY. I LEARNED THAT GROWTH CHANGES, SOMETHING NEW HAD OCCURRED TO MY BODY FOR THE FIRST TIME. I WAS REASSURED AND COMFORTED. SHE ALSO SAID TO ME, "CHRISTIAN YOU CAN NOW BECOME PREGNANT, DON'T LET ANY MAN OR BOY TOUCH YOU NOW, OKAY." AMEN!

I UNDERSTOOD EXACTLY WHAT MY MOTHER MEANT. I WAS A **VIRGIN** AT TWELVE YEARS OLD. MY MOTHER'S TEACHING ENCOURAGED ME NOT TO BE ENTICED TO HAVE PREMATURE SEXUAL RELATIONS AT MY GROWING AGE. MY MOTHER TOLD MY AUNTS AND IT BECAME A FAMILY MATTER.

MY AUNTS BECAME PROTECTIVE OF ME. I REMEMBER AS I WALKED IN OUR NEIGHBOURHOOD ONE EVENING AT DUSK WITH MY AUNT LUCY MY MOTHER'S SISTER, A YOUNG MAN BETWEEN THE AGES OF EIGHTEEN AND TWENTY STOOD AT A GATE AND YELLED OUT TO MY AUNT, HE KNEW MY AUNT BY HER FIRST NAME.

HE SAID, "CAN I HAVE THAT MISS WHO WALKS BESIDE YOU? MY AUNT REPLIED TO HIM AND SAID, "SHE IS TOO YOUNG FOR YOU." I SMILED WITHOUT UTTERING A WORD AT MY AUNTS REPLY.

MY BIOLOGICAL FATHER WAS IN FRANCE, AND FATHER FIGURES IN MY LIFE WERE NOT ALWAYS THERE FOR ME TO BOND WITH. MY MOTHER'S CONSTANT LOVE AND MY FAMILY'S LOVE NURTURED ME. I HAD ONE SPECIAL PRIMARY SCHOOL FRIEND HER NAME WAS OPHIA. WE LIVED IN THE SAME NEIGHBOURHOOD AND OFTEN WALKED TO AND FROM SCHOOL TOGETHER. OPHIA AND I TOOK AFTER SCHOOL PRIVATE LESSONS. SHE WAS VERY **BRIGHT** AND **INTELLIGENT.** SHE HAD A VISUAL IMPAIRMENT.

ONE DAY WHEN I WAS ENROLLED IN MY NURSING PROGRAM, I HEARD A FAMILIAR VOICE CALLED OUT TO ME AS I WALKED DOWN THE CORRIDOR OF THE SCHOOL, "CHRISTIAN CHILDS, IS THAT YOU?"

I TURNED TO SEE WHO IT WAS THAT RECOGNIZED ME AND IT WAS MY CHILDHOOD FRIEND OPHIA. I WAS VERY SURPRISED, YET IT WAS SO FITTING THAT WE WOULD MEET EACH OTHER AGAIN IN AN **EDUCATIONAL** SETTING. I ASKED HER, "WHEN AND HOW DID YOU ARRIVE IN FRANCE? SHE REPLIED TO MY QUESTION WITHOUT HESITANCE.

"I AM ENROLLED IN THE NURSING PROGRAM", I SHARED WITH HER. THEN SHE TOLD ME WHAT PROGRAM SHE WAS ENROLLED IN. I WAS SO BLESSED TO SEE HER AGAIN. I WAS ON MY WAY TO THE CLASSROOM AND I DIDN'T HAVE ADEQUATE AMOUNT OF TIME TO SHARE, COMMUNICATE AND REMINISCE WITH HER.

WE WERE BOTH HURRIED AND WE FORGOT TO

EXCHANGE PHONE NUMBERS AND I NEVER SAW HER AGAIN AFTER THAT DAY. I OFTEN THOUGHT ABOUT HER THOUGH. **I AM** WONDERING NOW IF SHE IS ON FACEBOOK. I REMEMBER HER LAST NAME. THIS PUTS A SMILE ON MY FACE. IT IS VERY HEALTHY FOR CHILDREN TO HAVE CHILDHOOD FRIENDS, COMPATIBLE FRIENDSHIPS.

CHILDREN MUST AVOID BULLYING, RIVALLING AND BAD COMPANY. A CHILD CANNOT EXCEL WITH FRIENDSHIPS THAT EXUBERATES THESE CHARACTERISTICS.

CHILDREN MUST BE ENCOURAGED SPIRITUALLY AND ACADEMICALLY TO GROW UP HEALTHY, STABLE, PRODUCTIVE AND SUCCESSFUL. **JESUS CHRIST** IS EVERYTHING HUMAN BEINGS NEED FIRST. AMEN!

CHILDREN MUST NOT CARRY GUNS TO SCHOOL, SWEARING ON SCHOOL PROPERTY SHOULD BE BANNED. FIGHTING, STEALING, SMOKING, SEXUAL ASSAULT, SEXUAL MOLESTATION, JEERING, JEALOUS BEHAVIOR EXPRESSED TOWARD OTHERS AND EVERY NEGATIVE ATTITUDE AND BEHAVIOUR ON SCHOOL PROPERTY MUST BE ADDRESSED AND BANNED BY SCHOOL POLICY IMMEDIATELY. **AMEN!**

"**THE HOLY BIBLE** DOES NOT HARM CHILDREN OR ADULTS, SO WHY DO YOU BAN ITS **WORDS** AND PRAYERS FROM THE **SCHOOL SYSTEM** MANKIND? WHY GOVERNMENT? WHY EDUCATIONAL DEPARTMENT? WHY POLITICIAN? WHY LAWYERS AND JUDGES? WHY PROVINCE AND STATE? WHY NATIONS? **WHY MAN-KIND?** IT IS A CRUCIAL TIME TO BE A **"KIND MAN"** TOWARDS THE **HOLY BIBLE. DON'T TURN AWAY LOVE. AMEN!**

WHEN I WAS IN THE PRIMARY SCHOOL SYSTEM, STUDENTS REVERENCED, RESPECTED AND HONOURED

THEIR TEACHERS AND PRINCIPALS. WHEN WE SAW THEM COMING WE KEPT SILENT UNTIL THEY PASSED BY.

WE WERE TAUGHT TO BE POLITE TO OUR TEACHERS AND ADULTS. WE NEVER DARED TALK BACK TO THEM DISRESPECTFULLY. DURING CLASS TIME WHENEVER A QUESTION WAS ASKED WE HAD TO RAISE OUR HAND AND WAIT FOR THE TEACHER TO ACKNOWLEDGE US.

WHEN THE TEACHER ACKNOWLEDGED US THEN WE STOOD UP POISED WITH CONFIDENCE WITH A GENTEEL ATTITUDE TO GIVE A REPLY TO THE TEACHER. WE WERE TAUGHT TO BE URBANE.

TEACHERS IN ST. LUCIA HAD AUTHORITY TO EXERCISE CORPORAL PUNISHMENT; DISCIPLINING STUDENTS WITH SLAPS IN THE PALM OF THEIR HAND BECAUSE OF RUDE BEHAVIOUR. **BAD** BEHAVIOR STEMS FROM **SIN**.

*****DIVINE WISDOM: LOVE! NO ONE CAN CONQUER HIM.** REWARD GOOD BEHAVIOUR IN SCHOOLS. WRITE IT IN THE SCHOOL POLICY. LET **STUDENTS VIE TO BE PREFECTS** OF GOOD BEHAVIOR IN SCHOOLS. AMEN! (SMILE).

WHEN A CHILD IS WELL NOURISHED, EMBRACED AND RAISED WITH **LOVE** AT HOME, WHEN THEY GO TO SCHOOL AND INTO PUBLIC PLACES THEY WILL EXUBERATE RECIPROCAL **LOVE** TO OTHERS. AMEN!

I STARTED TO ATTEND MY NEW CATHOLIC SCHOOL DURING THE WINTER MONTH OF JANUARY IN FRANCE.

I REMEMBER BEING ASKED A QUESTION BY THE TEACHER, HIS NAME WAS MR. BAPTISTE AND I STOOD UP TO REPLY TO HIM AND HE QUICKLY TOLD ME, "IT IS NOT NECESSARY FOR YOU TO STAND UP TO REPLY

TO ME CHRISTIAN." I REMEMBER THINKING, "AM I THE ONLY ONE WHO RESPECTS AND REVERENCED HIM." I REALIZED THAT THIS WAS NOT THE NORM IN FRANCE. USUALLY WHEN A CHILD IS REQUIRED TO STAND IN FRANCE'S CLASSROOM IT WAS TO STAND AND FACE THE WALL BECAUSE OF MISBEHAVING.

TEACHERS **LEARN** FROM THE **WISE TEACHINGS** AND EXAMPLES IN THIS BOOK. EMBRACE A CHILD WHO LOVES AND RESPECTS YOU, ENCOURAGE THE OTHERS TO DO THE SAME.

MINISTER(S) OF EDUCATION, SCHOOL SYSTEMS CAN BE IMITATED. HUMBLY WE CAN LEARN FROM OTHERS. YOU HAVE THE POWER AND AUTHORITY TO STOP THE HARMFUL BEHAVIOURS DIRECTED AT STUDENTS AND TEACHERS WITHIN YOUR SCHOOL SYSTEM. **IMITATE WISELY, POSITIVELY AND MANY HEARTS WILL BE JOYFUL.** AMEN!

IT WAS MY CULTURED UPBRINGING THAT DETERMINED HOW I SHOULD REPLY TO MY NEW FRENCH SCHOOL TEACHER. MR. BAPTISTE WAS A COMPASSIONATE AND SYMPATHETIC TEACHER. MY FIRST DAY AT MY NEW CATHOLIC SCHOOL WAS VERY LONELY FOR ME.

AT RECESS TIME EVERYONE LEFT THE CLASSROOM TO GO OUTSIDE EXCEPT ME AND MR. BAPTISTE. I SAT IN MY CHAIR AND WEPT AND MR. BAPTISTE CAME OVER TO ME AND SPOKE KIND WORDS TO ME. AFTER THE RECESS WAS OVER AND CLASS RESUMED MR. BAPTISTE SPOKE ABOUT "BEING COMFORTED WHEN YOU FEEL LONELY IN A NEW ENVIRONMENT." HE WAS A BLESSING TO ME. AMEN!

IN THE HOLY BIBLE. 2ND KINGS CHAPTER 5 VERSE 10 STATES: ELISHA SENT A MESSENGER TO HIM,

SAYING, "GO AND WASH IN THE JORDAN SEVEN TIMES, AND YOUR FLESH WILL BE RESTORED TO YOU AND YOU WILL BE CLEAN." AMEN!

CHILDREN MUST TAKE A BATH OR SHOWER DAILY FOR PREPARATION FOR SCHOOL. IN ST. LUCIA MY MOTHER HELPED ME ON THE WEEKENDS TO PREPARE FOR SCHOOL ON MONDAY MORNINGS. BATH TIME WAS LIKE A LEISURE ACTIVITY, LINGERING UNDER THE COOL RUNNING WATER WAS COMFORTING ON A HOT SUNNY DAY. OUR HOME WAS BUILT WITH A SHOWER AND NOT A BATHTUB. AN ADULT WAS ALWAYS AT HOME WHENEVER MY SISTERS, COUSINS AND I TOOK OUR SHOWERS. WE WERE NEVER LEFT UNATTENDED. I WORE STARCHED BLUE AND WHITE UNIFORM TO SCHOOL, MY UNIFORM SKIRTS WERE PLEATED AND WHEN THEY WERE IRONED THEY WERE PROMINENTLY DEFINED.

FOR PREPARATION TO GO TO SCHOOL MY HAIR WAS COMBED ON SUNDAY NIGHT AND I WOULD TIE MY HEAD WITH A HEAD SCARF. MY SHOES WERE POLISHED WITH BLACK SHOE POLISH. IF I WORE WHITE SNEAKER I WOULD WHITEN THEM ON SUNDAY EVENING WITH SHOE WHITENER.

MAKE-UP AND NAIL POLISH WAS NEVER A PART OF MY CHILDHOOD, NEITHER WAS HIGH HEELED SHOES. I WAS MY MOTHER'S LITTLE GIRL, A HUMBLE AND BRIGHT CHILD.

THE EMPHASIS OF MY LIFE AT THAT TIME WAS GOING TO SUNDAY SCHOOL, DOING MY HOMEWORK, HELPING MY MOTHER, AND PASSING MY TESTS. I LEARNED TO CROCHET BY THE AGE OF TWELVE. OCCASIONALLY DURING SUMMER HOLIDAYS MY MOTHER WOULD SEND

ME WITH RELATIVES TO VISIT OTHER RELATIVES IN THE RURAL COUNTRY AREAS.

I LOVED AND STILL LOVE THE RURAL COUNTRY SIDE COMMUNITIES. THEY ARE OVERGROWN WITH LUSH GREEN VEGETATION, BEAUTIFUL TROPICAL PLANTS, MANY RIVERS, WATER HOLES BUBBLING UP FROM THE GROUND AND AMIDST THEM IS THE ABUNDANCE OF MANY FRUIT TREES AND VEGETABLES WHICH IS A SPLENDID DISPLAY OF **GOD'S ABUNDANT BLESSINGS ON THE TROPICAL ISLAND COUNTRY.**

EVERY NATION, ISLAND-COUNTRIES BOW DOWN IN HUMILITY, RAISE YOUR HANDS AND VOICES TO **ALMIGHTY GOD** AND GIVE THANKS FOR YOUR BLESSED ABUNDANCE. AMEN!

GENESIS CHAPTER 1 VERSES 11 AND 12 STATES: THEN GOD SAID, "LET THE EARTH SPROUT VEGETATION: PLANTS YIELDING SEED, AND FRUIT TREES ON THE EARTH BEARING FRUIT AFTER THEIR KIND WITH SEED IN THEM", AND IT WAS SO. (VERSE 12) THE EARTH BROUGHT FORTH VEGETATION, PLANTS YIELDING SEED AFTER THEIR KIND, AND TREES BEARING FRUIT WITH SEED IN THEM, AFTER THEIR KIND; AND GOD SAW THAT IT WAS GOOD. AMEN!

I REMEMBER VISITING MY GRANDFATHER IN THE QUARTER WHERE MY FATHER WAS BORN IN ST. LUCIA FOR THE FIRST TIME. THE QUARTER'S RESIDENCE WERE FRIENDLY AND QUIET. HE LIVED AWAY FROM THE INFLUENCE OF BUSTLING TOURISM.

I RECALL GOING WITH MY FATHER'S NIECES, HIS SISTER'S CHILDREN TO VISIT OUR GRAND FATHER WHO WAS ALIVE AT THE TIME AND WAS BLIND. WE GREETED MY GRANDFATHER "PA" AND HE SMILED. HE

WAS A WIDOWER. MY COUSIN DALIAH WHO WAS MUCH OLDER THAN THE REST OF US HAD TO DESCRIBE MY APPEARANCE TO MY GRANDFATHER.

I REMEMBER HER SAYING TO "PA", "MORDECAI'S DAUGHTER CHRISTIAN IS HERE PA." MY GRANDFATHER ASKED HER, "WHO DOES SHE LOOK LIKE"? DALIAH REPLIED IN PATOIS DIALECT (CREOLE FRENCH), "LI GEN YON BANN SOUSI, BUSHY SOUSI RENMEN UNCLE MADOCHE." THIS IS WHAT DALIAH MEANT, "SHE HAVE A LOT OF EYEBROW, BUSHY EYEBROW LIKE UNCLE MORDECAI."

MY GRANDFATHER LIVED ON AN ELEVATED PIECE OF LAND, SURROUNDED BY MANY TREES AND UNDEVELOPED LANDSCAPE. HIS HOME WAS LIKE A LARGE DORMITORY MADE OF WOOD WITHOUT INDOOR PLUMBING. WE TOOK WATER FROM A LARGE STEEL BARREL. MY COUSINS AND I PLAYED, WE RAN AROUND AND AMONGST THE TREES, WE WENT UP AND DOWN THE HILL AND WHEN WE BECAME TIRED WE SAT DOWN UNDERNEATH THE SHADE OF THE TREES. AFTER SPENDING THE MEMORABLE SUMMER DAYS WITH MY GRANDFATHER AND COUSINS WE PREPARED AND RETURNED TO THE CITY OF CASTRIES.

TO COMMENCE THE NEW MONDAY MORNING SEPTEMBER SCHOOL DAY I WOULD GET UP BEFORE DAWN AND LIGHT THE KEROSENE OIL LAMP THAT WE USED, NOT EVERY ROOM ON MY GRANDPARENTS PROPERTY HAD ELECTRICITY. WE LIVED A SIMPLE LIFE. OUR CLOTHES WAS WASHED IN A CLOTHES WASHING BASIN.

A COAL STOVE OR A KEROSENE OIL STOVE WAS USED FOR COOKING. GAS STOVES AND MODERNITIES HAVE

REPLACED THE OLD COOKING STOVES. MANY TIMES I WAS SENT TO PURCHASE THE KEROSENE OIL THAT WE NEEDED. WHEN I WAS GROWING UP IT WAS ONLY MY UNCLE PAUL WHO OWNED A BLACK AND WHITE TELEVISION AND HAD A REFRIGERATOR.

OUR SHOWER WAS NOT ATTACHED TO OUR MAIN SLEEPING AREA THEREFORE I HAD TO GO OUTSIDE AT DAWN AND WALK A FEW FEET TO THE BATHROOM AREA. THERE WERE TIMES WHEN I WOULD BRING A CANDLE WITH ME. I KNEW WHERE EVERYTHING WAS LOCATED.

I DON'T LIKE SLEEPING IN A DARK ROOM. A NIGHT LIGHT OR A SMALL LAMP AT NIGHT COMFORTS ME **I ENJOY READING MY HOLY BIBLE** BEFORE GOING TO SLEEP. I LISTEN TO GOSPEL WORSHIP MUSIC OR PREACHING SERMONS AS I LAY IN BED NOW.

I WAS A CONFIDENT AND BRAVE CHILD. MOTHER TAUGHT ME TO COOK WHEN I WAS ABOUT TEN YEARS OLD. I STARTED OFF BY PREPARING SIMPLE MEALS. IT IS OKAY TO ASSIGN CHILDREN SIMPLE CHORES AND TASKS THAT IS AGE APPROPRIATE BUT THESE ASSIGNMENTS SHOULD NOT DENY THEM AN EDUCATION OR SUNDAY SCHOOL CLASSES.

THE HOLY BIBLE STATES IN PSALM 34 VERSE 8: O TASTE AND SEE THAT THE LORD IS GOOD; HOW BLESSED IS THE MAN WHO TAKES REFUGE IN HIM! AMEN!

I AM AN EXCELLENT COOK NOW, I ONLY PREPARE MEALS BAKED OR BOILED TO AVOID HIGH CHOLESTEROL. I ENJOY COOKING MEALS OF DIFFERENT CULINARY VARIETY SUCH AS CARIBBEAN ISLAND NATION MEALS AND OTHER MULTICULTURAL ETHNIC MEALS: CURRY GOAT! **YEA MON! IT TASTE GOOD!** "YEA MON" IS ENGLISH

BASED CREOLE (PATOIS), WHICH MEANS "WE SAY YES IN AGREEMENT."

I INTENTIONALLY WANT TO SHOW THE **"MULTICULTURAL ETHNICITY IN FRANCE** AND OTHER REGIONS.

THE EXOTICNESS OF THE **FRENCH** CUISINE MENU SUCH AS FROG LEGS, ROAST DUCK, RABBIT AND (ESCARGOTS) SNAILS COOKED WITH BUTTER AND GARLIC GIVES THE FRENCH THREE COURSE MEALS INTERNATIONAL NOTORIETY.

I RELISH THE TASTE OF NORTH AMERICAN GREEN VEGETABLES SUCH AS SPINACH AND COLLARD GREENS YUM! YUM! YUMMY!

ST. LUCIA, ISLAND NATIONS CITIZENS AND RESIDENCE ARE A BEAUTIFUL PEOPLE; EXCELLENT, OLYMPIC MEDALIST, **LAUREATES,** BILINGUAL, CREATIVE, FRIENDLY, HUMBLE, **CHRISTIANS** WITH A BEAUTIFUL HISTORY. **ENGLISH BASED CREOLE (PATOIS):** "DEM SEY WI DIS AN DEM SEY WI DAT," TRANSLATED MEANING: "THEY SAY WE ARE LIKE THIS, THEY SAY WE ARE LIKE THAT." **FRENCH BASED CREOLE (PATOIS):** YO DI NOU SE TANKOU SA A, YO DI NOU SE TANKOU SA. TRANSLATED MEANING: "THEY SAY WE ARE LIKE THIS, THEY SAY WE ARE LIKE THAT.

1ST. JOHN 4 VERSES 20 AND 21: STATES, IF SOMEONE SAYS, "I LOVE GOD," AND HATES HIS BROTHER, HE IS A LIAR; FOR THE ONE WHO DOES NOT LOVE HIS BROTHER WHOM HE HAS SEEN, CANNOT LOVE GOD WHOM HE HAS NOT SEEN. (VERSE 21) AND THIS COMMANDMENT WE HAVE FROM HIM, THAT THE ONE WHO LOVES GOD SHOULD LOVE HIS BROTHER ALSO. AMEN!

I WAS BEAUTIFULLY MOLDED FOR MY FIRST THIRTEEN YEARS OF LIFE IN MY COUNTRY'S MATRIX, IT IS THE ENVIRONMENT WHERE I HAVE MY ORIGIN. **BOB MARLEY** THE SINGER SANG **"ONE LOVE ONE HEART LET US GET TOGETHER…"** IT IS **THE LOVE AND THE HEART** THAT I DESIRE TO EMPHASIZE IN THE BOB MARLEY'S SONG. **LOVE ALL PEOPLE.** AMEN!

I AM PROUD OF MY HERITAGE. MY FATHER AND HIS WIFE WERE BOTH FROM ST. LUCIA. THE LAWS OF **FRANCE** REGARDING IMMIGRATION, ADOPTION **AND MARRIAGE** WERE DIFFERENT WHEN I FIRST ARRIVED IN FRANCE. MY FATHER HAD TO FILTER ME THROUGH AN ADOPTION PROCESS SO I COULD JOIN HIM.

THE HOLY BIBLE BOOK OF ST. MATTHEW CHAPTER 7 VERSE 1 STATES: DO NOT JUDGE SO THAT YOU WILL NOT BE JUDGED.

THE HOLY BIBLE IN ST. MATTHEW 19 VERSE 19 TEACHES US TO: "…LOVE YOUR NEIGHBOUR AS YOURSELF". WE MUST WORK TOWARDS ERADICATING SHOOTINGS, UNTIMELY DEATHS AND VIOLENCE IN EVERY NATIONS EDUCATIONAL SCHOOL SYSTEM. AMEN!

THE HOLY SPIRIT CALLED ME TO BE THE "HEAD AND NOT THE TAIL".

***NOW I WILL SPEAK TO THOSE WHO COMMIT VIOLENCE AGAINST MANKIND'S HEAD. DO YOU KNOW WHO IS THE "GOD-HEAD" OF MAN'S HEAD? "WHAT IS HIS NAME? HE IS THE CREATOR OF HEAD TO TOE. EYES HIS! HIS EYES SEES. EYES HIS! HIS EYES SEES! EYES HIS, HIS EYES SEES. I AM, EYES HIS, EYES HIS, I AM, I AM, SEES ETERNALLY. AMEN!**

***THE DEADLY VIOLENCE AGAINST MANKIND MUST

STOP IMMEDIATELY. STOP! STOP! STOP! THE CUT, CUT, CUT, CUTTING OFF OF MAN'S HEAD **NOW**. AMEN!

THE HOLY BIBLE IN EXODUS 20 VERSE 13, STATES "YOU SHALL NOT MURDER". "I AM" JESUS CHRIST ALMIGHTY GOD, EYES HIS. I GAVE YOU EYES TO SEE, EYES HIS, SAYS THE LORD. AMEN!***

PRAYER

DEAR LORD JESUS CHRIST, I REPENT AND CONFESS MY SINS. HUMBLY I COME BEFORE YOUR THRONE OF GRACE MY LORD AND GOD TO INTERCEDE FOR THOSE HELD CAPTIVE BEING LED TO THE SLAUGHTER. I PRAY FOR THOSE BEHIND PRISON BARS, THOSE WHO HAVE BEEN <u>ABDUCTED</u> AND LOCKED UP IN METAL CAGES AGAINST THEIR WILL. I PRAY FOR GOD'S CHILDREN. I PRAY FOR JOURNALIST, PRIESTS AND PASTORS. I PRAY FOR PRESIDENTS AND PRIME MINISTERS. I PRAY FOR SALVATION, SAFETY AND PROTECTION FOR THEM. BLESS THEM WITH WISE DECISION MAKING SKILLS. <u>ABBA</u> FATHER HEAR THE VOICE OF THOSE WHO ARE CRYING OUT TO YOU RIGHT NOW AND EACH BLESSED DAY. PROTECT THE ABDUCTEE FROM PREMATURE DEATH. TURN BACK THE HANDS OF SATAN FROM THAT SOUL FATHER. LORD JESUS CHRIST <u>STOP</u> THE HANDS OF THE BEHEADERS, GIVE THEM A HEART OF LOVE AND COMPASSION. REMOVE HATE LORD. SWORD OF THE SPIRIT DELIVER. I PRAY FOR DIVINE INTERVENTION AND MIRACLE DELIVERANCE FOR THOSE TARGETED TO BE KILLED. HAVE MERCY <u>ABBA</u> FATHER, ANOINT BODIES, HANDS AND FEET TO DO THY WILL. SEND HOLY ANGELS TO OPEN CAGES AND

SET THE ABDUCTEE THE CAPTIVES FREE. IN JESUS NAME I PRAY TO MY HEAVENLY FATHER. AMEN!

CHRISTIAN INSPIRATIONAL.
TITLE: UNMASK THE MASKER.

THOSE WHO ARE BOUND BEING LED TO THE SLAUGHTER, HAVING TO FACE THE BLACK BALACLAVA MASKER.

MASKER CLAD IN BLACK A DEPICTION OF HELL. FREE THEM LORD INTERVENE DIVINELY, STIR UP THYSELF HOLY FATHER.

GOD OUR ETERNAL MASTER. UNMASK THE MASKER, JESUS YOU SEE INTO THEIR HEARTS. YOU KNOW THEIR BEGINNING BIRTH AND FINAL END.

THE COLOUR OF FIRE IS BLACK, ORANGE, BLUE, YELLOW AND SOME RED. BLOOD SHED. CHRIST BLOOD WAS POURED FLOWED TO THE GROUND, THEY NEVER HURT HIS HEAD.

HEAD OF THE CHURCH, HEAD OF MAN. THE DISCERNING WISE UNDERSTAND. ORANGE IS FOOD. FOOD **GOD** GAVE FOR MAN'S MOUTH THAT ENTERS HIS HEAD. JESUS OUR ETERNAL BREAD.

JOURNALIST, PRIEST, PASTORS AND GOD'S CHILDREN CRY ALOUD. RESIST SATAN WITH THE SWORD, GOD'S HOLY WORD. I PRAYED AND INTERCEDE FOR DIVINE DELIVERANCE AND GOD HEARD EVERY WORD. AMEN!

GROWING UP IN ST. LUCIA AT CHRISTMAS TIME, WAS VERY BEAUTIFUL. WE NEVER GET SNOW. MANY PEOPLE FLOCK TO THE BEACH WITH FAMILY AND FRIENDS AT **CHRISTMAS TIME.**

JUST ABOUT EVERYONE REMEMBERS THE TRUE MEANING OF **CHRISTMAS** AND FLOCK TO THE **CHRISTMAS EVE AND CHRISTMAS DAY** CHURCH SERVICE IN THEIR NEW CLOTHES TO **CELEBRATE THE VIRGIN BIRTH OF CHRIST.** CHILDREN WERE ADORNED WITH PRETTY RIBBONS, HAIR CLIPS AND SKILLFULLY BRAIDED HAIR.

CHRISTMAS IS NOT ABOUT THE BUN AND CHEESE. CHRISTMAS IS NOT ABOUT THE PRESENT UNDERNEATH THE **CHRISTMAS** TREE. MY HOME NOW IS BEAUTIFULLY DECORATED EVERY CHRISTMAS AND I HAVE PURPOSED IN MY HEART TO MAINTAIN THE AMBIANCE AND SPIRIT OF CHRISTMAS IN MY HOME THROUGHOUT EACH DAY OF THE YEAR. **I WILL LEAD** THE CHRISTMAS CELEBRATION SERVICES FOR MY MINISTRY BY THE GRACE OF GOD EACH BLESSED YEAR. AMEN!

JESUS CHRIST IS THE FREE GIFT, THE BEAUTIFUL PRESENT THAT ALL OF MANKIND MUST JOYFULLY RECEIVE EVERYDAY OF THE YEAR, NOT ONLY ON DECEMBER 25TH. WE MUST **NOT "EX" CHRIST OUT, IT IS NOT "EX"-MAS.** THE **HOLIDAY** IS ONLY **"HAPPY"** BECAUSE OF **JESUS CHRIST** AND THE **JOY** HE BRINGS. **AMEN!**

CHRISTMAS, CHRIST—MAS MEANS "CHRIST" FOR THE (MASS)ES. JESUS CHRIST IS THE REASON FOR THE SEASON. THE SPRING, SUMMER, FALL AND WINTER SEASON. WHEN YOU TRY TO REMOVE, OMIT, ERASE AND NULLIFY **JESUS CHRIST** FROM SOCIETY AND ORGANIZATIONS, IN LIKE MANNER **JESUS** ERASES YOUR NAME OUT OF HEAVEN'S LAMB BOOK OF LIFE AND WILL CAST YOU AWAY FROM HIS PRESENCE THEN SEND YOU

TO HELL ETERNALLY, **THE CHILDREN OF GOD AGREES. AMEN!**

REVELATION CHAPTER 20 VERSE 15: STATES. AND IF ANYONE'S NAME WAS NOT FOUND WRITTEN IN THE BOOK OF LIFE, HE WAS THROWN INTO THE LAKE OF FIRE.

SOME PEOPLE SAY DECEMBER 25TH. WAS NOT WRITTEN AS **JESUS CHRIST** BIRTHDAY IN THE **HOLY BIBLE.** WELL! WE CHRISTIANS CHOSE **A DAY** TO CELEBRATE **JESUS CHRIST BIRTH** AND TO HONOUR THE TRUTH OF HIS BIRTH. WE KNOW THAT **JESUS CHRIST** WAS BORN ON **A DAY.** THEREFORE WE WILL NOT DENY THE TRUE FACT THAT **JESUS** CAME FROM HEAVEN TO EARTH **BY A VIRGIN BIRTH TO SAVE US FROM SIN.**

MARY SAW **JESUS.** THE DISCIPLES SAW **JESUS.** THE **LAND OF ISRAEL** SAW AND MET **JESUS CHRIST THE SON OF GOD, JESUS CHRIST ALMIGHTY GOD, JESUS CHRIST THE HOLY SPIRIT. AMEN!**

THE **WISE MEN** SAW **JESUS CHRIST.** I TELL YOU THE **TRUTH** IT IS THE **21ST. CENTURY** AND **I HAVE SEEN JESUS CHRIST TOO. JESUS CHRIST** IS THE **HOLY SPIRIT** AND I HAVE SEEN **JESUS** IN MANY DIVINE VISIONS THAT HE GAVE TO ME OF HIMSELF. **JESUS CHRIST** LIVES ETERNALLY. THE FIRST VISION I HAD OF **JESUS CHRIST** WAS SHORTLY AFTER I WAS BAPTIZED AND BECAME A **BORN-AGAIN CHRISTIAN.**

I WAS ON THE CHURCH CHOIR AT A LOCAL NEIGHBOURHOOD CHURCH IN FRANCE. I WAS PRACTISING A SONG FOR THE CHURCH CHRISTMAS CANTATA AND THE **LORD** OPENED MY EYES IN THE SPIRIT AND REVEALED HIMSELF TO ME. THE VISION

OF **JESUS CHRIST** WAS SO BEAUTIFUL. I SAW **JESUS** AS A BRILLIANT WHITE BRIGHT LIGHT.

JESUS PRESENCE ILLUMINATES THE HEAVENS AND THE UNIVERSE, I COULD ONLY LOOK AT THE VISION OF **JESUS** WITH MY SPIRITUAL EYES. THE PHYSICAL NATURAL EYES OF MAN CANNOT LOOK AT SUCH BRIGHTNESS. **JESUS** IS BRIGHTER THAN THE SUN MANY TIMES.

THE SECOND **VISION OF CHRIST** I HAD WAS AT A CHURCH **PRAYER** MEETING. AFTER AN INTENSIFIED ANOINTED PRAYER MEETING, I STOOD WITH MY BACK AGAINST THE WALL OF THE **SANCTUARY** AND WAS RESTING AND THE LORD OPENED MY **SPIRITUAL EYES** AND REVEALED HIMSELF TO ME ONCE AGAIN. I SAW **JESUS CHRIST AS A FIRE**.

WHEN I SAW CHRIST AS A **FIRE** HE SAID TO ME, **I AM** ABOUT TO COME, **I AM** VERY CLOSE TO APPEARING, TO REVEAL MYSELF TO MANKIND BUT BECAUSE SO MANY ARE STILL UNSAVED, I AM HOLDING MYSELF BACK AND BEING PATIENT, **I AM** GIVING MANKIND MORE TIME TO REPENT AND TURN TO ME." **GOD** IS **LOVE,** MERCIFUL, PATIENT AND KIND. AMEN!

THE THIRD VISION I HAD OF **CHRIST** WAS WHEN I SAW HIM ABOVE THE EARTH IN THE HEAVENS WALKING THROUGH THE ATMOSPHERE TO AND FRO LIKE FLASHES OF LIGHTENING, THE LORD PLACED IN MY HEART AND SPIRIT THAT DAY, TO MAKE HASTE, TO HURRY AND MOVE FORWARD TO **TEACH MANKIND HIS WORDS, HIS WISDOM.** HALLELUJAH! AMEN!

2ND PETER 3 VERSE 8, STATES. BUT DO NOT LET THIS ONE FACT ESCAPE YOUR NOTICE BELOVED, THAT

WITH THE LORD ONE DAY IS LIKE A THOUSAND YEARS AND A THOUSAND YEARS LIKE A DAY. AMEN!

*** THE WILL OF **GOD** IS FOR EVERY MAN TO GET TO KNOW HIM. **GOD** WANTS YOU TO REPENT AND CONFESS YOUR SINS TO HIM NOW AND **GET BAPTIZE THE JOHN THE BAPTIST WAY,** IN THE NAME OF THE **FATHER,** THE **SON** AND THE **HOLY SPIRIT.** AMEN!

EZEKIEL CHAPTER 1 VERSE 1 STATES: NOW IT CAME ABOUT IN THE THIRTIETH YEAR, ON THE FIFTH DAY OF THE FOURTH MONTH, WHILE I WAS BY THE RIVER CHEBAR AMONG THE EXILES, THE HEAVENS WERE OPEN AND I SAW VISIONS OF GOD.

HEBREWS CHAPTER 12 VERSE 29 STATES: FOR OUR GOD IS A CONSUMING FIRE.

PRAYER.

DEAR LORD JESUS CHRIST, HUMBLY I COME BEFORE YOU NOW, TO REPENT AND CONFESS ALL OF MY SINS TO YOU, I THANK YOU LORD THAT YOUR WILL FOR ME IS TO KNOW YOU PERSONALLY AS MY LORD AND SAVIOUR. I WANT TO GET BAPTIZE THE JOHN THE BAPTIST WAY, IN THE NAME OF THE FATHER, THE SON AND THE HOLY SPIRIT. GUIDE ME FOR MY BAPTISM TO THE NEAREST TRUE BORN AGAIN CHURCH SO THAT I CAN BECOME A BORN AGAIN CHRISTIAN. IN JESUS NAME I PRAY TO MY HEAVENLY ABBA FATHER. AMEN.

ST. MATTHEW 3 VERSES 13 AND 16 STATES: THEN JESUS ARRIVED FROM GALILEE AT THE JORDAN COMING TO JOHN, TO BE BAPTIZED BY HIM. (VERSE 16) AFTER BEING BAPTIZED, JESUS "CAME UP" IMMEDIATELY FROM THE WATER; AND BEHOLD, THE

HEAVENS WERE OPENED, AND HE SAW THE SPIRIT OF GOD DESCENDING AS A DOVE AND LIGHTING ON HIM.

***THE TRUTH THAT JESUS **"CAME UP"** OUT OF THE WATER AT THE JORDAN RIVER, IS A TESTIMONY THAT JESUS CHRIST WAS NOT SPRINKLED WITH WATER ON HIS FOREHEAD, HE WENT DOWN IN THE JORDAN RIVER THEN **"CAME UP."**

BAPTISM MUST ONLY BE DONE THE **JOHN THE BAPTIST WAY BY FULL IMMERSION IN A BODY OF WATER. THERE MUST NOT BE <u>VARIOUS WAYS</u> FOR WATER BAPTISM. JESUS CHRIST** WAS BAPTIZE TO SET THE PERFECT EXAMPLE FOR US TO FOLLOW.

WHEN WE FOLLOW **JESUS** WE ARE IN THE RIGHT WAY. FOLLOWING **JESUS** WAY MAKES US **RIGHT** WITH **GOD. JESUS** MAKES US **RIGHT**EOUS BEFORE HIM.

JESUS WAS NOT BAPTIZE BECAUSE HE HAD TO REPENT AND CONFESS ANY SINS. **JESUS** IS THE ONE WHO FORGIVES US AND SAVES MANKIND FROM SIN. PLEASE REMEMBER THIS DIVINE **TRUTH. JESUS CHRIST** WAS BORN TO SAVE MANKIND FROM SIN. AMEN!

ST. MATTHEW CHAPTER 1 VERSE 21: SHE WILL BEAR A SON; AND YOU SHALL CALL HIS NAME JESUS, FOR HE WILL SAVE HIS PEOPLE FROM THEIR SIN.

NOW REGARDING **CHRISTMAS DAY, DECEMBER 25TH.** AND THE BIRTH OF **CHRIST,** I WANT TO EMPHASIZE THIS POINT IF THE **HOLY SPIRIT, THE HOLY BIBLE WORDS OF GOD** WERE TO GIVE US THE DATE THAT **JESUS** WAS BORN MANKIND WOULD CALCULATE AND SAY THAT WE KNOW HOW OLD **GOD** IS AND TRY TO MAKE OURSELVES EQUAL WITH **GOD.**

DON'T ATTEMPT TO PRINT A BIRTH CERTIFICATE

FOR **ETERNAL ALMIGHTY GOD. THE HOLY BIBLE** IS NOT **GOD'S** AUTOBIOGRAPHY. **GOD** IS NOT TWO THOUSAND YEARS OLD. IF A "DATE" WAS GIVEN FOR **JESUS CHRIST** BIRTH SOME PEOPLE WOULD SAY **JESUS** IS AS OLD AS MY 6TH, GREAT,

GREAT, GREAT, GREAT, GREAT, GREAT, GREAT, GRANDFATHER. **JESUS CHRIST,** IS ETERNAL, WITHOUT AGE, THE ANCIENT OF DAYS. AMEN!

GOD GAVE ME THIS BOOK TO WRITE THEREFORE I HONOUR **GOD** WITH IT. **GOD** IS A PART OF EVERYTHING I DO. AMEN! **"I AM" THE AMEN."** SAYS THE **LORD.**

IT IS DIFFICULT TO AVOID NOSTALGIA ABOUT MY CHILDHOOD DAYS. I ENJOYED WALKING HOME FROM PRIMARY SCHOOL. HEAVY DOWN POURS OF RAIN FREQUENTLY ACCOMPANIED ME HOME, AFTER THE RAIN THE BEAUTIFUL **RAINBOW** WOULD SOMETIMES APPEAR. THE **RAINBOW** IS MADE BY **GOD.** COWS, DOGS AND GOATS WALKED ON THE SIDEWALKS JUST AS HUMAN BEINGS DID.

MANKIND NEEDS TO LEARN THE TRUE MEANING OF THE **RAINBOW.** THERE ARE SEVERAL SCRIPTURES IN THE **HOLY BIBLE** THAT TEACHES AND MAKES REFERENCE OF THE BRIGHT BEAUTIFUL, MULTICOLOURED **RAINBOW. GENESIS CHAPTER 9 VERSES 9 TO 17 EXPLAINS THE TRUE MEANING OF THE RAINBOW.**

GENESIS 9 VERSES 11 AND 13 STATES: "I ESTABLISH MY COVENANT WITH YOU; AND ALL FLESH SHALL NEVER AGAIN BE CUT OFF BY THE WATER OF THE FLOOD, NEITHER SHALL THERE AGAIN BE A FLOOD TO DESTROY THE EARTH." VERSE 13: I SET MY BOW IN THE CLOUD, AND IT SHALL BE FOR A SIGN OF A COVENANT BETWEEN ME AND THE EARTH.

GOD IS A COVENANT KEEPING **GOD**. A COVENANT IS AN **AGREEMENT OR PROMISE** AND **GOD** MADE A COVENANT PROMISE TO MANKIND, THE ANIMALS AND THE EARTH BY SAYING **"ALL FLESH SHALL NEVER AGAIN BE CUT OFF BY THE WATER OF THE FLOOD, NEITHER SHALL THERE AGAIN BE A FLOOD TO DESTROY THE EARTH."**

THIS IS WHAT THE **RAINBOW** SYMBOLIZES, THE **RAINBOW** IS A **SIGN SYMBOL** FROM **GOD** THAT **GOD** DISPLAYS TO MANKIND AFTER A **RAIN** SHOWER. **GOD** USES THE **RAINBOW** AS A REMINDER TO HIMSELF ABOUT THE COVENANT PROMISE HE MADE TO MANKIND, THE ANIMALS AND THE EARTH.

WHEN WE SEE THE **RAINBOW** AFTER THE **RAIN** WE MUST REMEMBER THAT IF **GOD** DOES NOT LIMIT THE LENGTH OF TIME THAT THE **RAIN** FALLS WE WOULD HAVE A **FLOOD. AMEN!**

GOD ALONE IS **WISE,** THERE IS NO **GOD** LIKE OUR **JESUS CHRIST. LUKE CHAPTER 2 VERSE 14 STATES: "GLORY TO GOD IN THE HIGHEST, AND ON EARTH PEACE AMONG MEN WITH WHOM HE IS PLEASED."** THE **LORD SPOKE** TO ME ONE DAY AND **SAID, "I AM WISDOM."**

WHEN IT RAINED I WOULD SOMETIMES MAKE PAPER BOATS FROM NEWSPAPER AND PLACED IT ON THE SURFACE OF THE WATER AND WATCHED IT FLOAT DOWN THE STREET ALONGSIDE THE SIDEWALK.

MY SISTER MARY AND I CUSTOMARILY WENT TO DO ERRANDS TOGETHER FOR OUR MOTHER MS. KAY, I TRIED TO RECALL CONVERSATIONS THAT MARY AND I HAD AS WE WALKED CLOSELY TOGETHER. I ALWAYS HUGGED MY SISTER MARY WHEN WE WENT ANYWHERE

TOGETHER. IF SHE WAS ON MY LEFT SIDE, MY LEFT HAND WAS STRETCHED ACROSS HER BACK AND RESTED ON HER LEFT SHOULDER.

THE HOLY SPIRIT HEARD MY HEARTS QUESTION REGARDING MY SISTER MARY AND **GOD** REMINDED ME THAT EVERY WORD THAT MANKIND UTTERS IN THIS LIFE IS REMEMBERED AND RECORDED BY **JESUS CHRIST. GOD DOES NOT FORGET. AMEN!**

GOD REPLIED TO ME AND SAID, **"ONE OF YOUR FREQUENT TOPIC OF DISCUSSION WITH YOUR SISTER AS YOU BOTH TRAVELLED ALONG IN THE HOT SUN WAS THE HEAT OF THE ROAD ASPHALT ON THE BOTTOM OF YOUR BARE FEET."**

MARY AND I HABITUALLY UTTERED, "HOWBEIT THAT THE SUN IS SO HOT." TRANSLATED IN CREOLE FRENCH, "MAKÒNEN KE SOLÈY LA SE CHO KONSA."

I AM IN AWE OF THE POWER OF **ALMIGHTY GOD JESUS CHRIST.** MANKIND, PLEASE LISTEN TO ME, PURPOSE IN YOUR HEART **NOW TO LOVE JESUS CHRIST,** HE HOLDS THE BREATH YOU BREATHE IN HIS ETERNAL HANDS.

JESUS CHRIST HOLDS THE UNIVERSE IN HIS POWERFUL MIGHTY HANDS. EACH TIME **GOD** SPEAKS TO ME HIS WORDS ARE **ETERNAL, DIVINE, HOLY, TRUE AND WISE WORDS.** AMEN!

IT WAS COMMON FOR CHILDREN TO BE BAREFOOTED DUE TO THE TROPICAL CLIMATE. I WOULD ONLY WEAR SHOES OR SLIP-

PERS WHEN I GO TO SCHOOL, WHEN I TAKE THE BUS OR WHEN I WENT SOMEWHERE IMPORTANT WITH MY MOTHER OR WITH AN ADULT. THE HOT ST.

LUCIAN TEMPERATURES ALLOWED ME TO WEAR LESS CLOTHING.

AFTER SCHOOL IN ST. LUCIA MY PLACE OF LEISURE AND REST WAS ON MY GRANDPARENT'S VERANDAH OR UNDERNEATH THE HUGE ACKEE TREE THAT HUNG OVER OUR PROPERTY. DOORS AND WINDOWS WERE NEVER LOCKED DURING THE DAY TIME, THEY WERE ONLY CLOSED AT NIGHTS.

I HAD A SAVINGS ACCOUNT AND A BANK BOOK WHEN I WAS IN PRIMARY SCHOOL. THE ST. LUCIAN MONETARY SYSTEM IS WELL ESTABLISHED WITH MANY LOCAL BANKS. THE AMERICAN DOLLAR IS USED IN THE ISLAND ALSO. SHARING WAS INCESSANT AND UNREMITTING AMONG MY FAMILY MEMBERS.

IN MY FAMILY NOTHING WAS THROWN AWAY THAT COULD BE USED. WHEN I DID OUTGREW AN ITEM OF CLOTHING IT WAS DONATED TO SOMEONE WHO WOULD WEAR IT. I LOVE MY SISTER MARY. MARY LIKES WORKING WITH HER HANDS.

FROM AN EAGLE'S BIRD EYE VIEW, I DELIGHTED MYSELF IN WHAT **GOD** CREATED WHEN I VIEWED THE MOUNTAINS OF ST. LUCIA, MOUNT GIMIE THE TALLEST, FROM A VOLCANIC ORIGIN IS COVERED WITH LUSH TROPICAL RAINFOREST. CURIOUS STEPS ON THE GROUND LEADS TO THE RAINFOREST ABODE. LAYERS AND BRANCHES OF LEAVES ENTWINED THE CLOSELY SPACED TREES.

ENTER THE WORLD OF THE EXOTIC PLANTS, ANIMALS AND BIRD SPECIES. OBSERVE THE DAZZLING MULTICOLOURED ST. LUCIAN PARROT. THE PARROT IS MAINLY GREEN IN COLOUR, HAS A BLUE FOREHEAD, TURQUOISED-GREEN CHEEK AND A RED BREAST.

THE ST. LUCIAN BIRD PERCHES ON WET TREE BRANCHES, FEEDS ON FRUITS AND NUTS THEN FLY TO NEARBY CHERRY TREES AND FILL IT'S UNIQUE BEAK WITH BRIGHT RED CHERRIES THAT **GOD** PROVIDES. THE BEAUTIFUL ST. LUCIAN PARROT IS FOUND NOWHERE ELSE IN THE WORLD AND IS KNOWN LOCALLY AS JACQUOT.

FERTILE BLESSED LANDSCAPE QUARTERS, FLORAL BLISS, FRUITFUL GARDENS AND THE CARIBBEAN SEA ARE ALL MASTERPIECES OF **GOD'S CREATION, WISDOM AND DESIGN.**

MOTHER CALLED WHILE I WAS PREPARING TO GO TO BED. SHE SENT ME A TEXT MESSAGE WITH MOTHER'S DAY GREETINGS A FEW DAYS AGO. "DO YOU REMEMBER LUCY? MY MOTHER ASKED ME. I VAGUELY REMEMBER THE "LUCY" THAT MY MOTHER MENTIONED.

I KNEW SHE WAS NOT REFERRING TO MY AUNT LUCY HER SISTER. "I DON'T REMEMBER HER VERY WELL." I ADMITTED TO MY MOTHER, EVEN THOUGH THE NAME WAS VERY FAMILIAR TO ME. I DID HAVE A FRIENDLY ACQUAINTANCE WITH THE NAME LUCY WHEN I WAS GROWING UP IN ST. LUCIA. "WHAT IS IT ABOUT LUCY? I ASKED MY MOTHER.

"EACH TIME LUCY SEES ME SHE ASKS ME ABOUT YOU, SHE WANTS TO KNOW HOW YOU ARE." I QUICKLY TRIED TO RECALL LUCY'S FACIAL FEATURES IN MY MIND.

BEFORE I COULD GIVE MY THOUGHTS ON LUCY MY MOTHER CONTINUED AND SHARED HER WEIGHT LOSS SUCCESS. "DO NOT REGAIN THE WEIGHT." I ENCOURAGED MY MOTHER.

THERE ARE MANY BENEFITS TO INCORPORATING

GINGER, LEMON, LIME AND GRAPEFRUIT INTO OUR DIET. I WAS VERY SUCCESSFUL LOSING WEIGHT ALSO BY DRINKING HOT GINGER TEA WITH LEMON JUICE TWO TO THREE TIMES PER DAY. BOILED EGGS ARE REGULAR PROTEINS INCLUDED IN MY DIET. I LIMITED MY SUGAR INTAKE AND DRANK MORE WATER.

I CONSUME MORE FRUITS AND VEGETABLES AT MEAL TIME AND USED MORE OATMEAL AND WHOLE WHEAT PRODUCTS. WHEN I WASH MY DISHES I HAVE THE OPTION OF USING THE DISHWASHER OR THE SINK. I HAVE TWO FAVOURITE DISH WASHING LIQUID, ONE THAT STATES ON THE LABEL, **"WITH LEMON"** AND THE OTHER LABEL DISPLAYS **"ANTIBACTERIAL."**

THE ONE WITH **LEMON REMOVES AND CUTS AWAY THE GREASE AND OIL** FROM THE DISHES. THIS IS WHY I KNOW THAT IF **I INGEST LEMON AND CITRUS FRUITS** IT WOULD GIVE ME THE SAME RESULTS OF REMOVING AND REDUCING SUBCUTANEOUS FAT UNDERNEATH MY SKIN AND VISCERAL FAT AROUND THE ORGANS IN MY BODY AND EVENTUALLY I WOULD LOSE WEIGHT. I WAS SUCCESSFUL, YOU WILL BE TOO, NOW TRY IT. I DON'T LIKE TO TRAVEL ANY DISTANCE TO GET TO A GYM SO I EXERCISE AT HOME TWO TO THREE TIMES PER WEEK FOR THIRTY MINUTES. I USE INDIVIDUAL TWO POUND ARM WEIGHT LIFTS, I DO MY SIT-UPS ON MY BED AND I WALK FIFTEEN MINUTES TO AND BACK FROM THE NEIGHBOURHOOD GROCERY STORE.

I INCORPORATED FOOT MUSCLE STRENGTHENING EXERCISE IN MY EXERCISE ROUTINE. I HAVE A **BEAUTIFUL** SMILE. I WAS VICTORIOUS WITH MY DIET AND EXERCISE. I HAVE MAINTAINED MY DESIRED ACHIEVED WEIGHT OF UNDER ONE HUNDRED AND SIXTY POUNDS. I DID

NOT HAVE TO PAY ANY ENORMOUS COST TO LOSE THE WEIGHT. I THANK **GOD**, AMEN!

"WISDOM DOES WHAT WISDOM SEES." I WAS PERSISTENT AND DISCIPLINED WITH MY DIET AND NEVER ALLOWED ANYONE TO ENTICE OR FORCE ME TO EAT WHAT I KNOW WAS UNHEALTHY FOR ME. HERE IS A VERSE IN THE **HOLY BIBLE THAT STATES IN LEVITICUS CHAPTER 4 VERSE 31: "THEN HE SHALL REMOVE ALL ITS FAT JUST AS THE FAT WAS REMOVED..." GOD** KNOWS BEST HOW TO TAKE CARE OF US. AMEN!

IT IS **GOD** WHO MADE THE GINGER, LIME, LEMON AND GRAPEFRUIT. TRUST **GOD.** EVERYTHING THAT **GOD** TAUGHT US IN THE **HOLY BIBLE** IS FOR OUR BENEFIT AND IT IS GOOD FOR ALL OUR DAYS. WHEN WE OBEY **BIBLE TEACHINGS** THEY LEAD TO ETERNAL LIFE. AMEN!

I REMEMBERED NOW THAT MY MOTHER TOLD ME THAT LUCY ASKS ABOUT ME SO I INTENTIONALLY INTERJECTED LUCY INTO OUR CONVERSATION. I SAID TO MOTHER, "IT WAS VERY KIND AND THOUGHTFUL OF LUCY TO ASK ABOUT ME." "HOW IS SHE DOING? "IS SHE MARRIED?

MOTHER KNEW MORE ABOUT LUCY THAN I EXPECTED TO HEAR. "I WILL PRAY FOR HER AND KEEP HER IN MY PRAYERS." I TOLD MY MOTHER. "I LOVE YOU MOTHER." I ALWAYS END MY CONVERSATIONS WITH MY MOTHER BY TELLING HER THAT I LOVE HER.

AFTER THAT PHONE CALL I THOUGHT ABOUT MY SON AND MY DAUGHTER AND WONDERED WHERE THEY ARE AND WHAT THEY ARE DOING. I HAVE BEEN UNABLE TO CONTACT THEM BY PHONE THEREFORE I DECIDED TO WRITE THEM A LETTER.

WHEN OBASI WAS SEVENTEEN YEARS OLD HE CAME TO VISIT ME IN THE EAST COAST FROM THE WEST COAST OF FRANCE. ONE DAY OBASI WOKE UP AND AFTER HAVING A SHOWER AND GETTING DRESSED FOR THE DAY HE BEGAN TO QUERY ME. "MOM, WHY DON'T YOU LEAVE THIS HOUSE AND MOVE TO OUR HOUSE AND LIVE WITH US." HE SAID, "YOU ARE MISSING, COME BACK TO DAD." I REPLIED TO MY SON, "THE DIVORCE IS FINAL PLUS I HAVE **ESTABLISHED MY BEAUTIFUL BORN AGAIN CHRISTIAN MINISTRY** AND I MUST ATTEND TO IT."

MANY THOUGHTS WERE IN MY MIND AT THAT TIME. I HAVE NEVER TOLD MY CHILDREN THE TRUE REASONS FOR OUR DIVORCE. I WANTED THEM TO BE HAPPY. I DECIDED TO SHOW MY WILLINGNESS AND DESIRE TO BE CLOSER TO THEM.

I TOLD OBASI, "IF IT IS **GOD'S** WILL I COULD SECURE MY OWN ACCOMMODATION IN WESTERN FRANCE JUST TO BE CLOSER TO YOU AND RENEE."

"WE HAVE SPACE FOR YOU IN OUR HOUSE." HE SAID, AS I WALKED TOWARDS THE KITCHEN TO MAKE BREAKFAST. OBASI WALKED BEHIND ME AND SAID, "MOM, WHY DON'T YOU BECOME A MUSLIM? IT WOULD BE BETTER FOR ALL OF US, WE COULD BECOME A FAMILY AGAIN."

AT THAT POINT I FELT **THE HOLY SPIRIT** PRESENCE EMBRACED ME AND I KNEW **GOD** WAS SAYING, THAT SATAN WILL NOT HAVE HIS WAY WITH YOU. I REMEMBER LOOKING AT OBASI AND TEARS SWELLED IN MY EYES AND I WANTED TO WEEP BUT I HELD BACK THE TEARS. HE WAS A YOUNG ADULT AND MY SON DID NOT KNOW **JESUS CHRIST** AS I DID.

AT SEVENTEEN YEARS OLD MY SON WAS MUCH

TALLER THAN I WAS. I HAD TO EXHUBERATE **CHRIST TO HIM, I HAD TO SHOW HIM JESUS LOVE AND COMPASSION** INSTEAD OF ARGUING AND DEBATING WITH MY SON ABOUT MY CHRISTIAN FAITH. "I AM" HIS MOTHER AND HIS **SPIRITUAL** MOTHER. SO **I USED WISDOM, DIVINE WISDOM,** IT WAS NEEDED NOW MORE THAN EVER.

IMMEDIATELY I REMEMBERED A FORMER CONVERSATION I HAD WITH OBASI ON THE TELEPHONE IN WHICH I DISCUSSED SALVATION AND EXPLAINED THE MEANING OF WATER BAPTISM TO HIM.

AFTER LISTENING TO MY TEACHING ON **SALVATION AND WATER BAPTISM,** OBASI HAD SAID, "I CAN **BAPTISE** MYSELF, I JUST HAVE TO GO TO THE MEDITERRANEAN BEACH AND DUNK MYSELF."

I REMINDED OBASI OF THAT FORMER CONVERSATION. I EXPLAINED TO HIM THE ORDINANCE OF WATER BAPTISM.

I TOLD HIM THAT HE CANNOT BAPTIZE HIMSELF BUT A BORN AGAIN PASTOR OR A BORN-AGAIN CHRISTIAN MUST BAPTIZE HIM.

THEY CAN EXPLAIN THE TRUE MEANING OF BAPTISM BY IMMERSION. THERE MUST BE A TESTIMONY IN THE SPIRIT. THE **BORN-AGAIN CHRISTIAN WHO SERVES JESUS CHRIST KNOWS AND COMMUNICATES WITH JESUS CHRIST IN THE SPIRIT AND IS A WITNESS OF HIS SPIRIT, PRESENCE AND TRUTH. AMEN!**

I CONTINUED TO ENCOURAGE MY SON OBASI I TOLD HIM, **"BAPTISM** CAN BE DONE ANYWHERE THERE IS A BODY OF WATER FOR FULL IMMERSION, LET ME BAPTIZE YOU IN THE BATHTUB UPSTAIRS, THIS

IS WHAT THE ENTIRE FAMILY NEEDS TO DO INSTEAD OF ME BECOMING A MUSLIM." OBASI LISTENED TO MY ENCOURAGEMENT THEN SAID, "MOM DO YOU KNOW HOW TO MAKE SCRAMBLED EGGS? "PLEASE MAKE ME SOME."

SCRAMBLE! SATAN SCRAMBLE! SCRAMBLE SATAN! LOUDER! SCRAMBLE! SCRAMBLE! PLEASE PRAY FOR MY SON OBASI AND MY DAUGHTER RENEE. GOD BLESS YOU AND THANK YOU.

JESUS LOVES YOU OBASI. JESUS LOVES EVERYONE. GOD LOVES THE WHOLE WORLD, GOD IS NOT PARTIAL, GOD DOES NOT HAVE FAVOURITES.

ABBA FATHER DOES NOT HATE PEOPLE. JESUS THE SON OF GOD MADE ALL OF MANKIND IN HIS IMAGE AND LIKENESS. GOD HATES SIN.

***SATAN IS SIN. GOD HATES THE DEVIL. SATAN USES PEOPLE TO COMMIT SIN AGAINST GOD, AGAINST THEMSELVES AND AGAINST THEIR FELLOW HUMAN BEINGS.

GOD PUNISHES SIN, (THE DEVIL) BECAUSE IT, (HE) HURTS US AND OTHER HUMAN BEING, SIN GRIEVES THE HOLY SPIRIT, GOD HAS A HEART. GOD IS A SPIRITUAL PERSON, THE HOLY SPIRIT.

JESUS CHRIST ALMIGHTY GOD LOVES YOU MANKIND, MAN, WOMAN AND CHILD. GET TO KNOW JESUS CHRIST AND EMBRACE HIS ETERNAL LOVE FOR YOU, WELCOME LOVE, DESIRE GOD'S LOVE, SEEK JESUS LOVE FOR YOU NOW. YOU ARE LOVED. AMEN!

RECENTLY DURING THE SUMMER TIME OBASI VISITED ME, HE JOURNEYED TO SEE ME AND HIS FATHER'S RELATIVES. HE TOOK ME SHOPPING AND

SAID, "MOM, BUY THE BEST, LOOK YOUR BEST, CHOOSE ANYTHING YOU WANT."

I LOVE MY SON OBASI VERY MUCH AND I DID NOT WANT HIM TO OVERSPEND, I WANTED OBASI TO SPEND WITHIN A BUDGET AND SAVE. I WANT MY CHILDREN TO LEARN AND DEVELOP WISE INVESTMENT FINANCIAL PRINCIPLES.

I WANTED TO BE AN EXCELLENT EXAMPLE TO MY SON THEREFORE I DECIDED TO CHOOSE QUALITY AND DURABLE CLOTHING ITEMS TO BUY. I WAS FILLED WITH JOY ON THIS PARTICULAR DAY BECAUSE WHEN OBASI ARRIVED I WAS WAITING ON THE **LORD** TO GIVE ME INSTRUCTIONS REGARDING MOVING.

GOD BLESSED MY CHILDREN WITH EMPLOYMENT. OBASI IS VERY VOCAL AND SHARES HIS THOUGHTS WITHOUT RESERVATIONS. I LOVE YOU RENEE. RENEE ANSWERS TO QUESTIONS WHEN I ASK. THIS IS A DIFFERENCE THAT I OBSERVE ABOUT MY SON AND DAUGHTER.

I LOVE BOTH OF MY CHILDREN AND SOMETIMES THE THINGS THEY SHARE REALLY TOUCHES MY HEART. ONE DAY OBASI SAID TO ME, "MOM, WHEN YOU WERE NOT WITH US EVERY DAY, RENEE HELPED ME."

I THANK **GOD** THAT HE GAVE RENEE THE WISDOM TO KNOW WHAT TO DO FOR OBASI. I TOLD RENEE THAT OBASI SHARED THIS WITH ME. I ALSO TOLD HER HOW MUCH I LOVED HER BECAUSE SHE WAS MY DAUGHTER AND SHE SHOWED LOVE TOWARDS HER BROTHER.

RENEE I BLESS YOU AGAIN FOR YOUR KINDNESS AND LOVE TOWARDS YOUR BROTHER OBASI. MAY JESUS CHRIST IN HIS LOVE AND MERCY REMEMBER

YOU BOTH WITH HIS BLESSED SALVATION, ETERNAL LIFE. AMEN!

I WANT THE BEST FOR BOTH RENEE AND OBASI. **JESUS CHRIST IS THE BEST** I CAN GIVE TO THEM, NOT SILVER AND GOLD. OBASI **IS EXCELLENT** WITH TECHNOLOGY AND LIKES PHOTOGRAPHY AND SHOWED ME SOME PICTURES HE TOOK ON HIS CELL PHONE.

OBASI WAS FASHIONABLY DRESSED, HE WORE DESIGNER QUALITY CLOTHES THE LAST VISIT I HAD WITH HIM. **I AM** PROUD OF MY SON. WHEN I ASKED HIM ABOUT ONE PARTICULAR PHOTOGRAPH THAT HE SHOWED ME, HE REPLIED, "MOM THE GIRLS LIKE IT THAT WAY."

I KEPT SILENT, WITH GOOD REASONS. **I AM** GLAD **HE WANTS TO ATTRACT GIRLS.** MY SON IS TALL AND HANDSOME, HE IS A YOUNG MAN NOW.

OBASI AND I HAD AN INTIMATE DIALOGUE A FEW YEARS AGO AND HE TOLD ME, "MOM I WANT TO GET MARRIED AND HAVE A DAUGHTER AND NAME HER CHRISTIAN JUST LIKE YOU."

THAT IS A WONDERFUL DESIRED PLAN AND NAME CHOICE." I ENCOURAGED HIM.

SOME PEOPLE ARE NAMED AFTER BEAUTIFUL FLOWERS LIKE A ROSE, LILLY, PETUNIA OR PRIMROSE. MICHAEL THE ARCHANGEL WAS SENT FROM **GOD. I AM** CLOSE TO **GOD.** I PRAYED TO **JESUS CHRIST ALMIGHTY GOD** AND ASKED HIM TO BLESS OBASI WITH THE DESIRES OF HIS HEART. AMEN!

"I AM" NOT AFRAID, "I AM" A LEADING PASTOR. I WILL NOT INCORPORATE FEAR INTO MY HEART. I UPHOLD JESUS CHRIST NAME, JESUS CHRIST UPHOLDS

ME. I ONLY KNOW THE POWER OF GOD MANIFESTED IN MY LIFE. JESUS ALWAYS TELLS ME "DO NOT BE AFRAID." GOD SPOKE TO ME DIRECTLY AND IT SHALL BE KNOWN..." THAT THE SON OF GOD GAVE ME WISDOM TO RELEASE TO MANKIND. I HUMBLY EMBRACE RECOGNITION FOR THE WISDOM GOD TAUGHT ME... WISDOM OVERIDES FEAR. DO NOT FEAR CHURCH, ONLY PRAY AND BELIEVE IN GOD'S ETERNAL POWER. AMEN!

MY SPIRITUAL GIFT OF DISCERNMENT EMPOWERS ME TO **KNOW AND AVOID.** DIVINE INSIGHT LETS ME UNDERSTAND IN THE SUPERNATURAL. **HOLY ANGELS** SURROUNDS ME. **LAWS,** JUSTICE AND SAFETY FOR INDIVIDUALS WORLDWIDE MUST BE UPHELD. AMEN!

CHAPTER 3

YOUNG ADULTHOOD

MY YOUNG ADULTHOOD, PUBERTY STARTED AT THE AGE OF TWELVE YEARS OLD. WHEN I ARRIVED IN FRANCE AT THE AGE OF THIRTEEN YEARS OLD THE WARM AMBIANCE OF THE **CHRISTMAS SPIRIT** WELCOMED ME IN MY FATHER'S HOME AS I EMBRACED MY NEW FRENCH ENVIRONMENT.

I REMEMBERED I HAD DISTRIBUTED THE GIFTS THAT MOTHER SENT ME WITH. SOME OF THE GIFTS WERE BAKED BY ONE OF OUR NEIGHBOUR IN ST. LUCIA. EVERYONE WAS HAPPY, THANKFUL AND ENJOYED THEM.

THE GIFTS WERE WRAPPED AND PLACED IN A BEAUTIFUL HAND CRAFTED STRAW BASKET. THE BASKET HAD A HANDLE. **CHRISTMAS DAY** WAS COLD. THERE WAS SNOW ON THE GROUND. THE BALCONY RAILS WERE COVERED WITH SNOW.

MY FATHERS HOME WAS BRIGHTLY LIT. THE DINING TABLE WAS PREPARED FOR OUR **CHRISTMAS** MEAL. WE GATHERED AT THE TABLE. I SAT HUMBLY WITH BOTH HANDS ON MY KNEES WAITING PATIENTLY THEN

PARTICIPATE IN THE BLESSED MEAL THAT **GOD** HAD PROVIDED FOR OUR FAMILY.

MY FORMATIVE YOUNG ADULT YEARS WERE DEVELOPED IN FRANCE AND MEXICO IT IS AT THIS AGE THAT A CHILD BEGINS TO TAKE ON THE FORMATION OF ADULTHOOD. THEIR VOICE CHANGES, GIRLS BEGIN TO APPEAR PEAR SHAPED AND HAIR GROWTH BEGINS IN VARIOUS PLACES.

A **GIRLS MAMMARY GROWTH BEGINS TO PROTRUDE** AND HER MENSTRUAL CYCLE USUALLY BEGINS AT THIS TIME. BOYS SOMETIMES GROWS A BEARD. I REMEMBER THE FIRST TIME I HEARD MY SON SAY, "MOM I NOW HAVE A BEARD."

WHEN **GOD** MADE THE FIRST HUMAN BEINGS HE MADE THEM AS ADULTS. ADAM AND EVE WERE CREATED AS ADULTS NOT AS BABIES, SO THAT THEY COULD QUICKLY REPRODUCE AND MULTIPLY AND POPULATE THE EARTH. I WILL REPEAT THIS TRUTH, **GOD** DID NOT MAKE ADAM AND EVE AS BABIES. AMEN!

GENESIS CHAPTER 1 VERSE 27: STATES. GOD CREATED MAN IN HIS OWN IMAGE IN THE IMAGE OF GOD HE CREATED HIM MALE AND FEMALE.

YOUNG ADULT NEEDS LESS PHYSICAL HANDS ON CARE FROM THEIR PARENTS. AT TWELVE YEARS OF AGE I COULD COMB MY OWN HAIR, CHOOSE MY CLOTHING TO WEAR, SELECT MY SCHOOL FRIENDS, DRESS MYSELF, WASH MY OWN CLOTHING AND MAKE MY OWN SIMPLE MEALS.

IT IS A BEAUTIFUL TIME TO DISCOVER YOUR **TRUE SELF AND IDENTITY.** AS YOU GO THROUGH THE TRANSITION FROM DEPENDENCE TO INDEPENDENCE.

THINK ABOUT THE DAY YOU WERE BORN, THE **GENDER** YOU WERE BORN WITH IS YOUR TRUE IDENTITY. YOUR TRUE SELF IS YOUR SOUL, YOUR **SOUL** IS YOU **ETERNALLY.**

YOUR PHYSICAL **ANATOMY** IS THE PERSON WHO **GOD** CREATED YOU TO BE ON THIS EARTH; IT IS **PHYSICALLY** YOU **EX**TERNALLY. YOUR **SOUL IS** THE **INVISIBLE PART** OF YOU LIKE THE OXYGEN BREATH YOU BREATHE. OXYGEN IS INVISIBLE WITHIN EVERY LIVING HUMAN BEING WE CANNOT LIVE WITHOUT IT.

GOD DETERMINES WHO YOU ARE AND WHO YOU WERE GOING TO BE BEFORE HE CREATED THE EARTH AND THE UNIVERSE. WHO YOU ARE DID NOT BEGIN IN YOUR MIND OR THINKING AFTER YOU WERE BORN. YOU DID NOT MAKE YOURSELF, OUR LIFE CAME FROM **JESUS CHRIST ALMIGHTY GOD.**

THE WILL, POWER, MIND, AND SOVEREIGN THOUGHTS OF JESUS CHRIST ALMIGHTY GOD PREDETERMINED AND DETERMINED OUR BEING AND EXISTENCE. AMEN!

YOUR MOTHER AND FATHER HAD NOTHING TO DO WITH YOU, **JESUS CHRIST ALMIGHTY GOD** HAD EVERYTHING TO DO WITH YOU. AMEN!

THERE ARE TWO SPIRITUAL THOUGHT PATTERNS. THE FIRST IS **DIVINE AND GODLY** THOUGHTS. KIND, LOVING, AND PEACEFUL THOUGHTS ARE THOUGHTS THAT LETS YOU LOVE YOUR NEIGHBOUR AS YOURSELF. **GODLY** THOUGHTS ENCOURAGES YOU TO LOVE AND PROTECT YOURSELF AND YOUR BODY.

THE SECOND THOUGHT PATTERN IS UNGODLY, EVIL AND WICKED. SATANIC THOUGHTS ENCOURAGES HUMAN BEINGS TO HARM THEMSELVES, DESTROY

PEOPLE AND THINGS. EVIL THOUGHTS ARE DESTRUCTIVE AND SELF DESTRUCTIVE.

GET A FULL LENGTH MIRROR AND LOOK AT YOUR REFLECTION IN THE MIRROR. YOU ARE BEAUTIFULLY MADE IN THE IMAGE OF **GOD.** YOU RESEMBLE YOUR PARENTS BUT YOU ARE CREATED IN THE IMAGE OF **GOD.**

JESUS CHRIST WAS BORN AS A **HUMAN BEING.** YOU WERE BORN AS A **HUMAN BEING,** YOU LOOK LIKE **JESUS CHRIST** AS A **HUMAN BEING,** YOU WERE NOT BORN LOOKING LIKE A CHIMPANZEE.

EACH SPECIES ON EARTH PRODUCES IT'S OWN KIND. MANKIND DID NOT EVOLVE FROM PRIMATE MONKEYS. EVOLUTION IS A LIE FROM THE DEVIL. AMEN! IT WAS NOT YOUR PARENTS WHO CREATED, KNITTED, JOINED AND CONNECTED YOUR BODY PARTS IN YOUR MOTHERS WOMB, IT WAS **GOD. JESUS CHRIST** DID THE MIRACULOUS WORK ON YOU. AMEN!

"WHICH MAN ON EARTH CAN MAKE THE HUMAN BODY OR BRAIN? NO MAN CAN! AMEN!

GOD SPOKE TO ME RECENTLY ABOUT **MAN**-NEQUINS, THOSE **THREE** DIMENSIONAL REPRESENTATION OF THE HUMAN FORM DISPLAYED IN STORES. **GOD SAID, "THOSE WHO MAKE THEM MAKE THEM!** ANOTHER DAY, **GOD SAID, "THEY WILL NEVER MOVE IN STORES."** AMEN!

GOD CREATED **MAN**KIND WITH A SOUL, SPIRIT, AND A BODY. YOU WERE CREATED AS **THREE** IN ONE, HAVING ONE BODY. **GOD IS THREE IN ONE, FATHER, SON AND HOLY SPIRIT.** TRUTH IS PARALLEL. AMEN! THE CREATED **HUMAN BODY** IS NOT A STATIONARY MANNEQUIN DUMMY. AMEN!

AN EGG FOR EXAMPLE HAS THE OUTER EGG SHELL, THE EGG WHITE AND THE YELLOW YOKE. ALL **THREE** PARTS MAKE UP **ONE** WHOLE EGG.

LIFE IS WITHIN THE EGG. **GOD IS TRIUNE THREE IN ONE** FROM THE **HOLY BIBLE BOOK OF GENESIS TO REVELATION. AMEN! ETERNAL LIFE IS GOD, MAN'S LIFE IS FROM GOD. AMEN!**

HERE IS ANOTHER EXAMPLE: AN **ORANGE** HAS THE ORANGE OUTER SKIN, THE JUICE AND THE ORANGE SEED. THE ORANGE IS **THREE IN ONE**. AMEN! TAKE A CLOSER LOOK AT THE MAPLE LEAF FOUND IN SEVERAL REGIONS OF THE WORLD.

TRAVEL SOUTHEAST OF FRANCE TO CAMPOBASSO ITALY AND THERE IS A HUGE VARIETY OF MAPLE TREES. IT IS ONE LEAF WITH THREE SEPARATED SERRATED DESIGN IN THE ONE LEAF. **GOD** REVEALS HIMSELF IN THE THINGS HE CREATES.

THE **HOLY TRINITY** IN UNITY, OUR TRIUNE **THREE IN ONE GOD** DISPLAYS HIMSELF AND HIS POWER BY CREATING CREATION AS THREE IN ONE. THIS IS UNDEBATABLE! IRREFUTABLE WISDOM! AMEN!

SCIENTIST HAVE TO BEGIN WITH AN **ORIGINAL** ORGANISM OR ITEM IN ORDER TO GENETICALLY MODIFY IT. TO MODIFY MEANS TO ALTAR OR CHANGE SOME ASPECT, QUALITY OR FORM OF SOMETHING.

GOD MADE EVERYTHING **"ORIGINALLY PERFECT"**. MEN WERE MADE WITH SPERMS AND **ORANGES** WERE MADE WITH SEEDS. "ARE THE SCIENTIST AND DOCTORS ATTEMPTING TO CHALLENGE AND COMPETE WITH OUR **GOD AND CREATOR?** EVERYTHING MANKIND WANTS TO KNOW AND DISCOVER **GOD ETERNALLY KNOWS.**

TURN TO **GOD**, PRAY TO **GOD**, ASK **GOD**, SEEK **GOD**, **ALL WISDOM AND TRUTH IS FROM JESUS CHRIST ALMIGHTY GOD. AMEN!**

CHILDREN MUST BE TAUGHT SPIRITUAL WISDOM AT SUNDAY SCHOOL AND AT HOME IF THEIR PARENTS ARE TRULY **BORN AGAIN CHRISTIANS.**

CHILDREN SHOULD NOT BE DENIED THEIR **GOD GIVEN RIGHTS TO PRAY AT SCHOOL.** YES! MY SPIRITUAL LIFE BUDDED WHEN I WAS A SUNDAY SCHOOL CHILD. WHEN I WAS A YOUNG ADULT MY **MAJOR CONCERN IN SCHOOL** WAS PASSING MY TEST AND EXAMS.

AT PRIMARY SCHOOL IN ST. LUCIA BOYS AND GIRLS OFTEN STAND IN ROWS AND LINES. PRAYING WAS A PART OF OUR UPBRINGING. BOYS BEGAN SHOWING INTEREST IN ME IN MY TEENAGE YEARS AND MY STEP-BROTHER HAD A FIFTEEN YEAR OLD FRIEND NAMED SOLOMON. SOLOMON LIKED ME. MY FATHER HAD A TOTAL OF TWO STEP-CHILDREN.

SOLOMON WAS SPANISH, TWO YEARS OLDER THAN I AND WAS GOOD LOOKING. SOLOMON INVITED ME TO HIS MOTHER'S HOUSE FOR A FAMILY CELEBRATION ONCE AND HIS MOTHER INSISTED THAT WE WERE NOT TO BE ALONE UPSTAIRS IN SOLOMON'S BEDROOM.

MY FATHER'S WIFE DID NOT LIKE SOLOMON. SHE CRITICIZED HIM AND SHE WAS NOT LOVING AND KIND TOWARDS ME EITHER. MY STEPMOTHER DID NOT LOVE ME.

MY STEPMOTHER REGULARLY WOKE ME FROM SLEEP AT NIGHTS TO COMB HER HAIR. MY FATHER ALSO WORKED FULL TIME NIGHT SHIFTS.

I REMEMBER ONCE DURING A HEATED ARGUMENT WITH MY FATHER, MY STEPMOTHER YELLED AT MY

FATHER AND SAID, "SEND HER BACK TO ST. LUCIA! SHE WANTED MY FATHER TO RETURN ME TO ST. LUCIA. I FELT LIKE CINDERELLA.

GOD DOES EMBRACE THE REJECTED AND THE UNLOVED. **GOD** EMBRACES ME. **GOD** GAVE MY FATHER WISDOM. I WAS CONFERRED A FRENCH CITIZENSHIP. MY FATHER MUST HAVE FELT THE ANGUISH THAT **ABRAHAM** FELT WHEN HE HAD TO SEND HAGAR AWAY WITH **ISHMAEL** HIS SON FROM THE PRESENCE OF SARAH HIS WIFE. **HOLY BIBLE VERSE OF GENESIS CHAPTER 21 VERSE 11 STATES: THE MATTER DISTRESSED ABRAHAM GREATLY BECAUSE OF HIS SON.**

THE DIFFERENCE WAS THAT I WAS **GOD'S CHOSEN CHILD** AND NOT THE OUTCAST. **GOD CHOSE ME TO HONOUR HIM BEFORE I WAS FORMED IN MY MOTHER'S WOMB.**

GOD SELECTED ME FROM THE CROWD. JESUS CHRIST CALLED ME INTO THE HIGHEST DIVINE CALLING JUST LIKE MOSES. AMEN!

GOD SENT A DISTANCE RELATIVE OF MY FATHER FROM MEXICO TO VISIT US WHEN THERE WAS UNCERTAINTY REGARDING OUR FAMILY UNION IN MY FATHER'S HOUSE.

SOLOMON AND I WOULD SIT ON THE GRASS OUTSIDE THE BACK OF OUR CONDOMINIUM BUILDING DURING THE SUMMER TIME AND ENJOYED EACH OTHERS COMPANY. WE ROLLED ON THE GRASS, WE LAUGHED AND SMILED AT EACH OTHER. SOLOMON WAS MY YOUNG ADULT COMPANION HE MADE ME FEEL LOVED AND I REMAINED A VIRGIN WHILE I WAS SOLOMON'S FRIEND.

I WAS ALLOWED TO VISIT MY SCHOOL FRIENDS ANGÈLE AND ARIEL OCCASIONALLY BUT I WAS NEVER ALLOWED TO STAY AT THEIR HOMES OVERNIGHT OR ON THE WEEKENDS. MY FATHER ASKED ME ONE DAY, "CHRISTIAN, WOULD YOU LIKE TO SPEND SOME TIME IN MEXICO WITH MY RELATIVES? "YES! I WOULD." I AGREED TO MY FATHER'S QUESTION.

I SPENT SEVERAL YEARS IN MEXICO ON TWO SEPARATE OCCASION WITH MY FATHERS RELATIVES AND LIVING INDEPENDENTLY ON MY OWN. ONE OF MY FAVOURITE CITY IS MEXICO CITY.

THE CHRISTIAN FAITH IS NUMBER ONE (NÚMERO UNO) IN MEXICO. I DID MISS MY DAD AND WROTE HIM LETTERS AND HE DID SEND ME MONEY FOR MY NEEDS. I ATTENDED **HIGH SCHOOL IN MEXICO** AND WAS ENROLLED IN A VOLUNTARY CADET SERVICE TRAINING COURSE.

IN EVERY SCHOOL SYSTEM THERE SHOULD ONLY BE **ACADEMIC** EMPHASIS IN THE SCHOOL CURRICULUM. THERE IS A CORRELATION BETWEEN WHAT STUDENTS ARE TAUGHT, TRAIN TO DO AND HOW STUDENTS BEHAVE TOWARDS PARENTS, AUTHORITIES AND SCHOOL OFFICIALS.

STUDENTS MUST NOT LEARN COMBAT AND HOW TO HANDLE WEAPONS IN AN **ACADEMIC** SETTING. THIS WILL LESSEN THE PARALLELISM AND INTERCONNECTION BETWEEN SCHOOLS AND HAND GUN VIOLENCE.

THE VIOLENCE THAT IS PERPETRATED IN MANY SCHOOLS IS DEMONIC. IT IS A DESTROYING SPIRIT SENT INTO SCHOOLS TO KILL BECAUSE THERE IS **NO PRAYER PROTECTIVE COVERAGE INTERNALLY OR POLICY THAT IS EFFECTIVE TO PROTECT** SCHOOL CHILDREN AND

STAFF. ANOINT YOUR SCHOOL PROPERTY WITH OLIVE OIL AND REINSTATE PRAYERS. PRAYER HELPS EVERYONE ESPECIALLY WHEN VIOLENCE IS OCCURRING. AMEN!

THE MURDEROUS COMBATIVE DEADLY ATTITUDE OF MANY INDIVIDUALS AND STUDENTS IN SOCIETY WITH ACCESS TO HANDGUNS WOULD DIMINISH IF THEY WERE **DRILLED** FIRST WITH THE **HOLY BIBLE COMMAND**-MENTS SUCH AS: **EXODUS 20 VERSE 13: "YOU SHALL NOT MURDER." AND LEVITICUS 19 VERSE 18: "YOU SHALL LOVE YOUR NEIGHBOUR AS YOURSELF." AMEN!**

***RECENTLY **JESUS CHRIST, THE HOLY SPIRIT SPOKE TO ME AND SAID, "I HAVE AFFLICTED AMERICA BECAUSE THEY HAVE TURNED THEIR BACKS ON ME,"** ***

A POSITIVE LOVING RECIPROCAL RELATIONSHIP IS NEEDED BETWEEN **GOD** AND MANKIND. LET ME REMIND EVERYONE OF **GOD'S TRUTH: GOD IS LOVE. GOD** HAS A HEART, **GOD** IS THE **HOLY SPIRIT, GOD IS A SPIRIT PERSON. GOD DESIRES FOR MANKIND TO LOVE HIM, BECAUSE HE FIRST LOVES US.** AMEN!

LET THIS AMERICAN MOTTO, **"IN GOD WE TRUST," REMAIN WRITTEN ON EVERY HEART. GOD** WE LOVE AND **GOD WE TRUST. AMEN!**

WHEN YOU LIVE IN A MULTI-CULTURAL SOCIETY WITH DIFFERENT FAITH BELIEFS DO NOT QUICKLY GET RID OF **YOUR OWN FAITH BELIEFS** TO ACCOMMODATE THEM. LEAVE THE DOOR OPEN TO FREEDOM TO **CHOOSE.** LET EVERYONE SERVE THEIR CHOSEN **GOD** AND **REMEMBER** ON WHAT FAITH OUR NATION WAS BUILD, BECAME STRONG AND WAS ALWAYS VICTORIOUS. LET EVERYONE REMEMBER, **"IN GOD, THE HOLY BIBLE WE TRUST STILL." AMEN!**

ST. JOHN 3 VERSE 16 STATES: "FOR GOD SO LOVE THE WORLD, THAT HE GAVE HIS ONLY BEGOTTEN SON, THAT WHOEVER BELIEVES IN HIM SHALL NOT PERISH BUT HAVE ETERNAL LIFE".

DON'T EVER SAY, "IF **GOD** DID **LOVE** ME I WOULD NOT HAVE THAT BAD EXPERIENCE." **GOD LOVES** YOU AND WANTS YOU TO **LOVE AND OBEY** HIM. YOU MUST RESPECT **GOD** AND HONOUR **GOD**. **GOD** REWARDS THE RIGHTEOUS WHO LOVES HIM AND **GOD** PUNISHES SINNERS WHO HATES HIM.

REMEMBER GOD IS A SPIRIT PERSON WITH A HEART, A HEART FULL OF ETERNAL LOVE FOR YOU AND ME. AMEN!

DEUTERONOMY CHAPTER 7 VERSES 9 AND 10 STATES: "KNOW THEREFORE THAT THE LORD YOUR GOD, HE IS GOD, THE FAITHFUL GOD, WHO KEEPS HIS COVENANT AND HIS LOVING KINDNESS TO A THOUSANDTH GENERATION WITH THOSE WHO LOVE HIM AND KEEP HIS COMMANDMENTS; (VERSE 10) BUT REPAYS THOSE WHO HATE HIM TO THEIR FACES, TO DESTROY THEM; HE WILL NOT DELAY WITH HIM WHO HATES HIM, HE WILL REPAY HIM TO HIS FACE. AMEN!

GOD IS A JUST **GOD**. LOOK AT OUR JUSTICE SYSTEM. IT DOES PUNISH SINNERS WHO KILL. REMEMBER **GOD** SAID, "THOU SHALL NOT KILL." OUR LEGAL JUSTICE SYSTEM IS BASED ON **THE HOLY BIBLE**.

MEXICO HAS TWO CADET TRAINING LOCATIONS. FEMALE CADET RECRUITMENT TRAINING CONSISTS OF PHYSICAL AND EDUCATIONAL TEST, MARCHING AND OBSTACLE COURSES.

MEXICO'S MILITARY CAREER SCHOOL HAS PROGRAMS SUCH AS **NURSING,** ADMINISTRATION, MILITARY DOCTOR AND DENTIST. FEMALE CADETS ARE NOT ALLOWED TO STUDY WEAPONRY AS A CAREER. CADETS ARE CHOREOGRAPHED, UNIFORMED.

I COMPLETED MARCHING DRILLING SESSIONS. I REMEMBERED OUR **STARTING COMMANDS** GIVEN, A RAISED VOICE SAID, "FALL IN, ATTENTION, **FORWARD,** MARCH! EVERYONE STARTED TO MARCH FORWARD IN A STRAIGHT LINE.

I STARTED TO SWEAT, WHICH DIRECTION NEXT? I TRIED TO QUICKLY REMEMBER MY CHOREOGRAPHED STEPS AND COMMANDS.

"ONWARD **CHRISTIAN SOLDIER** MARCHING AS TO **WAR** WITH THE **CROSS** OF **JESUS** GOING ON BEFORE, **CHRIST** THE ROYAL **MASTER LEADS** AGAINST THE FOE FORWARD INTO BATTLE, SEE HIS BANNERS **GO...**" THIS BEAUTIFUL CHRISTIAN SONG WAS WRITTEN BY SABINE BARING-GOULD, 1834-1924. **"GO, GO, GO FOR ME SAYS THE LORD."**

ARMAGEDDON! ARM AGE DON(E)! ARM-AGE-DDON! I LOVE THAT CHRISTIAN SONG, CHRISTIANS AROUND THE WORLD LOVE THAT SONG. "WOULD I HAVE RECEIVED A HIGH GRADE IN MY TRAINING PROGRAM IF I HAD TRULY SUNG THAT SONG?

I YELLED, **STOP! STOP! EVERYONE HALTED, EVERYONE STOPPED.** GLANCING AT THE SQUAD LEADER I WALKED AWAY QUIETLY WITHOUT GIVING AN EXPLANATION.

I DID THE BEST I COULD, I WAS A TEENAGER. I NEVER COMPLETED THAT PROGRAM IN MEXICO. THE NURSING

AREA OF TRAINING INTERESTS AND APPEALED TO ME. I ADMIRE BEAUTIFUL CHOREOGRAPHED MILITARY MARCHING FORMATIONS.

I LIKE THE ABOUT FACE MARCHING COMMAND, THE RIGHT FACE, LEFT FACE AND LEFT FLANK MARCH, RIGHT FLANK MARCH AND READY FRONT MARCHING COMMAND. I ALSO LIKE THE RIGHT STEP MARCH AND COLUMN RIGHT MARCHING.

THE HOLY BIBLE WORDS AND COMMAND-MENTS I NEVER FORGET NOW AND I DO WALK IN STEPS WITH THEM EVERYDAY NOW. HOLY! AMEN! PLEASE PRAY FOR THOSE IN THE MILITARY, NAVY, AIR FORCE AND MARINE AROUND THE WORLD TODAY. AMEN!

PRAYER.

DEAR LORD JESUS CHRIST I REPENT AND CONFESS ALL OF MY SINS. I PRAY FOR THOSE IN THE MILITARY, NAVY, AIR FORCE AND MARINES AROUND THE WORLD TODAY. I PRAY FOR PILOTS AND THE UNSAVED.

BLESS THEM WITH PROTECTION, SHIELD THEM FROM PREMATURE DEATH, BLESS THEM WITH MERCY AND GRACE AND SALVATION. BLESS THEIR FAMILIES ALSO. IN JESUS NAME I PRAY TO MY HEAVENLY FATHER. AMEN!

THE HOLY BIBLE PSALM 37 VERSE 23 STATES: THE LORD MAKES FIRM THE STEPS OF THE ONE WHO DELIGHTS IN HIM."

I VISITED ORANGE ORCHARDS AND LAKE CHAPALA IN MEXICO. LAKE CHAPALA IS WITHIN SIX MEXICAN MUNICIPALITIES. THE REGION IS POPULATED WITH

MEXICANS AND INTERNATIONAL RESIDENTS. IT IS MEXICO'S LARGEST FRESH WATER LAKE. I SPENT TIME IN THE LAKE WITH FRIENDS. I WAS NOT A SWIMMER AND I WOULD NEVER ENTER INTO THE WATER ALONE.

ONE DAY BECAUSE MY FRIENDS WERE WITH ME WHO KNEW HOW TO SWIM I GATHERED UP CONFIDENCE AND ENTERED INTO THE LAKE. I DID NOT WEAR A LIFE JACKET BUT I SHOULD HAVE HAD ONE ON AS A NON-SWIMMER FOR SAFETY REASONS. THERE IS SOMETHING AWESOME AND SPIRITUAL ABOUT A LARGE BODY OF WATER SUCH AS A LAKE, THE RIVER AND THE OCEAN. THE POWERS THAT THESE BODIES OF WATER EXUBERATE IS SUPERNATURAL. THEY MOVE BY THE POWER OF **GOD. AMEN!**

I REMEMBER AS I ENTERED LAKE CHAPALA FOR THE FIRST TIME MY FRIENDS WERE A FEW FEET OUT INTO THE WATER. I SHOUTED OUT TO THEM, "I CANNOT SWIM! THEY ENCOURAGED ME TO COME TO WHERE THEY WERE. "COME! THEY SAID.

I WALKED TOWARDS THEM IN THE WATER NOT REALIZING HOW DEEP THE LAKE BECOMES JUST A FEW FEET FROM THE SHORE. I MADE A FEW MORE STEPS TRYING TO REACH THEM QUICKLY BUT SUDDENLY I COULD NOT FEEL THE LAKE BOTTOM UNDER MY FEET AND DREAD CAME UPON ME. IN MY EFFORT TO STABILIZE MYSELF AND GAIN CONTROL, THE WATER LIFTED ME UP AND I BEGAN TO FLOAT DUE TO THE POWER OF ITS BUOYANCY.

I STARTED TO MOVE MY HANDS IN A SWIMMING MOTION, I KEPT MY HEAD OUT OF THE WATER. I CALLED OUT TO MY FRIENDS AGAIN, "I DON'T KNOW HOW TO SWIM! I KNEW THEY THEY HEARD ME BECAUSE THEY

STOPPED WHAT THEY WERE DOING AND THEY BOTH TURNED IN MY DIRECTION AND FIXED THEIR EYES ON ME. THEY NEVER MOVED FROM WHERE THEY WERE AND THEY NEVER CAME TOWARDS ME EITHER.

THEY WATCHED ME GET CLOSER TO THEM IN MY EFFORTS UNTIL I FINALLY REACHED THEM. I DID NOT QUICKLY LEARN TO SWIM THIS WAY. MY FRIENDS NEVER LEFT MY SIDE. WE STAYED IN CLOSE PROXIMITY AND WHEN THE TIME CAME THEY ASSISTED ME BACK TO THE SHORE.

I WOULD LIKE TO TAKE THIS OPPORTUNITY TO ENCOURAGE NON SWIMMERS: IF YOU ARE PLANNING TO VISIT A LARGE BODY OF WATER AND INTENDS TO GET INTO IT BE PREPARED. DON'T GO ALONE, LET OTHERS KNOW THAT YOU CANNOT SWIM. KNOW WHERE THE SHALLOW AND DEEP ENDS ARE AND WEAR A LIFE JACKET. DON'T LET ANYONE ENTICE YOU TO GO TO THE DEEP END ALONE. STAY CLOSE TO A SWIMMER AND KEEP YOUR HEAD OUT OF THE WATER. PRAY THAT GOD WILL KEEP YOU AND OTHERS SAFE.

I KNEW THAT **GOD** WAS WATCHING OVER ME THAT DAY AT THE LAKE AND KEPT ME SAFE. I LOVE LARGE BODIES OF WATERS. **I AM** ALWAYS DRAWN TO THE WATER NOT ONLY TO PERFORM **WATER BAPTISMS NOW BUT I HAVE A NATURAL LOVE FOR THE OCEAN.** I LOVE LIVING NEAR THE WATER.

I TAKE PLEASURE IN A MOUNTAINOUS ENVIRONMENT LIKE **ISRAEL. GOD'S** CREATED EARTH IS FRUITFUL, FLORAL AND BEAUTIFULLY POPULATED WITH PEOPLE, SPECIES OF ANIMALS, REPTILES AND BIRDS. AMEN!

WATER IS NOT A TOY. WE ALLOW CHILDREN TO PLAY IN WATER BUT THEY MUST BE MONITORED

CONSTANTLY ESPECIALLY AROUND A LARGE BODY OF WATER TO AVOID DROWNING ACCIDENTS. **WATER AND WORDS** HAS A RELATIONSHIP WITH MANKIND, IT IS LIKE A MARRIAGE, THEY COMPLIMENT EACH OTHER. WE CANNOT LIVE WITHOUT EITHER WATER OR A COMMUNICATION METHOD.

IF WE ARE SEPARATED FROM WATER WE CRY OUT FOR IT AND WE GO SEEKING FOR IT. WATER IS VERY POWERFUL AND CAN BE FRIGHTENING DURING A HURRICANE OR A TROPICAL STORM. WATER HYDRATES, REASSURES AND COMFORTS US DAILY.

WATER LIFTS AND CARRIES MANKIND AND WHEN IT DOES WE HAVE NO CONTROL, WE CANNOT HOLD UNTO WATER, IT IS SELF DETERMINED. IF YOU DON'T KNOW HOW TO SWIM OR HOW TO LIVE RIGHTEOUSLY AND LOVINGLY THE NATURAL AND THE SPIRITUAL WATER CAN HARM YOU.

IN THE **HOLY BIBLE JESUS CHRIST** IS THE LIVING **WATER. IN THE HOLY BIBLE BOOK OF REVELATION CHAPTER 22 VERSE 17 IT STATES: THE SPIRIT AND THE BRIDE SAY, "COME." AND LET THE ONE WHO IS THIRSTY COME; LET THE ONE WHO WISHES TAKE THE WATER OF LIFE WITHOUT COSTS.**

THE FIRST TIME I WENT TO MEXICO I WAS ALMOST FOURTEEN YEARS OLD AND I SPENT A FEW MONTHS THEN RETURNED TO SCHOOL IN FRANCE TO BEGIN GRADE EIGHT. AFTER I COMPLETED GRADE ELEVEN AT SEVENTEEN YEARS OLD AT MY FRENCH **SECONDARY SCHOOL** I RETURNED TO MEXICO.

DURING MY SECOND VISIT TO MEXICO, I MET A WONDERFUL ST. LUCIAN FAMILY WHO HAD CHILDREN MY AGE AND IT WAS AT THAT TIME I BEGAN DATING.

I GOT A JOB IN A LOCAL OLD AGE HOME AS A NURSES AID IN THE SMALL COMMUNITY. THE JOB HELPED TO COVER MY EXPENSES. THE TOWN WAS VERY SMALL WITHOUT PUBLIC TRANSPORTATION AND HAD ONE HOSPITAL. ONE OF MY FAMILY MEMBER DECIDED TO MOVE FROM THE SMALL TOWN COMMUNITY TO A LARGER CITY WHICH HAD AN AIRPORT AND I WENT WITH HER.

SHE IS NOW A **BORN-AGAIN CHRISTIAN.** WE LIVED TOGETHER FOR A SHORT TIME THEN I SECURED MY OWN APARTMENT AND WAS EMPLOYED AGAIN IN ANOTHER OLD AGE HOME. I ENTERED INTO A COMMITTED RELATIONSHIP WITH A MAN I MET LOCALLY. WE ENJOYED FISHING TOGETHER, VISITING THE FLEA MARKETS AND VISITING THE RIVERS AND THE OCEAN.

I WORKED THE EVENING 3 TO 11 p. m. SHIFT AT THE OLD AGE HOME. MY FORMER BOYFRIEND DROVE ME HOME FROM WORK EACH NIGHT. WE LIVED TOGETHER.

MY DIET WAS RICH WITH SEAFOOD AND **ORANGES,** I HAD BUCKETS OF FISH TO EAT AND BASKETS FILLED WITH ORANGES. THEY WERE NEVER BOUGHT IN A GROCERY STORE. MY FORMER BOYFRIEND HELPED ME LEARN HOW TO DRIVE AND I GOT MY FIRST DRIVER'S LICENSE IN MEXICO. MY FIRST CAR WAS BOUGHT IN MEXICO.

I AM ALWAYS KIND TO MY MOTHER, IN **GOD** WE TRUST. **GOD** HAS BLESSED YOU, **GOD** BLESSED US. TURN BACK TO THE **HOLY BIBLE** AND LET **JESUS CHRIST** CONTINUE TO BLESS YOUR BASKETS AND BUCKETS. REMEMBER **"IN GOD WE TRUST." AMEN!**

THE SCHOOL ENVIRONMENT WAS SAFE IN MEXICO WHEN I ATTENDED HIGH SCHOOL.

I NEVER HAD FEAR WHILE ATTENDING HIGH SCHOOL. THE THOUGHT OF SOMEONE GOING ON A RAMPAGE THROUGH THE SCHOOL WITH A GUN WAS UNHEARD OF, IT NEVER ENTERED MY MIND. THE YELLOW SCHOOL BUS PICKED US UP AND DROPPED US OFF AT THE DESIGNATED PICK UP AND DROP OFF POINT MONDAY TO FRIDAY AND WE TRAVELLED SAFELY.

SOMETIMES POSITIVE AND NEGATIVE EVENTS OCCUR DURING ONE'S CHILDHOOD AND YOUNG ADULTHOOD YEARS, WHETHER THEY LIVE WITH BOTH PARENTS, A SINGLE PARENT, A FOSTER PARENT, AN ADOPTIVE PARENT OR NO PARENT.

ADULTS AND SENIOR CITIZENS DOES EXPERIENCE DIFFICULTIES SOMETIMES IN THEIR LIFE AND RELATIONSHIPS. WHEN TRIALS ENTER INTO YOUR LIFE SEEK **GOD** FIRST. SEEK **GOD** NOW AND DON'T WAIT UNTIL YOU ARE EXPERIENCING TROUBLE BEFORE YOU DECIDE THAT YOU WANT **GOD** TO HELP YOU AND BE A PART OF YOUR LIFE.

I WAS WITHOUT PARENTAL GUARDIANSHIP IN MEXICO AND IN A SMALL TOWN EVERYBODY KNOWS EVERYBODY. IN A SMALL TOWN PEOPLE KNOWS WHEN SOMEONE IS NEW TO THE NEIGHBOURHOOD. THE SHARING OF TRANSPORTATION WAS COMMON BECAUSE NOT EVERYONE OWNED A CAR IN MY COMMUNITY.

SOME OF THE PEOPLE I MET ON MY SECOND VISIT TO MEXICO WERE WILY AND NONE OF THE PEOPLE THAT I KNEW THEN WERE **BORN-AGAIN CHRISTIANS.**

I WANT TO ENCOURAGE YOUNG PEOPLE TO PRESERVE THEIR BODIES FOR THEIR FUTURE HUSBANDS AND WIVES. DON'T ALLOW ANYONE TO MISUSE YOUR PRECIOUS BODIES PREMATURELY AND LUSTFULLY.

AVOID PORNOGRAPHY. MANY PEOPLE IN SOCIETY ARE SEXUAL PREDATORS AND SEEKS RELATIONSHIP WITH A YOUTH. SOME SAY, "SIXTEEN PLUS." SOME SAY, "BELOW THE AGE OF EIGHTEEN."

THE TEENAGE YEARS ARE SEXUAL FORMATIVE YEARS. YOUR BODY IS GROWING AND GLOWING. YOU ARE IMPRESSIONABLE AND VULNERABLE. YOU ARE ALMOST FULLY RIPE FOR THE MARRIAGE PICKING, WAIT FOR THE MARRIAGE DAY. DON'T LOOK BACK YEARS LATER AND HAVE REGRETS ABOUT YOUR SEXUAL RELATIONSHIP AND CHOICES OF THE PAST.

MARRY YOUR WIFE OR HUSBAND WHO LOVES YOU AND LET IT BE THE ONE YOU LOVE ALSO. AMEN! WHEN I WENT TO MEXICO FOR THE FIRST TIME, I WAS A VIRGIN. AFTER SPENDING TIME IN MEXICO ON MY SECOND VISIT, I LOST MY SEXUAL INNOCENCE. LOVE MUST LEAD TO MARRIAGE SEX FULLFILLS THAT LOVE. TEENAGERS PROTECT YOUR CHASTITY FROM SEXUAL PREDATORS. AMEN!

ALWAYS BRING UP THE **TOPIC OF MARRIAGE WITH THE OPPOSITE SEX** IF YOU LOVE AND DESIRE THEM. LET THEM KNOW HOW YOU TRULY FEEL ABOUT THEM SO THAT THEY MAY CONSIDER YOU IN THEIR FUTURE PLANS. KEEP EVERYONE AT ARM'S LENGTH WHO ONLY WANTS SEXUAL INTIMACY WITHOUT A COMMITMENT TO MARRY YOU. **LOVE** HAS NO COLOUR, EVERY HUMAN BEING IS WORTHY TO BE LOVED.

PRAY AND ASK **GOD** TO SEND YOU THE RIGHT COMPATIBLE PERSON FOR YOU TO LOVE AND MARRY. PRAY THAT THEY WILL LOVE YOU ALSO. LOVE IS RECIPROCAL AND CANNOT BE ONE WAY. **TWO PEOPLE, MALE AND FEMALE** MUST BE HONEST ABOUT WHETHER

OR NOT THEY TRULY LOVE EACH OTHER BEFORE MARRIAGE.

DO NOT DECEIVE ANYONE. DO NOT GO THROUGH A DIVORCE BECAUSE ONE PARTNER DID NOT LOVE THE OTHER. **GOD** WILL PUNISH THOSE WHO ENTER INTO A MARRIAGE ONLY FOR MONEY, IMMIGRATION REASONS OR CONVENIENCE AND NOT FOR TRUE PASSIONATE LOVE AMEN! AVOID JEALOUS MEN AND WOMEN.

SOMEONE WHO IS CONSUMED WITH JEALOUSLY TOWARDS YOU CAN BECOME VIOLENT AND HARMFUL TO YOU. AVOID SUCH A PERSON. MY EX-BOYFRIEND IN MEXICO WAS JEALOUS AND POSSESSIVE. SOMETIMES I WOULD AVOID HIM BECAUSE OF HIS EXTREME JEALOUSY.

I ESCAPED BEING PHYSICALLY HARM BY HIM BY THE GRACE AND POWER OF **ALMIGHTY GOD.** ONE DAY I WENT TO WORK AT THE OLD AGE HOME TO DO A MORNING SHIFT. MY WORK SHIFT WAS OCCASIONALLY ROTATED.

I HAD SPENT THE NIGHT WITH ONE OF MY FEMALE COWORKERS AT HER HOME BECAUSE I HAD TO SHUN, DODGE AND ESCAPE FROM MY JEALOUS BOYFRIEND. WE DROVE TO WORK TOGETHER THAT MORNING. I WAS TIMOROUS OF MY EX-BOYFRIEND. HE WAS FREQUENTLY UNEASY, ANGUISHED AND UNNECESSARILY SUSPICIOUS.

UNKNOWN TO ME ON THAT PARTICULAR DAY WAS THAT MY FORMER BOYFRIEND WAS ON MY WORKPLACE PROPERTY WAITING TO WAYLAY ME AT THE END OF MY WORK SHIFT. HE CAME WITH THE INTENT TO HARM. AS I STEPPED OFF THE ELEVATOR AND PROCEEDED A FEW STEPS TOWARD THE EXIT WITH MY FRIEND. I FELT A HAND GRABBED ME AND PUSHED ME FORWARD. I TRIED TO STOP THE UNEXPECTED PUSH BUT I COULD NOT.

I TURNED MY HEAD TO SEE WHO IT WAS, IT WAS MY FORMER BOYFRIEND, HE WAS BEHIND ME.

I WAS FRIGHTENED AND SCARED AT WHAT WAS HAPPENING TO ME. MANY EMPLOYEES WERE COMING INTO THE BUILDING TO START THEIR SHIFT WHILE OTHERS WERE LEAVING THE FACILITY.

MY EX-BOYFRIEND WAS MUSCULAR AND PHYSICALLY STRONGER THAN I. HE PERSISTENTLY COMPELLED ME FORWARD, I COULD NOT LOOSE MYSELF FROM HIM, HE HAD A FIRM STRONG GRIP ON MY UNIFORM.

WHEN I REALIZED THE DANGER AND SERIOUSNESS OF WHAT WAS REALLY HAPPENING TO ME I CRIED OUT TO MY FRIEND AND YELLED, "LORIA, CALL THE POLICE." "LORIA DO NOT HESITATE." "CALL THE POLICE QUICKLY, DO IT NOW." "CALL THE POLICE." LORIA HAD STOPPED, WITNESSED AND SHOCKINGLY WATCHED THE WHOLE SCENE.

LADIES THIS IS THE KIND OF MAN YOU DO NOT WANT TO ATTRACT OR MARRY. HE PROCEEDED TO FORCE ME OUTSIDE THE BUILDING INTO THE PARKING LOT AND INTO HIS CAR, THEN SLAMMED THE DOOR SHUT AND SPED OFF. I WAS ABDUCTED FROM MY WORKPLACE. **GOD** WAS WITH ME IN THE CAR THAT DAY.

I PLEADED WITH MY EX-BOYFRIEND AND I SOBBED. TEARS RUNNING DOWN MY FACE, I ASKED HIM TO STOP THE CAR AND LET ME OUT. I TOLD HIM I WAS WITH MY FRIEND "LORIA" WHO GOT OFF THE ELEVATOR WITH ME. HE WOULD NOT LISTEN BUT ONLY HAD INTENT TO DO EVIL. HE DROVE THROUGH TRAFFIC, IT WAS A BUSY TIME OF DAY ON THE ROAD AND I DID NOT RECOGNIZED THE ROUTE HE HAD TAKEN.

HE DROVE QUICKLY TO AN ISOLATED AND DESERTED PART OF THE CITY, THERE WERE NO HOUSES OR BUSINESSES AROUND. THERE WERE A LOT OF TALL SHRUBS AND BUSHES. HE PARKED THE CAR ON THE UNPAVED ROAD AND CAME AROUND TO THE OTHER SIDE AND OPENED THE DOOR AND SAID, "GET OUT! I WAS ALARMED AND SHAKING.

AS I STOOD BEFORE MY EX-BOYFRIEND OFF THE SIDE OF THE DIRT ROAD AMONGST THE CLOISTERED BUSHY AREA, I TREMBLED. I REMEMBERED **GOD,** AT THAT TIME AND I CRIED OUT TO **GOD** AND SAID, "O **LORD** PLEASE HELP ME, DON'T LET HIM HARM ME." I WAS IN DIRE NEED OF IMMEDIATE **DIVINE INTERVENTION. AMEN!**

I DID NOT SEE WHERE HE TOOK THE WEAPON FROM BUT SUDDENLY HE THRUST IT THEN STEPPED BACKWARDS. **GOD** DIVINELY ORDAINED A DISTANCE BETWEEN US. THE FORCE OF THE WEAPON DID NOT PENETRATE BUT BOUNCED OFF. I WAS STILL STANDING AND CRYING WHILE HE HELD THE WEAPON IN HIS HAND. THE POWER OF **GOD SHIELDED ME** THAT DAY.

AS HE REMAINED BEFORE ME I THOUGHT ABOUT MY FRIEND LORIA AND WONDERED IF SHE HAD CALLED THE POLICE. I KEPT LOOKING TOWARDS THE DIRT ROAD FOR A SIGN OF HELP. I WAS NOT YET A **BORN-AGAIN CHRISTIAN** BUT I ALWAYS DID BELIEVE IN THE **HOLY BIBLE.** I WAS **CHRISTENED AND DEDICATED TO GOD** AT SEVEN MONTHS OLD AS A BABY. IN MY SOUL I KNEW I WAS NOT GOING TO DIE THAT DAY. I WAS COMFORTED BECAUSE OF MY BELIEF IN **GOD.**

I DID NOT KNOW HOW I WOULD BE VICTORIOUS THROUGH THIS ORDEAL BUT I KNEW I WOULD BE BECAUSE **I HAD FAITH IN GOD.** I REMEMBER FEELING

DIVINE PRESENCE AROUND ME, I CANNOT EXPLAIN IT BUT I REALLY DID **BELIEVE** IN MY HEART THAT **GOD** SAW ME AND WAS WATCHING OVER ME DURING THIS DANGEROUS SITUATION. MY **"FAITH BELIEF" IN JESUS CHRIST ALMIGHTY GOD REASSURED ME.**

THOUGHTS OF **GOD'S PRESENCE** ENLIVENED MY HEART. I FELT HEARTENED IN MY SPIRIT. THEN I BEGAN TO THINK ABOUT LORIA MY CO-WORKER WHILE MY SOUL CRY OUT TO **GOD** FOR HELP. WHILE I THOUGHT OF LORIA, I SAW A CAR SLOWLY PULLED UP AND DROVE PAST MY EX-BOYFRIEND'S CAR. I THOUGHT IT WAS JUST A COMMUTER DRIVING BY. THEN I SAID SILENTLY IN MY HEART, "**GOD** PLEASE LET THEM COME BACK, LET THEM RETURN."

THEN SUDDENLY THE CAR STOPPED AND REVERSED AND MY EYES AND THE DRIVERS EYES LOCKED FIXED TOGETHER AS ONE. **JESUS CHRIST ALMIGHTY GOD SENT THE TWO MEN.**

MY INTENSE STARE ENCOURAGED THE DRIVER TO STOP. SATAN WAS DEFEATED. AMEN!

WHEN MY EX-BOYFRIEND REALIZED THAT THE CAR WAS STOPPED HE QUICKLY THREW THE WEAPON INTO THE BUSHES BEFORE THE MEN COULD SEE IT. WHEN THE TWO CAUCASIAN MEN CAME OUT OF THEIR VEHICLE THEY DID NOT SPEAK, THEY STOOD CALM AND STILL LOOKING AT ME DIRECTLY WHILE MY EX-BOYFRIEND'S BACK WAS TURNED TO THEM. THE TWO MEN DID NOT WEAR A POLICE UNIFORM THEY WERE DRESSED IN PLAIN CLOTHES.

I MAINTAINED EYE CONTACT WITH THE MEN, THEN SUDDENLY I GAIN COURAGE AND DASHED PAST MY EX-BOYFRIEND TOWARDS THE TWO MEN AND SCREAMED

OUT SEVERAL TIMES, "HE TRIED TO HARM ME!" "HE TRIED TO HARM ME!" "HE HAD A WEAPON AND HE THREW IT INTO THE BUSHES WHEN HE SAW YOU!" "PLEASE HELP ME!" "HE TRIED TO HARM ME!" "WHERE DID HE THREW THE WEAPON?" ONE OF THE MEN ASKED ME. "OVER THERE!" I SAID.

THEN I POINTED MY FINGER TO SHOW THEM THE LOCATION. ONE OF THE GENTLEMAN WALKED TO THE LOCATION WHERE I POINTED AND FOUND THE WEAPON AND SEALED IT INTO A PLASTIC BAG. THEN THE TWO MEN PULLED OUT THEIR PISTOLS AND POINTED IT AT MY EX-BOYFRIEND AND SAID, "DON'T COME NEAR!" "YOU STAND BEHIND US!" THEY SAID TO ME AND I MOVED BEHIND THEM.

THIS WAS WHEN I REALIZE THAT THESE MEN WERE NOT JUST COMMUTERS THEY CAME WITH A PURPOSE. **GOD** INTERVENED. I WAS VERY THANKFUL AND GRATEFUL TO **GOD** FOR THEIR PRESENCE. **GOD** SENT THEM AT THE PERFECT TIME. THEY WERE DETECTIVES IN AN UNMARKED DETECTIVE VEHICLE.

THE DETECTIVES HELD MY EX-BOYFRIEND OFF AT BAY AND THEY CALLED FOR MORE HELP. WITHIN SECONDS OTHER POLICE VEHICLES WERE ON THE SCENE, THEY HANDCUFFED AND ARRESTED MY EX-BOYFRIEND AND DROVE AWAY AS HE SAT IN THE BACK OF THEIR CAR LOOKING BACK AT ME.

THE DETECTIVES ASKED ME SOME PERTINENT QUESTIONS. I THANKED THEM WITH A HEART FILLED WITH GRATITUDE THEN THEY DROVE ME HOME. THE CIRCUMSTANCES THAT SURROUNDED ME THAT DAY WAS PUBLISHED. FAMILY MEMBERS, I CHOSE TO SHIELD SO THAT YOUR JOY WOULD REMAIN, THE EVENT OCCURRED

OVER TWENTY YEARS AGO. AMEN! **GOD** PRESERVED ME FOR A PURPOSE AND I THANK **GOD**. AMEN!

PSALM CHAPTER 91 IS A BEAUTIFUL CHAPTER TO USE AS A PRAYER FOR **SAFETY**. **PSALM 91 VERSE 15 STATES: "HE WILL CALL UPON ME AND I WILL ANSWER HIM; I WILL BE WITH HIM IN TROUBLE; I WILL RESCUE HIM AND HONOUR HIM.**

GOD SENT HELP, **GOD** HEARD MY CRY AND HEARD MY HEART SPEAKING TO HIM ALONG THE WAY THAT DARK DAY. WHEN THERE IS DARKNESS WE MUST HAVE HOPE FOR THE LIGHT. DON'T GIVE UP WHEN IT IS DARK. CRY OUT TO **GOD** WHEN IT IS DARK. CRY OUT TO **GOD** THE LIVING LIGHT. AMEN!

IF YOU HAVE DOUBT ABOUT THE EXISTENCE OF **GOD,** PLEASE READ THIS BOOK TO THE END. DOUBT WILL LEAVE YOU. I PROMISE IT WILL BECAUSE **GOD IS TRUE AND WISE. AMEN!**

GOD DOES HEAR YOU WHEN YOU PRAY AND TALK TO HIM. IF YOU ARE NOT YET A **BORN-AGAIN CHRISTIAN** AND YOU TURN YOUR FAITH TOWARDS **JESUS CHRIST** AND START PRAYING TO HIM HE DOES HEAR YOUR EVERY WORD. **GOD** RECORDS EVERY EVENT OF OUR LIVES ON THIS EARTH. EVERYTHING WE DO AND SAY **GOD** KNOWS ABOUT IT.

GOD WORKS IN A MYSTERIOUS WAY! A FEW DAYS AFTER MY ABDUCTION AND THE ARREST OF MY EX-BOYFRIEND, HIS BROTHER AND HIS WIFE CONTACTED ME. THEY WERE ALWAYS LOVING AND KIND TO ME DURING MY RELATIONSHIP WITH MY EX-BOYFRIEND. WE OFTEN ATE MEALS TOGETHER, THEY LOVED FISH ALSO. THEY WERE UNHAPPY BECAUSE OF THE EVIL THAT HAD MANIFESTED ITSELF.

MY EX-BOYFRIEND BROTHER ASKED ME HUMBLY AND GENTLY TO DROP THE CHARGES AND SET MY EX-BOYFRIEND FREE. I WAS INEXPERIENCED WITH THE LEGAL SYSTEM AND DID NOT KNOW EXACTLY WHAT TO DO. HIS BROTHER EXPLAINED THE REQUIRED PROCEDURES TO ME.

I DID **LOVE** HIS BROTHER AND HIS WIFE SO I THOUGHT ABOUT THEIR REQUEST FOR A FEW DAYS, THEN HIS BROTHER AND I ARRANGED TO GO AND HAVE THE NECESSARY PAPER WORK DONE TO REMOVE THE CHARGES. **I FORGAVE** MY EXBOYFRIEND AND SIGNED THE PAPERS TO **SET HIM FREE.** IT IS EASY TO FORGIVE WHEN YOU **FIRST LOVE. AMEN!**

ST. MATTHEW CHAPTER 6 VERSES 14 AND 15 STATES: FOR IF YOU FORGIVE OTHER PEOPLE WHEN THEY SIN AGAINST YOU, YOUR HEAVENLY FATHER WILL ALSO FORGIVE YOU. BUT IF YOU DO NOT FORGIVE OTHERS THEIR SINS, YOUR FATHER WILL NOT FORGIVE YOUR SINS.

SHORTLY AFTER I RELEASED MY EX-BOYFRIEND, I MOVED AWAY FROM MEXICO. **GOD** SHOWED ME HIS **LOVE FIRST,** THEN I SHOWED MY EX-BOYFRIEND **GOD'S LOVE** THROUGH ME. **AMEN!** WHEN **GOD** SAVES YOU, REACH OUT TO ONE DESTINEDTO HELL AND SAVE THEM ALSO. **AMEN!**

IT IS VERY IMPORTANT TO CHRISTEN AND DEDICATE A NEW BORN BABY TO **GOD.** MOTHER, MS. KAY ENSURED THAT I WAS BLESSED THIS WAY. THE DEDICATION BLESSING I RECEIVED FROM **GOD** WAS STILL WORKING AND OPERATING THROUGHOUT MY CHILDHOOD, TEENAGE AND YOUNG ADULTHOOD YEARS. MY SALVATION BLESSING PLUS MY DEDICATION BLESSING

IS STILL WORKING FOR ME TODAY AND WILL CONTINUE TO REST UPON ME FOR ALL OF MY LIFE. AMEN!

ISAIAH 54 VERSE 17 STATES: NO WEAPON THAT IS FORMED AGAINST YOU WILL PROSPER AND EVERY TONGUE THAT ACCUSES YOU IN JUDGEMENT YOU WILL CONDEMN. THIS IS THE HERITAGE OF THE SERVANTS OF THE LORD, AND THEIR VINDICATION IS FROM ME, DECLARES THE LORD.

PLEASE PRAY AGAIN FOR ALL THE POLICE OFFICERS AND DETECTIVES IN THE WORLD TODAY. **GOD** DOES USE THEM TO PROTECT AND BRING LAW AND ORDER IN SOCIETY EACH DAY. AMEN!

PRAYER.

DEAR LORD JESUS I REPENT AND CONFESS MY SINS. I PRAY FOR THE SALVATION OF ALL POLICE OFFICERS AND DETECTIVES TODAY. I ALSO PRAY FOR EACH OF THEIR FAMILY MEMBERS. PROTECT THEIR LIVES FROM DANGERS, VIOLENCE AND HARM. GIVE THEM WISDOM, KNOWLEDGE, UNDERSTANDING AND A DISCERNING SPIRIT DURING EVERY ENCOUNTER AND HELP THEM TO MAKE LIFE SAVING DECISIONS. IN JESUS NAME I PRAY TO MY HEAVENLY FATHER. AMEN!

THE HOLY BIBLE BOOK OF PROVERBS CHAPTER 24 VERSE 11 STATES: DELIVER THOSE WHO ARE BEING TAKEN AWAY TO DEATH AND THOSE WHO ARE STAGGERING TO SLAUGHTER OH HOLD THEM BACK.

***THIS IS MY CALLING THIS IS WHAT GOD WANTS ME TO DO TO HELP MANKIND. I AM TO HELP YOU TO KNOW JESUS CHRIST. ONE DAY THE LORD SPOKE TO ME AND JESUS CHRIST SAID, "YOU MUST TEACH MANKIND

MY WISDOM". I REPLIED, "YES LORD." IN OBEDIENCE TO JESUS CHRIST I WILL. AMEN!

I AM TO TEACH YOU GOD'S WISDOM FOR ALL OF MY DAYS UNTIL THE LORD TAKES ME HOME TO HEAVEN. I AM TO DELIVER YOU FROM SATAN'S LIES AND DECEPTION. SATAN HAS TOLD A LOT OF LIES ABOUT WHO JESUS CHRIST REALLY IS. "I HAVE, I WILL ERASE, NULLIFY, OMIT, WIPE OUT, CANCEL AND MELT AS WAX BEFORE THE FIRE EVERY LIES OF SATAN." SAYS JESUS CHRIST MY LORD. AMEN!

THE DEVIL TELL LIES ABOUT THE TRUE HOLY BIBLE. THE DEVIL TELL LIES TO THOSE WHO BELIEVE FALSE FAITH DOCTRINES. THE DEVIL TELL LIES TO THOSE WHO ARE RELIGIOUS AND NOT HOLY SPIRIT FILLED MEN AND WOMEN. THE DEVIL TELL LIES TO SOME DOCTORS AND PSYCHIATRISTS AND THE DEVIL TELL LIES TO HIS OWN FOLLOWERS. AMEN!

*IF THE DEVIL TELL LIES TO HIS OWN FOLLOWERS, THE DEVIL WILL TELL WORSE DECEPTIVE LIES TO HIS ADVERSARIES, NON FOLLOWERS. THE DEVIL TELL LIES TO THOSE WHO SAY, "I HAVE NO RELIGION." THE DEVIL TELL LIES TO MANY SECULAR RULERS AND LEADERS IN SOCIETY. AMEN! COME AND BE FILLED WITH GOD'S TRUTH AND UNCOMMON WISDOM. YOU WILL DRINK AND THIRST NO MORE. AMEN!

REMOVE DOCTRINAL ERRORS FROM YOUR MINISTRY THAT LEADS YOUR MEMBERS TO HELL INSTEAD OF GIVING THEM THE ASSURANCE OF ETERNAL LIFE.

I WILL SHOW YOU YOUR ERRORS AND HELP YOU TO REPLACE IT WITH GOD'S INTENDED TRUTH. AMEN! COME TO JESUS CHRIST OUR ETERNAL WISE GOD AND TEACHER. AMEN!

ST. JOHN CHAPTER 8 VERSE 44 STATES: YOU ARE OF YOUR FATHER THE DEVIL AND YOU WANT TO DO THE DESIRE OF YOUR FATHER. HE WAS A MURDERER FROM THE BEGINNING AND DOES NOT STAND IN THE TRUTH BECAUSE THERE IS NO TRUTH IN HIM. WHENEVER HE SPEAKS A LIE HE SPEAKS FROM HIS OWN NATURE, FOR HE IS A LIAR AND THE FATHER OF LIES. AMEN!

"THE KING JAMES VERSION HOLY BIBLE IS ONE OF THE TRUE VERSIONS OF THE HOLY BIBLE." I WILL ONLY HONOUR THE **KING OF KINGS OF HEAVEN. AMEN!**

JAMES CHAPTER 1 VERSE 1 STATES: JAMES A BOND SERVANT OF GOD AND OF THE LORD JESUS CHRIST, TO THE TWELVE TRIBES WHO ARE DISPERSED ABROAD: GREETINGS.

THERE ARE NINE GIFTS OF THE **HOLY SPIRIT** AND SPEAKING IN TONGUES IS ONE OF THE NINE GIFTS. **GOD GIVES SPIRITUAL GIFTS TO EACH ONE INDIVIDUALLY AS HE WILLS.**

NOT EVERY **BORN-AGAIN CHRISTIAN** SPEAKS IN TONGUES. **IN THE HOLY BIBLE BOOK OF 1ST. CORINTHIANS CHAPTER 12 VERSE 11: IT STATES: BUT ONE AND THE SAME SPIRIT WORKS ALL THESE THINGS, DISTRIBUTING TO EACH ONE INDIVIDUALLY JUST AS HE WILLS.**

THE **CORE** FAITH BELIEFS IN SOME CHURCH ORGANIZATIONS IS INCORRECT AND DECEPTIVE: IT MUST BE TRUE.

THE **CORE** FAITH BELIEF OF EVERY CHURCH ORGANIZATIONS MUST LEAD TO SALVATION, ETERNAL LIFE. THE ORDINANCE OF WATER BAPTISM MUST BE PERFORMED THE **JOHN THE BAPTIST WAY <u>ONLY</u> BY**

EVERY <u>TRUE</u> BORN-AGAIN CHURCH. THERE MUST NOT BE VARIATIONS IN HOW BAPTISM IS PERFORMED.

MANY CHRISTIAN BELIEVERS ARE FOLLOWING DOCTRINAL DELUSIONS. **"CHRIS-LAM"** IS NOT THE SOLUTION. **CHRISLAM IS WRONG.** SOME CHRISTIANS ARE GATHERING IN "HOME-CHURCHES," AND NOT HAVING TO PAY FOR THE COST OF A BUILDING OR SPACE IS NOT THEIR MAIN REASON FOR AVOIDING SOME ESTABLISHED CHURCHES.

HOME CHURCHING REMINDS ME OF **HOME SCHOOLING** THERE IS AN INTENTIONAL EFFORT TO AVOID FALSE TEACHINGS. IN THE ESTABLISHED CHURCHES, INCURRED COST IS COVERED BY CHURCH MEMBERS AND EVERY MEMBER BENEFITS.

THE PASTOR OVERSEES THE CARE AND PARTICIPATE IN EVERY RELATED MATTER CONCERNING CHURCH SPACES. THE CHURCH BUILDING IS FOR THE BODY OF CHRIST.

ESTABLISHED REGISTERED CHURCH ORGANIZATIONS IN MANY COUNTRIES ABIDES BY GOVERNMENT LEGAL REGULATORY LAWS AND POLICIES REGARDING FINANCIAL DONATIONS. HOME CHURCHES ARE NOT GOVERNED REGARDING FINANCIAL GIVING AND ACCOUNTABILITY.

COME AND GATHER IN **JESUS CHRIST PRESENCE.** WE HAVE NO DOCTRINAL DECEPTION AND WE ARE TAUGHT DIRECTLY BY THE **HOLY SPIRIT.**

I NEVER WENT TO A **BIBLE** SEMINARY TO LEARN ABOUT THE **HOLY BIBLE.** AFTER I WAS BAPTIZED, **GOD** CALLED ME INTO THE MINISTRY FROM MY NURSING CAREER AND TAUGHT ME HIMSELF. REMEMBER WHEN

JESUS CHRIST CALLED HIS TWELVE DISCIPLES TO FOLLOW HIM HE NEVER SAID TO THEM, "GO TO THE UNIVERSITY, COLLEGE OR SEMINARY."

JESUS CHRIST TAUGHT HIS DISCIPLES HIMSELF, **JESUS IS THE HOLY SPIRIT. ST. MATTHEW 4 VERSE 19: AND HE SAID TO THEM, "FOLLOW ME, AND I WILL MAKE YOU FISHERS OF MEN."** WHEN YOU LEARN FROM ME," SAID THE **LORD.** "YOU WILL BE QUALIFIED UNIVERSITY SEMINARY PROFESSORS, YOU WILL BE KNOWN BIBLE SCHOLARS, YOU WILL BE QUALIFIED FOR EVERY PHD'S, MASTERS AND DEGREES." AMEN!

THE YOUTH WHO LEARN FROM ME WILL **BE A MASTER OF TRUTH** AND THE OLD MAN WILL TRULY BE WISE. YOU WILL BE SOUGHT AFTER. YOU WILL BE REVERENCED AND KNOWN TO BE WISE. "COME! COME! COME! TO **JESUS CHRIST AND LEARN FROM ME."** SAID **THE LORD.**

A FEW YEARS AGO THE **HOLY SPIRIT** SAID TO ME, "GET READY FOR THE... AND BRING THE... TO ME." THIS **I AM** ALSO DETERMINED TO DO FOR THE LORD. **AMEN!** VICTORY IN **JESUS CHRIST. AMEN!**

WORSHIPPING **GOD** ON SATURDAYS ONLY DOES NOT GUARANTEE YOUR SALVATION. **GOD** WANTS US TO WORSHIP HIM IN **SPIRIT** AND IN **TRUTH** SEVEN DAYS PER WEEK. THIS QUESTION IS FOR THE CHURCHES. "WHO WAS IT THAT ORDAINS MARRIAGES? "WAS IT **GOD** OR A CHURCH ESTABLISHMENT?

I AM TO IMPART **GOD'S TRUTH** WHICH WILL ENCOURAGE YOU TO REPENT AND CONFESS YOUR SINS AND GET BAPTIZED **THE JOHN THE BAPTIST WAY IN THE NAME OF THE FATHER, THE SON AND THE HOLY SPIRIT. AMEN!**

GOD DOES NOT WANT YOU TO BE SLAUGHTERED TO DEATH **JESUS CHRIST** SAID, IN **ST. JOHN 10 VERSE 10.** **"THE THIEF COMES ONLY TO STEAL AND KILL AND DESTROY, I CAME THAT THEY MAY HAVE LIFE AND HAVE HAVE IT ABUNDANTLY".**

LIFE AND ABUNDANCE IS ALWAYS BETTER. AMEN! UNSAVED PEOPLE, NONE **BORN-AGAIN CHRISTIAN** INDIVIDUALS ARE PRONE TO SIN, THEY ARE POSSESSED, HELD CAPTIVE BY DEMONS IN THOUGHTS AND BEHAVIOUR. SIN CONTROLS THE UNSAVED PERSON. AMEN!

ONE DAY I WONDERED WHY WAS IT THAT SOME UNSAVED PEOPLE EXHUBERATE BEHAVIORAL MADNESS AND ARE ADMITTED TO MENTAL HEALTH INSTITUTIONS WHILE SOME UNSAVED INDIVIDUALS HAVE A CAREER, A FAMILY AND RAISE CHILDREN.

I WANTED TO KNOW WHAT MAKES THEM DIFFERENT. THE LORD GAVE ME THE ANSWER AND SAID, "THOSE WHO HAVE FAMILIES AND CAREERS ARE "THE DISCIPLINED UNSAVED." THE LIFESTYLE AND THE DESIRES OF THE UNSAVED PERSON IS THAT OF THE WORLD.

UNSAVED PEOPLE MUST BE ENCOURAGED TO PRAY AND ATTEND CHURCH SERVICES. THEIR MIND AND THOUGHTS ARE NOT ON **JESUS CHRIST ALMIGHTY GOD** FREQUENTLY AND THEY RARELY TALK ABOUT **GOD**.

MANY TIMES THEY DON'T WANT TO HEAR **JESUS CHRIST** NAME MENTIONED; UNFORTUNATELY SOME ARE OFFENDED AT **JESUS** NAME. SOME NON-CHRISTIANS EVEN TRY TO DISCOURAGE CHRISTIAN BELIEVERS AND **BORN-AGAIN CHRISTIANS** FROM SERVING **GOD**.

THE LIFESTYLE OF THE NON-CHRISTIAN MANY TIMES LEADS TO TRAGEDY, SADNESS AND DISAPPOINTMENTS. WHEN I LIVED IN MEXICO, **I DID BELIEVE IN GOD** BUT I WAS NOT YET BAPTIZED **THE JOHN THE BAPTIST WAY BY FULL IMMERSION UNDERNEATH A BODY OF WATER.**

IT DOES MAKE A DIFFERENCE WHEN AN INDIVIDUAL BECOMES **A BORN-AGAIN CHRISTIAN.** THEIR LIFESTYLE, DESIRES AND CONVICTIONS ARE DIFFERENT FROM THE UNSAVED PERSON. THEY HAVE ETERNAL **JOY FROM THE HOLY SPIRIT** THAT NO ONE CAN TAKE AWAY. AMEN!

THE **BORN AGAIN CHRISTIAN** LIVES A HOLY LIFE, LOVES **JESUS CHRIST,** OUR **HEAVENLY FATHER** AND THE **HOLY SPIRIT** AS THE **TRIUNE, THREE IN ONE GOD.** I AM NOW A **BORN-AGAIN CHRISTIAN** PASTOR BY DIVINE CALLING.

I WAS NOT BORN AUTOMATICALLY KNOWING OUR **TRIUNE GOD.** I NEVER HEARD **GOD'S** VOICE AS A BABY BUT **GOD** KNEW ME BEFORE HE CREATED ME IN MY MOTHER'S WOMB. **BORN-AGAIN CHRISTIANS** THRIVE TO IMITATE **JESUS CHRIST** IN THE SPIRIT DAILY.

WE OBEY **GOD** AND HATE SATAN-SIN. WE AVOID THE DEVIL. DO NOT WORSHIP HIM, RUN FROM HIM.

THE **HOLY BIBLE STATES IN ST. JOHN 8 VERSE 23,** **"AND HE WAS SAYING TO THEM, YOU ARE FROM BELOW, I AM FROM ABOVE; YOU ARE OF THIS WORLD, I AM NOT OF THIS WORLD."** THE CHILDREN OF **GOD** DOES NOT LIVE LIKE THE CHILDREN OF THE DEVIL. THE CHILDREN OF **GOD** TALKS TO **GOD** DAILY BY PRAYING WITHOUT CEASING. WE HEAR **GOD'S** VOICE DAILY.

A TRUE **BORN-AGAIN CHRISTIAN** CAN TESTIFY AND SAY TO YOU, "THE **LORD** SPOKE TO ME AND **SAID,**

I LOVE YOU." SATAN WILL NEVER TELL YOU THAT HE LOVES YOU. SATAN WILL TELL YOU TO HATE PEOPLE AND DO HARM TO OTHERS, YOUR PARENTS OR YOUR NEIGHBOUR. DON'T LET SATAN HARM, DESTROY OR STEAL FROM YOU. AMEN!

REMEMBER WHAT I SAID BEFORE, SATAN IS SIN, SATAN EQUALS SIN, SATAN LOOKS LIKE SIN, YOU CANNOT SEPARATE THE DEVIL FROM SIN, SIN IS HIM, **SINISM**. WHEN YOU LOOK IN A MIRROR YOU SEE THE EXACT RESEMBLANCE OF YOURSELF RIGHT! IT IS NOT A PHOTOCOPY OF YOU, YOUR MIRRORED REFLECTION IS EXACTLY YOU. IF YOU WERE TO PUT SATAN BEFORE A MIRROR YOU WOULD SEE THE LETTERS S. I. N. **AMEN!**

THE DEVIL IS NOTHING TO BEHOLD, DON'T DESIRE HIM, HE WILL HARM YOU AND TAKE YOU QUICKLY TO HELL. I WILL SHARE A TESTIMONY WITH YOU NOW. A FEW YEARS AGO WHEN I LIVED IN FRANCE I WAS ON MY WAY HOME FROM THE CHURCH ESTABLISHMENT WHERE I STARTED MY MINISTRY.

I WAS ALONE AND GOT OFF THE TRAMCAR. A TRAMCAR IS BUILT LIKE A BUS BUT IT RUNS ON RAILS. I WALKED TO A NEARBY CHINESE RESTAURANT FOR DINNER. SHORTLY AFTER I SAT DOWN THE **HOLY SPIRIT** SHOWED ME A VISION OF SATAN THE DEVIL.

REMEMBER! **I AM** NOW A **BORN-AGAIN CHRISTIAN PASTOR.** THE VISION OF THE DEVIL WAS DREADFUL AND TERRIBLE. IT WAS TERRIFYING AND ALARMING. IT WAS WORSE THAN ANY "SCARY" MOVIE. **I AM** GLAD THAT **GOD** DID NOT SAY TO ME, "**I AM** GOING TO SHOW YOU A VISION OF SATAN! IF HE DID I PROBABLY WOULD HAVE SAID, "**LORD,** PLEASE DON'T SHOW HIM TO ME." THE VISION CAME SUDDENLY AND UNEXPECTEDLY.

WHEN THE LORD OPENED MY SPIRITUAL EYES I SAW SATAN. HUMAN WORDS CANNOT EXPLAIN WHAT I SAW. SATAN IS GRUESOME LOOKING. HE HAS THE APPEARANCE THAT LOOKS WORSE THAN A MILLION HALLOWEEN MASK PUT TOGETHER. THE DEVIL IS THE SPIRIT BEHIND HALLOWEEN.

WHEN I SAW THE VISION I COULD NOT MOVE FROM MY CHAIR. THE **HOLY SPIRIT'S** POWER PREVENTED ME FROM MOVING AND RUNNING. MY MOUTH WAS WIDE OPEN AND I TRIED TO SCREAM BUT NO SOUND CAME FROM MY MOUTH. I WAS SPIRITUALLY FASTENED TO THE RESTAURANT'S CHAIR SO THAT I WOULD ENDURE LOOKING AT THE VISION. NO HUMAN BEING WOULD HAVE BEEN ABLE TO MOVE ME AT THE MOMENT WHEN I SAW THE VISION OF SATAN. THE HAND OF **GOD** WAS UPON ME.

GOD IS POWERFUL. I REMAINED SPEECHLESS AS BOTH OF MY HANDS WENT UP INTO THE AIR AND I ROCKED BACK AND FORTH IN MY CHAIR UNDER THE **POWER OF GOD.**

IF I WAS ALLOWED TO MOVE FROM MY CHAIR THAT DAY IN THE CHINESE RESTAURANT THE ROOF AND WALLS WOULD BE DEMOLISHED. THERE WOULD BE A TOTAL COLLAPSE OF EVERY PHYSICAL STRUCTURE. I WOULD RUN FASTER THAN A SUPERSONIC JET CONCORD AIR PLANE AND THE DAMAGE WOULD HAVE BEEN GRADED ABOVE TWENTY ON THE RICHTER SCALE THAT MEASURES **EARTHQUAKES**. (EMPHASIS ADDED). THE DEVIL IS VERY FRIGHTENING TO LOOK AT. DON'T DESIRE TO SEE HIM, HE IS SIN AND SIN LEADS TO DEATH. AMEN!

MANKIND **REMEMBER** WHO SENDS THE **EARTHQUAKES. REMEMBER JESUS DEATH ON THE CROSS** FOR YOU.

REMEMBER **JESUS LOVE FOR YOU. AMEN! BORN-AGAIN CHRISTIAN** ARE NOT AFRAID OF SATAN. BECAUSE THE **HOLY BIBLE STATES IN 1ST. JOHN 4 VERSE 18,** "**THERE IS NO FEAR IN LOVE; BUT PERFECT LOVE CAST OUT FEAR, BECAUSE FEAR INVOLVES PUNISHMENT, AND THE ONE WHO FEARS IS NOT PERFECTED IN LOVE.**"

PSALM 23 VERSE 4 STATES: EVEN THOUGH I WALK THROUGH THE VALLEY OF THE SHADOW OF DEATH I FEAR NO EVIL FOR YOU ARE WITH ME; YOUR ROD AND YOUR STAFF THEY COMFORT ME.

IT IS USUALLY WHEN A PERSON DIES AS A SINNER THEY SEE THE DEVIL THAT THEY WERE SERVING IN THIS EARTHLY LIFE. THE REASON WHY A SINNER ENDS UP SEEING THE DEVIL INSTEAD OF **JESUS CHRIST** AT DEATH IS BECAUSE SATAN IS THE ONE WHO TAKES THEM TO HELL AND PUT THEM INTO THE HELL FIRE.

WHEN A CHILD OF **GOD, A BORN AGAIN CHRISTIAN** WHO SERVES **GOD** ALL OF THEIR LIFE DIES, IT IS THE **HOLY ANGELS** WHO TAKE THEIR SOUL INTO **THE PRESENCE OF GOD,** THEY SEE **JESUS CHRIST** THE **GOD** THAT THEY WERE SERVING WHILE THEY WERE ALIVE. THE **HOLY SPIRIT** SAID TO ME ONE DAY, "WHEN A PERSON DIE AND THEIR SOUL LEAVES THEIR BODY, THEY SEE THE **GOD** THAT THEY WERE SERVING IN THEIR LIFETIME, HE WELCOMES THEM." THE DEVIL IS NOT REALLY A **GOD** BUT HE TRIES TO LIKEN HIMSELF LIKE **THE MOST HIGH GOD, JESUS CHRIST. AMEN!**

PRAYER.

DEAR LORD JESUS CHRIST HUMBLY I COME TO YOU FOR MERCY AND GRACE. I REPENT AND CONFESS ALL MY SINS, PLEASE FORGIVE ME. I DECLARE AND DECREE THAT YOU LORD ARE THE MOST HIGH GOD, THE HIGH AND THE LOFTY GOD, THE TRUE ALPHA AND OMEGA THE BEGINNING AND THE END, THE FIRST AND THE LAST, YOU ARE THE "I AM" LORD, YOU ARE THE AMEN! THERE IS NO GOD BUT YOU LORD. IN JESUS NAME I PRAY TO MY HEAVENLY FATHER JEHOVAH. AMEN!

AGAIN! WHEN YOU SERVE AND WORSHIP **JESUS CHRIST** IN THIS LIFE AS **A BORN-AGAIN CHRISTIAN** AND YOU WERE BAPTIZED BY FULL IMMERSION UNDERNEATH THE WATER IN THE NAME OF **THE FATHER, THE SON, AND THE HOLY SPIRIT,** YOU WILL SEE **JESUS CHRIST** WHEN YOUR SOUL SEPARATES FROM YOUR BODY. IF YOU WERE NOT SERVING **JESUS CHRIST,** YOU WILL SEE SATAN BECAUSE HE IS THE FALSE **GOD** OF EVERY FALSE RELIGION. AMEN!

THERE IS GOOD AND EVIL IN THIS WORLD: **JESUS CHRIST IS GOD AND GOD IS GOOD.** THE DEVIL IS THE EVIL ONE. WHEN YOU MENTION AND REFER TO **"THE HIGH-ER POWER"** IN YOUR TEACHING AND REFERENCES I WOULD LIKE FOR YOU TO REMEMBER THAT **JESUS CHRIST SPOKE TO ME ONE DAY AND SAID: "I AM THE HIGH AND THE LOFTY ONE".**

PSALM 100 VERSE 5 STATES: FOR THE LORD IS GOOD: HIS LOVINGKINDNESS IS EVERLASTING AND HIS FAITHFULNESS TO ALL GENERATIONS.

YOUR SOUL IS WHO YOU REALLY ARE, IT IS THE **SPIRIT-UAL** INVISIBLE PART OF YOU THAT NEITHER YOU

OR ANYONE ELSE CAN SEE WITH THE NATURAL EYE. **ONLY JESUS CHRIST CAN SEE YOUR INVISIBLE SOUL WITH HIS EYES.** I STUDIED ANATOMY AND PHYSIOLOGY IN NURSING SCHOOL, WE WERE ALLOWED TO EXAMINE AND STUDY CADAVERS. CADAVERS ARE DEAD HUMAN BODIES USED FOR MEDICAL TEACHING PURPOSES.

WHEN I LOOKED AT THE MALE CADAVER IN NURSING SCHOOL, I SAW THE INTESTINES, LUNGS, STOMACH AND OTHER ORGANS. THESE WERE THE PHYSICAL ANATOMY OF THE MAN WHOSE SOUL WAS NO LONGER WITHIN HIM. THE SOUL, THE REAL PERSON HAS LEFT IT'S FLESHLY COVERING THE BODY AND IS NOW IN HIS ETERNAL DWELLING ABODE.

YOU MAY ASK, "HOW CAN I PROVE THAT I HAVE A SOUL AND THAT **I AM** NOT JUST FLESH AND BLOOD? YOU ARE ALIVE BECAUSE YOUR SOUL IS STILL WITHIN YOUR BODY. AT DEATH YOUR SOUL EXIT YOUR BODY. THE **SOUL IS "LIFE" WITHIN MANKIND.**

A CADAVER IS WITHOUT LIFE, "DEAD" FLESH. YOUR SOUL LETS YOU BLINK YOUR EYES, YOUR SOUL LETS YOU SHIFT AND MOVE YOURSELF ON YOUR BED. YOUR SOUL LETS YOU SIT UP ON YOUR BED. CADAVERS DON'T DO ANY OF THESE LIVING "LIFE" FUNCTIONS. THE SOUL IS THE INVISIBLE SPIRITUAL ASPECT OF MANKIND. AMEN!

THE HOLY BIBLE STATES IN 1ST. CORINTHIANS 15 VERSE 50: "NOW I SAY THIS BRETHREN THAT FLESH AND BLOOD CANNOT INHERIT THE KINGDOM OF GOD..."

WHEN THE **LORD** STATES, **"FLESH AND BLOOD"** CANNOT INHERIT (RECEIVE) THE KINGDOM OF **GOD.** "WHAT DOES HE MEAN? WHAT IS **"FLESH AND BLOOD?** FLESH AND BLOOD IS THE PHYSICAL, TANGIBLE-TOUCHABLE, ANATOMICAL ASPECT OF MAN.

THEREFORE WHEN **GOD** PROMISED ETERNAL LIFE TO MANKIND IN HEAVEN, THIS PROMISE IS NOT TO OUR TOUCHABLE-TANGIBLE FLESH BUT TO OUR UNTOUCHABLE-INTANGIBLE SELF, OUR **SOUL. GOD IS WISE. AMEN!**

JESUS CHRIST, CAME TO THE EARTH IN THE FLESH, BECAUSE THE EARTH IS INHABITED BY THE **"FLESH".** THEY PIERCED **JESUS CHRIST** HANDS ON THE CROSS AT **CALVARY. JESUS "BLOOD"** WAS SHED. **JESUS** RETURNED TO **HEAVEN** AS **A SPIRIT** WHERE ONLY **SPIRIT-UAL** BEINGS LIVE AND INHABITS. AMEN! REMEMBER **JESUS CHRIST IS THE HOLY SPIRIT.**

EVERYBODY SHOULD DESIRE TO GO TO HEAVEN. THERE IS ONLY ONE WAY TO GET TO HEAVEN. **JESUS IS THE WAY TO HEAVEN. YOU MUST BECOME A BORN-AGAIN CHRISTIAN** AND ONE DAY THE **HOLY ANGELS OF GOD,** WILL ESCORT YOU TO HEAVEN. AMEN!

SKYDIVING OFF THE HIGHEST MOUNTAIN WILL NOT GET YOU TO HEAVEN. "CAN YOUR FEET WALK TO A PLACE WHERE THERE IS NO GRAVITY? "DO YOU KNOW THE DISTANCE FROM EARTH TO HEAVEN, HAVE YOU EVER CALCULATED IT? "HOW MANY HOURS WOULD IT TAKE YOU TO TRAVEL TO HEAVEN? **AMEN!**

YOUR SOUL IS SPIRITUAL AND IS NOT LIMITED BY GRAVITY. YOUR MIND IS ALSO SPIRITUAL, YOU CAN IMAGINE AND THINK ABOUT LIMITLESS THINGS. NO PHYSICAL BARRIER CAN STOP OR LIMIT YOUR THOUGHTS. WE EXISTS IN THE PRESENCE OF **GOD** DAILY.

GOD IS OMNIPRESENT, GOD IS SPIRIT, GOD IS THE HOLY SPIRIT. TO ENTER INTO GOD'S HEAVENLY PRESENCE WE MUST GO WITHOUT FLESH AND BLOOD, WE MUST LEAVE OUR BODIES AND BE ESCORTED BY

GOD'S HOLY ANGELS INTO THE HOLY PRESENCE OF **ALMIGHTY GOD.** THIS IS AWESOME AND **TRUE. AMEN!**

GOD IS POWERFUL. YOU CAN BEGIN TO UNDERSTAND THE POWER OF **GOD** BY LOOKING AT CREATION. AMEN! LOOK CLOSELY AT AN UNPEELED CORN ON THE COB THEN PEEL AWAY AND REMOVE THE HUSK LAYER BY LAYER WHICH IS THE DRY EXTERNAL COVERING OVER THE CORN.

BEFORE YOU REACH THE CORN ITSELF YOU WILL SEE THE AWESOME POWER OF **GOD,** THE CORN IS SECRETLY HIDDEN BY THE INTRICATE SHAPE AND CLOSENESS OF THE HUSK OUTER COVERING. THE CORN BENEATH THE HUSK IS PROTECTED FROM THE ELEMENTS AND ANIMALS WHO MAY OTHERWISE GET TO IT BEFORE WE DO. **GOD IS A MIRACLE WORKING GOD. AMEN!**

THE HOLY BIBLE STATES IN PSALMS 139 VERSE 14: "I WILL GIVE THANKS TO YOU FOR I AM FEARFULLY AND WONDERFULLY MADE; WONDERFUL ARE YOUR WORKS AND MY SOUL KNOWS IT VERY WELL."

YOUR PHYSICAL NATURAL SELF COVERS YOUR SOUL LIKE A WINTER JACKET COVERS YOUR FLESH. AT DEATH, YOUR SOUL RETURNS TO **GOD** AND YOU STAND BEFORE **GOD** TO ANSWER AND GIVE AN ACCOUNT FOR THE LIFE THAT YOU WERE LIVING IN YOUR LIFETIME.

GOD WILL JUDGE YOU, THIS IS YOUR **JUDGEMENT DAY.** WE MUST REALLY GET TO KNOW OURSELVES FIRST BEFORE WE DECIDE TO KNOW SOMEONE ELSE. WE SOMETIMES SPENDS A LOT OF TIME GETTING TO KNOW OTHERS AND WE DON'T REALLY KNOW OURSELVES, MANY PEOPLE DON'T REALLY KNOW WHO THEY ARE.

FIND OUT ABOUT YOURSELF. GET INQUISITIVE ABOUT YOURSELF, INVESTIGATE YOURSELF FIRST. LOOK IN THE MIRROR AGAIN, **SMILE** AT YOURSELF, BLESS YOURSELF, LOVE YOURSELF, TAKE GOOD CARE OF YOURSELF, LOOK YOUR BEST EVERYDAY.

SOMETIMES PEOPLE WONDER AND ASK THEMSELVES THESE QUESTIONS **"WHO AM I?** "WHY WAS I BORN? "WHERE DID I COME FROM? "WHY AM I HERE? "IS THERE A **GOD? "WHO IS THE TRUE GOD?** THE ANSWER TO ALL THESE QUESTION IS FOUND IN **THE HOLY BIBLE. AMEN!**

I REALLY DID NOT KNOW MYSELF UNTIL I BECAME **A BORN-AGAIN CHRISTIAN.** I KNEW I HAD GREAT POTENTIAL TO EXCEL ACADEMICALLY AND IN MY FORMER NURSING CAREER BUT THAT DID NOT MEAN THAT I REALLY KNEW WHO I WAS AS A HUMAN BEING CREATED IN THE IMAGE OF **GOD.** I HAD IGNORANT FEARS ABOUT THINGS THAT WERE REALLY A BLESSING AND ENHANCING TO ME.

AFTER I BECAME A **BORN AGAIN CHRISTIAN, GOD** SHOWED ME THAT MY AREAS OF FEAR WERE REALLY THINGS THAT WERE A PERSONAL BLESSING.

BELIEVE AND TRUST IN THE LORD JESUS CHRIST DON'T DIE IN SIN AND END UP IN THE PRESENCE OF SATAN IN HELL'S LAKE OF FIRE WHERE THERE WILL BE WEEPING, WAILING AND GNASHING OF TEETH. AMEN!

FLEE SEXUAL IMMORALITY, RUN FROM SIN, RUN FROM HIM QUICKLY. AMEN! I KNOW THAT **GOD** WATCHES OVER ME BECAUSE OF THE DIFFICULTIES HE HELPED ME OVERCOME THROUGHOUT MY LIFE. AMEN! **GOD'S** EYES ARE ON YOU TOO. AMEN!

IN THE HOLY BIBLE BOOK OF PSALMS CHAPTER 1 VERSE 1: IT STATES, HOW BLESSED IS THE MAN WHO DOES NOT WALK IN THE COUNSEL OF THE WICKED NOR STAND IN THE PATH OF SINNERS NOR SIT IN THE SEAT OF SCOFFERS.

REFRAIN FROM THE SINS OF SEXUAL PROMISCUITY, RAPE, DRUGS, INFIDELITY-ADULTERY, UNFAITHFULNESS, JEALOUSIES, ALCOHOL, PORNOGRAPHY, ABORTION, MURDER AND VIOLENCE. AMEN!

ON A PARTICULAR TWILIGHT EVENING IN THE SMALL TOWN WHERE I LIVED IN MY TEEN YEARS IN MEXICO I WAS WALKING HOME ON A QUIET STREET FROM A FRIEND'S HOME WHEN SUDDENLY A YOUNG MAN ON A BICYCLE PULLED UP ALONGSIDE ME. I THOUGHT HE WAS FRIENDLY BECAUSE HE SMILED. "WHERE ARE YOU GOING?" HE ASKED ME. "I AM WALKING HOME." I REPLIED. "WOULD YOU LIKE A RIDE? HE ASKED ME. I WAS APPROXIMATELY TEN MINUTES AWAY FROM HOME.

I HESITATED AT FIRST BECAUSE I DID NOT KNOW HIM AS A PERSONAL FRIEND. HIS FACE SEEMED FAMILIAR AND I ASUMED THAT HE LIVED IN THE NEIGHBOURHOOD. OKAY! "I WILL LET YOU RIDE ME HOME." I TOLD HIM.

I GOT ON THE BICYCLE AND SAT SIDEWAYS ON IT IN FRONT OF HIM THEN HE PEDALLED OFF GENTLY. AFTER PEDALLING A FEW FEET, HE SUDDENLY TURNED OFF ONTO A DUSTY SIDE STREET THAT LEADS OPPOSITE FROM THE DIRECTION THAT I WANTED TO GO IN. HE QUICKLY PROPELLED THE BICYCLE FASTER, WHILE I LISTENED TO HIS HASTED BREATHING. THEN I SAID TO HIM ANGRILY, STOP! "WHAT ARE YOUR INTENTIONS? "WHERE ARE YOU GOING? HE DID NOT REPLY TO MY

QUESTIONS. IT WAS BECOMING DARKER AND THE STREET WAS LONESOME.

WHEN I INSISTED THAT HE STOPPED, HE BRAKED THE BICYCLE WITH A SUDDEN JERK CAUSING ME TO FALL TO THE GROUND. THE BICYCLE FELL ON IT'S SIDE OPPOSITE ME, THEN HE CAME OVER ME BEFORE I WAS ABLE TO STAND UP AND HE ATTEMPTED TO UNDO MY BUTTON ON MY JEAN PANTS. HIS INTENTION WAS TO RAPE ME. I RESISTED HIM, PUSHED HIM AWAY AND SCREAMED. HE QUICKLY PULLED AWAY WHEN I SCREAMED. **GOD WAS WATCHING OVER ME AGAIN. AMEN!**

I GOT UP STILL FULLY DRESSED IN MY BLUE JEANS AND SLEEVELESS WHITE T-SHIRT AND RAN AWAY FROM HIM, TO THE MAIN STREET WHERE I MET HIM, HE DID NOT FOLLOW ME, AS I GOT CLOSER TO THE MAIN STREET I SAW ONE OF MY FRIEND WHO WENT WITH ME TO THE LAKE. I YELLED OUT TO MY FRIEND THREE TIMES. HE WAS WALKING AT A DISTANCE AHEAD OF ME THEN HE HEARD ME AND STOPPED AND I RAN TO JOIN HIM. MY FRIEND WAS MUCH TALLER THAN I AND TALLER THAN THE YOUNG MAN WHOM TRIED TO RAPE ME.

GOD AGAIN SENT MY FRIEND JUST IN TIME. MY FRIEND'S PRESENCE COMFORTED ME AND I KNEW HIS PRESENCE WOULD DETER ANOTHER ATTEMPT OF THAT OTHER YOUNG MAN. I CONTINUED ON HOME IN SAFETY THAT NIGHT AND I NEVER SAW THE YOUNG MAN WHO TRIED TO RAPE ME AGAIN. THANK **GOD.** AMEN!

YOUNG ADULTS, THE **HOLY BIBLE STATES IN 1ST. CORINTHIANS 15 VERSE 33: "DO NOT BE DECEIVED BAD COMPANY CORRUPTS GOOD MORALS."** CHOOSE YOUR FRIENDS WISELY. GET TO KNOW THE PEOPLE THAT YOU PLAN TO GO PLACES WITH. KNOW THEIR CHARACTER

AND FAMILY MEMBERS. KNOW IF THEY ARE PEOPLE OF INTEGRITY. KNOW THEIR REPUTATION. KNOW THEIR FRIENDS, BEFORE MAKING THEM A PRIMARY FRIEND. KNOW IF THEY ARE SEXUAL PREDATORS. NEVER TAKE A RIDE FROM SOMEONE JUST BECAUSE THEY SMILE AT YOU ESPECIALLY IF IT IS DUSK OR SUNDOWN.

A SMILE DOES NOT ALWAYS MEANS THAT THEY ARE FRIENDLY. YOUR BODIES ARE PRECIOUS AND YOU ARE BECOMING MORE DESIRABLE TO THE OPPOSITE SEX. WAIT FOR MARRIAGE BEFORE HAVING SEXUAL INTERCOURSE. CHERISH YOUR BODY WHILE YOU ARE YOUNG. KNOW THE POWER AND ABILITY WITHIN YOU TO ATTRACT THE BEST INTO YOUR **BLESSED GOD GIVEN LIFE. AMEN!**

DO NOT ALLOW ANYONE TO TAKE DISADVANTAGE OF YOUR BODY. DO A COMPLETE SELF EXAMINATION. INCREASE IN KNOWLEDGE ABOUT YOURSELF. BE ADAMANT TRUTHFULLY ABOUT YOUR BIOLOGICAL GENDER.

WHEN I WAS A TEENAGER I ASSUMED MANY THINGS ABOUT MY REPRODUCTIVE ORGANS. AFTER I STUDIED ANATOMY AND PHYSIOLOGY I REALIZED HOW WISELY **GOD CREATED AND DIFFERENTIATED OUR MANY BODY PARTS. AMEN!**

YOUR BODY BELONGS TO YOU AND NOT TO ANYONE ELSE WHEN YOU ARE UNMARRIED. YOUTH IS DESIRABLE AND EACH DAY YOU LIVE YOU BECOME OLDER AND GRADUALLY YOUR YOUTH FADES AWAY. IT WILL NEVER RETURN. PLASTIC SURGERY AND THOSE YOUTH PARAPHERNALIAS DOES NOT RESTORE YOUTH PERMANENTLY. TAKE GOOD CARE OF YOUR PHYSICAL APPEARANCE.

DRINK A LOT OF WATER AND EAT A HEALTHY DIET OF FRUITS AND VEGETABLES, WASH YOUR FRUITS AND VEGETABLES FIRST. EXERCISE TWO TO THREE TIMES PER WEEK. TAKE A SHOWER OR A BATH DAILY, COMB YOUR HAIR AND WEAR SOME FORM OF DEODORANT.

USE Q-TIPS TO CLEAN YOUR EARS. BRUSH YOUR TEETH TWICE DAILY, FLOSS YOUR TEETH BEFORE GOING TO BED. SEE YOUR DENTIST TWICE PER YEAR.

WEAR CLEAN CLOTHES DAILY, IF YOU DON'T LIKE TO IRON YOUR CLOTHE, BUY WASH AND WEAR CLOTHING. FEMALES DISPOSE OF SANITARY NAPKINS DISCRETELY WRAP THEM IN BROWN PAPER OR PLACE THEM INTO A DISPOSABLE BIN. GET A HAIR CUT WHEN YOU NEED ONE. GROOM YOURSELF THE BEST WAY YOU CAN. DRESS MODESTLY.

IF YOU CANNOT AFFORD TO PAY FOR BRAND NEW CLOTHING, GO TO THE SECOND HAND CLOTHING STORE OR TO THE DROP IN CENTRE WHERE YOU CAN GET FREE USED CLOTHING, TOILETRIES, WINTER CLOTHING AND FREE SHOES. AMEN!

YOUNG PEOPLE DO YOUR LAUNDRY ONCE PER WEEK AND KEEP YOUR LIVING ENVIRONMENT CLEAN. DO NOT FOLLOW THE CROWD. MAKE IT YOUR DUTY TO HELP YOUR PARENTS IN THE HOME. HELP THE INDIVIDUAL WHOM **GOD** ORDAINS TO BE YOUR GUARDIAN OR CARE PROVIDER. PRAY FOR THEM AND ASK **GOD** TO MAKE THEM LOVE YOU. ASK **GOD** TO HELP YOU TO LOVE THEM ALSO. FOLLOW **JESUS CHRIST** AND LIVE SUCCESSFULLY AND HAPPILY. AMEN!

IF YOUR PARENTS ARE POOR DO NOT CONDEMN THEM. DO NOT COMPARE YOUR PARENTS TO OTHER ADULTS. HAVE A DESIRE FOR HIGHER EDUCATION OR

LEARN A SKILL THAT WILL GENERATE INCOME FOR YOU. OBTAIN PART-TIME EMPLOYMENT IF YOU CAN OR START A BUSINESS, BECOME SELF EMPLOYED. THIS WILL **BLESS** YOUR FAMILY. **BORN-AGAIN CHRISTIAN YOUTH GOD NEEDS WORKERS TO GO OUT INTO THE VINEYARD. SEEK GOD'S WILL PRAYERFULLY FOR YOUR LIFE AND FUTURE. GOD NEEDS MANY FISHERS OF MEN. HOOK THEM WITH DIVINE WISDOM.**

DO VOLUNTEER WORK WHICH WILL ENABLE YOU TO ACHIEVE VALUABLE WORK EXPERIENCE. WHEN I WAS A TEENAGER LIVING WITH MY DAD IN FRANCE I WAS EMPLOYED AT ONE OF FRANCE'S AMUSEMENT THEME PARK. I WAS ALSO EMPLOYED IN A HOTEL GIFT SHOP AS A CASHIER. MY TEENAGE EMPLOYMENTS WERE A BLESSING.

HAVING THE PRESENCE AND AWARENESS OF **JESUS CHRIST** AT A YOUNG AGE IS VERY WISE. I REMEMBER THERE WAS A SMALL COMMUNITY CHURCH IN OUR SMALL MEXICAN NEIGHBOURHOOD WHERE I LIVED AND I ATTENDED THE SERVICE THERE ONE SUNDAY MORNING AND IT FELT VERY GOOD TO BE IN **GOD'S** HOUSE THAT DAY. AMEN!

ST. MATTHEW 5 VERSE 6 STATES: BLESSED ARE THOSE WHO HUNGER AND THIRST FOR RIGHTEOUSNESS, FOR THEY SHALL BE SATISFIED."

YOUNG PEOPLE, MANKIND, LET YOUR SOULS HUNGER AND THIRST FOR **GOD** AND CRY OUT TO **GOD** NOW FOR YOUR SALVATION, DELIVERANCE AND HELP. **JESUS CHRIST** DOES HEAR YOU WHEN YOU PRAY AND TALK TO HIM. **GOD IS A SPIRIT, JESUS CHRIST IS THE HOLY SPIRIT. AMEN!**

WHEN I BECAME AN OLDER TEENAGER I MET SOME PEOPLE WHO WERE WILEY. I WOULD NOT MAKE

PEOPLE WITH SUCH CHARACTERISTICS MY PRIMARY FRIENDS TODAY. I SHARE THE EVENTS OF MY LIFE TO ENCOURAGE, TO HELP YOU KNOW THAT WHATEVER YOUR BACKGROUND AND LIFE EXPERIENCES MAY ENTAIL **GOD** IS ABLE TO TURN YOUR DARKNESS INTO LIGHT AND YOUR SORROWS INTO JOY. AMEN!

GOD IS ABLE TO DELIVER YOU FROM EVERY UNPLEASANT AND DANGEROUS SITUATION THAT YOU MAY ENCOUNTER IN THIS LIFE. DON'T WAIT UNTIL WHEN TROUBLE COMES BEFORE YOU TURN TO **JESUS CHRIST** FOR HELP. **GOD** WANTS TO INTERACT WITH YOU NOW ON A DAILY BASIS. AMEN!

JESUS CHRIST WANTS TO TALK TO YOU. **JESUS** WANTS YOU TO HEAR HIS VOICE GUIDING YOU EACH DAY. **GOD** WANTS YOU TO TURN TO HIM AND NOT TO ANYONE ELSE FOR ALL YOUR NEEDS WHETHER BIG OR SMALL. AMEN!

THE HOLY BIBLE STATES IN EXODUS 34 VERSE 14; "FOR YOU SHALL NOT WORSHIP ANY OTHER GOD FOR THE LORD WHOSE NAME IS JEALOUS IS A JEALOUS GOD.

JESUS DOES NOT WANT YOU TO LOVE ANY OTHER **GOD** BUT ONLY HIM. YOU MAY WONDER WHY IS **GOD JEALOUS?** WELL IT IS BECAUSE **JESUS CHRIST IS ALMIGHTY GOD WHO** CREATED YOU AND GAVE YOU YOUR LIFE AND YOUR BEING. IF **GOD** DID NOT MAKE YOU, YOU WOULD NOT EXIST. AMEN!

THIS IS WHY **GOD IS JEALOUS** OVER HIS CREATION. HE MADE YOU IN YOUR MOTHER'S WOMB THEREFORE LIVE FOR **JESUS CHRIST.** PRAISE AND WORSHIP **JESUS** DAILY. THANK **GOD** FOR MAKING YOU AND GIVING YOU LIFE. IF YOU ARE UNSAVED I WANT TO ENCOURAGE YOU TO BECOME A **BORN AGAIN CHRISTIAN. AMEN!**

WHEN I BECAME A **BORN-AGAIN CHRISTIAN** I WAS IN MY MIDDLE THIRTIES. I HAD DEEP REGRETS FOR NOT TURNING TO **GOD** AND SURRENDERING TO **JESUS** MUCH SOONER IN MY LIFE.

I REMEMBER I CRIED AND SAID, **"JESUS, I AM** SORRY I WAITED SO LONG TO GET BAPTIZE AND TO KNOW YOU PERSONALLY AS MY **LORD AND SAVIOUR."** DON'T WAIT AS LONG AS I DID TO BECOME **A BORN-AGAIN CHRISTIAN** AVOID WASTING TIME AND DO IT NOW. AMEN!

THE HOLY BIBLE STATES IN 2ND. CORINTHIANS 6 VERSE 2 "...NOW IS THE ACCEPTABLE TIME; BEHOLD NOW IS THE DAY OF SALVATION." HAVE THE JOY OF SALVATION EARLY IN YOUR LIFE AND LIVE A BLESSED LIFE. AMEN!

MAKE **JESUS CHRIST** YOUR BEST FRIEND FIRST. **HE IS A FRIEND THAT STICKS CLOSER THAN A BROTHER, JESUS SAID ALSO IN THE HOLY BIBLE, JOSHUA I VERSE 5, "...I WILL BE WITH YOU I WILL NOT FAIL YOU OR FORSAKE YOU."**

BETWEEN THIRTEEN AND SEVENTEEN YEARS OF AGE I WAS ENROLLED IN THREE DIFFERENT HIGH SCHOOLS IN THREE DIFFERENT COUNTRIES. IN ST. LUCIA I WAS ENROLLED IN THE CATHOLIC GIRL HIGH SCHOOL, IN MEXICO I WAS ENROLLED IN A PUBLIC HIGH SCHOOL AND IN FRANCE I WAS ENROLLED IN A BOY AND GIRL PUBLIC HIGH SCHOOL.

WHEN I RETURNED TO FRANCE AFTER MY FIRST VISIT WITH MY FATHERS RELATIVES IN MEXICO, MY FATHER BECAME A BACHELOR AGAIN AND WE LIVED ALONE. ONE DAY I WENT TO VISIT OUR FORMER HOME. IT WAS NOSTALGIC BUT I FELT NO JOY IN THE HOME. I

WAS TOLD THAT SOLOMON AND HIS FAMILY MOVED TO MEXICO WHILE I WAS AWAY.

AS TIME PASSED, SOLOMON RETURNED FOR A VISIT TO FRANCE AND FOUND OUT WHERE I WAS LIVING WITH MY FATHER. MY FATHER LIKED SOLOMON. I BELIEVE THAT IF WE WERE BOTH OLDER AT THAT TIME SOLOMON WOULD HAVE MARRIED ME, HE LOVED ME. MY FATHER WORKED NIGHT SHIFT AT A LARGE HOSPITAL.

I REMEMBER MY FATHER SAYING TO SOLOMON WHEN HE VISITED, "I WILL NOT LEAVE YOU IN THE HOME ALONE WITH CHRISTIAN, MOREOVER I HAVE TO LEAVE FOR WORK BY 9:00 p. m."

PARENTS STOP AND THINK ABOUT YOUR OWN TEENAGE CHILDREN, THEY NEED **GOD,** THEY NEED YOU. THEY NEED WISE **GODLY** COUNCIL NOW TO BE SUCCESSFUL REGARDING MAKING RELATIONSHIP CHOICES, LIFESTYLE CHOICES AND FUTURE CHOICES. **HELP THEM!** DON'T LET THEM WONDER AIMLESSLY WITHOUT A PURPOSE AND **BLESSED** PATH. AMEN!

DON'T LET YOUR TEENAGERS BUDDING YEARS BE MARRED WITH MANY REGRETTABLE SCARS. RENEE AND OBASI PLEASE FORGIVE ME, I LOVE YOU BOTH. LOOKING BACK NOW I REALIZED HOW MUCH I NEEDED LOVING AND KIND, PARENTAL GUIDANCE AND COUNCIL IN MY EARLY TEEN TO YOUNG ADULT YEARS, THE AGES BETWEEN THIRTEEN AND NINETEEN YEARS OLD. I FELT LIKE I GREW UP ALONE, NOT ALWAYS HAVING CONSTANT PARENTAL PRESENCE, SUPPORT AND ADVICE. IT DOES HURT WHEN A CHILD LIVES THIS WAY.

WHEN **GOD** GETS INVOLVED FORTUNATELY THE BROKEN AREAS CAN BE HEALED, RESTORED AND

MENDED ESPECIALLY WHEN FAMILY MEMBERS ARE STILL ALIVE AND WILLING TO WORK ON THEIR RELATIONSHIP. AMEN!

I PRAY AND ASK **JESUS CHRIST ALMIGHTY GOD** DAILY NOW TO BRING RESTORATION IN MY FAMILY RELATIONSHIPS WHERE IT IS NEEDED. **I AM** REASSURED THAT **GOD** DOES HEAR AND ANSWER PRAYERS. AMEN.

YOUNG PEOPLE MUST RESPECT ADULTS. GET PERMISSION FROM AN ADULT BEFORE VISITING THEIR HOME. ASK YOUR FRIEND'S PARENT FOR AUTHORIZATION BEFORE VISITING THEIR HOME. I MUST ADMIT THAT WHEN SOLOMON CAME TO VISIT ME AND MY DAD I DON'T REMEMBER HIM CALLING US FIRST. I ONLY REMEMBER HEARING A KNOCK ON THE DOOR AND MY FATHER LET HIM IN. SOLOMON WAS HUMBLE IN SPIRIT BUT DETERMINED.

REMEMBER THIS HOLY BIBLE VERSE: IN THE HOLY BIBLE BOOK OF ECCLESIASTES CHAPTER 12 VERSE 1 IT STATES. REMEMBER ALSO YOUR CREATOR IN THE DAYS OF YOUR YOUTH, BEFORE THE EVIL DAYS COME AND THE DAYS DRAW NEAR WHEN YOU WILL SAY, "I HAVE NO DELIGHT IN THEM".

PARENT'S MUST ENCOURAGE THEIR CHILDREN POSITIVELY, TELL THEM THAT THEY ARE BEAUTIFUL AND HANDSOME, TELL THEM THAT THEY CAN EXCEL ACADEMICALLY. TELL YOUR CHILDREN TO FIRST SEEK **GOD** EARLY IN THEIR LIFE. PARENTS BECOME YOUR CHILD'S FIRST CONFIDANT.

KNOW YOUR CHILDREN BETTER THAN ANYONE ELSE. LET YOUR CHILDREN KNOW ALL THE DETAILS ABOUT YOU BEFORE YOUR FRIENDS OR STRANGERS DO. SHARE WITH YOUR CHILDREN. IF YOU ARE AN

ADOPTIVE PARENT LOVE THAT CHILD WHOM IS MADE IN THE IMAGE OF **GOD.** LOVE THAT CHILD AS IF YOU HAD GIVEN HIM OR HER BIRTH. **LOVE** YOUR TEENAGE CHILDREN, BE A POSITIVE EXAMPLE TO THEM AND DESIRE THE BEST FOR YOUR CHILDREN. AMEN!

FORGIVE YOUR TEENAGE CHILDREN. DO THE BEST YOU CAN FOR YOUR CHILDREN, GET HELP WHEN YOU DON'T KNOW WHAT TO DO. **GODLY SPIRITUAL HELP IS ALWAYS NEEDED FIRST.** DON'T COMPARE YOUR STEP-CHILD, WITH YOUR BIOLOGICAL CHILDREN, DO NOT DEMEAN YOUR STEPCHILDREN. AVOID FAVOURITISM.

A THIRTEEN YEAR OLD CHILD DOES NOT FULLY UNDERSTAND AN ADULT'S MOTIVE AND INTENTIONS WHEN AN ANGRY STEPPARENT SAYS TO THEM, "I WILL GET THIS CONDOMINIUM AND NOT YOU." JEALOUSY IS VERY DAMAGING. I HAVE FORGIVEN BY THE GRACE OF **GOD. AMEN!**

CHAPTER 4

ADULTHOOD

MANY COUNTRIES DEFINES LEGALLY WHEN **A CHILD** IS DEEMED AN ADULT. IN **FRANCE** THE LAW STATES THAT WHEN A CHILD BECOMES EIGHTEEN YEARS OLD **HE OR SHE** IS CONSIDERED AN ADULT. IN FRANCE THERE IS A KNOWN **LEGAL AGE** YOU HAVE TO BE BEFORE YOU CAN BUY CERTAIN PRODUCTS.

I WANT TO DISCOURAGE THE USE OF ALCOHOL AND TOBACCO NO MATTER WHAT AGE YOU ARE. TOBACCO, ALCOHOL AND ILLEGAL DRUGS ARE NOT NOURISHMENTS FOR YOUR BODIES, THEY DO NOT HAVE VITAMINS IN THEM. THESE HARMFUL SUBSTANCES DOES NOT BUILD YOU UP THEY TEAR YOU DOWN QUICKLY AND HARM YOU. THEY ARE AN ENEMY TO YOUR SOUL, LIFE AND HEALTH. AMEN!

THE HOLY SPIRIT SAYS IN THE HOLY BIBLE, LUKE 1 VERSE 15, "...AND HE WILL DRINK NO WINE OR LIQUOR AND HE WILL BE FILLED WITH THE HOLY SPIRIT..." AMEN!

IF YOU EVER HAD AN ENEMY IN YOUR LIFE, A REAL PERSON, **I AM** SURE THAT ALL THEY DID WAS TEAR YOU

DOWN AND NEVER BUILD YOU UP. AN ENEMY DOES NOT **BLESS YOU** BUT CURSES YOU ALWAYS.

SATAN IS YOUR FIRST ENEMY AND HE IS A CUNNING EVIL SPIRIT. THE DEVIL USES MANY DEVISES SUCH AS SCHEMES, LAWS, POLICIES, ISMS, SCHISMS, POLITICS, MONEY, DRUGS, SEX, IMMORALITY, POWER AND UNHEALTHY EATING TO CREATE HAVOC AND TO DESTROY MANKIND.

THE HOLY BIBLE STATES IN JAMES 4 VERSE 7: "SUBMIT THEREFORE TO GOD RESIST THE DEVIL AND HE WILL FLEE FROM YOU."

BECOME A SERVANT AND FRIEND OF **JESUS CHRIST ALMIGHTY GOD. JESUS CHRIST IS THE LIVING WATER. JESUS CHRIST** QUENCHES YOUR SPIRITUAL AND NATURAL THIRST. AMEN!

DO NOT BECOME A FRIEND OF SATAN. HE IS LIKE DRINKING POISON. THE DEVIL LEADS TO DESTRUCTION, DEATH AND HELL. TO **GET RID OF SATAN** YOU MUST BECOME A **BORN-AGAIN CHRISTIAN.**

YOU MUST REPENT AND CONFESS YOUR SINS TO **JESUS CHRIST** AND GET **BAPTIZE THE JOHN THE BAPTIST WAY BY IMMERSION IN THE WATER IN THE NAME OF THE FATHER, THE SON AND THE HOLY SPIRIT. AMEN!**

PRAYER.

DEAR LORD JESUS, I REPENT AND CONFESS MY SINS, PLEASE SET ME FREE FROM SATAN AND SIN, DELIVER ME FROM MY ADDICTION. I REALIZE THAT THE DEVIL COME TO STEAL, KILL AND TO DESTROY AND I WANT TO LIVE ETERNALLY AWAY FROM HIM, PLEASE HELP

ME LORD JESUS CHRIST TO DEFEAT THIS ADDICTION PROBLEM AND DEMON. IN JESUS NAME I PRAY TO MY HEAVENLY FATHER JEHOVAH. AMEN!

I AM ALLERGIC TO CIGARETTE SMOKE. I NEVER SMOKED AND I DON'T DRINK ALCOHOL. I HAVE NEVER USED ILLEGAL DRUGS. ALCOHOL WILL DESTROY YOUR LIVER AND OTHER ORGANS IN YOUR BODY. I DRINK WATER THROUGHOUT EACH DAY. THIS HELPS ME TO REMAIN HYDRATED AND FLUSHES IMPURITIES AND TOXINS FROM MY BODY.

I ENJOY THESE NATURAL TEAS, PEPPERMINT, GINGER AND LIME LEAF TEA. LIME LEAF TEA IS DELICIOUS. IN ST. LUCIA LIME TREES ARE ABUNDANT. I WOULD LIKE TO ENCOURAGE MY SISTER MARY; YOU CAN LOSE THE WEIGHT AND WIN THE BATTLE OVER OBESITY. AMEN!

VISCERAL FATS SURROUNDS THE ORGANS IN YOUR BODY AND SUBCUTANEOUS FATS ARE DIRECTLY UNDERNEATH YOUR SKIN. THE LEMON, LIME, GRAPEFRUIT AND GINGER USED REGULARLY IN YOUR DIET IS EFFECTIVE AT ERADICATING AND REMOVING THE FATTY GLOBULE DEPOSITS IN YOUR BODY. BE PATIENT TO LOSE WEIGHT.

THE HOLY BIBLE STATES: IN 1ST. CORINTHIANS CHAPTER 13 VERSE 4: LOVE IS PATIENT, LOVE IS KIND AND IS NOT JEALOUS; LOVE DOES NOT BRAG AND IS NOT ARROGANT. AMEN!

PRAYER

DEAR LORD JESUS CHRIST, I REPENT AND CONFESS MY SINS TO YOU LORD. PLEASE HELP ME TO LOSE WEIGHT AND EXERCISE ACCORDING TO MY ABILITY 2-3

TIMES PER WEEK. GIVE ME VICTORY OVER MY OBESITY. HELP ME TO EAT HEALTHY AS YOU TAUGHT MANKIND IN YOUR WORDS THE HOLY BIBLE. GIVE ME THE WILL POWER TO AVOID TEMPTATION OF UNHEALTHY EATING. KEEP ME AWAY FROM FRIED OILY FOODS, EXCESS SUGAR, FOODS FILLED WITH ARTIFICIAL FOOD COLOURINGS, PROCESSED FOODS AND PRESERVATIVES IN FOODS. HELP ME TO EAT ORGANIC FOODS ONLY. THANK YOU LORD IN ADVANCE FOR MY SUCCESS. IN JESUS NAME I PRAY TO MY HEAVENLY FATHER. AMEN.

MY DIET IN THE MORNINGS CONSISTS OF A MEDIUM SIZE BOWL OF OATMEAL PORRIDGE, TWO HARD BOIL EGGS, 1 CUP LEMON GINGER TEA, ONE SLICE OF MULTI-GRAIN BROWN BREAD AND A RIPE BANANA OR ANOTHER CHOICE OF FRUIT. SOMETIMES I USE SUGAR IN MY TEA AND OATMEAL. I AVOID EATING FRIED FOODS. I BAKE OR BOIL ALL MEATS, I DON'T USE BUTTER, CHEESE, MARGARINE OR SALAD DRESSING AND I ONLY DRINK SKIM MILK. I INCORPORATE IRON RICH FOODS IN MY DIET.

IN THE HOLY BIBLE BOOK OF LEVITICUS CHAPTER 7 VERSE 23 IT STATES: "SPEAK TO THE SONS OF ISRAEL SAYING, "YOU SHALL NOT EAT ANY FAT FROM AN OX, A SHEEP OR A GOAT."

WE MUST OBEY **GOD** AND AVOID EATING FAT. ONE BEAUTIFUL SUMMER DAY WHEN I WAS LIVING IN PARIS FRANCE I HAD A DISCUSSION WITH A LADY WHO WAS FROM AFRICA, I WAS BROUGHT TO HER HOME BY ONE OF HER FRIEND. THE THREE OF US SAT DOWN TO HAVE LUNCH. I COULD NOT EAT SOME OF WHAT WAS SERVED BECAUSE OF THE OIL CONTENT. SO WE STARTED TO DISCUSS THE BEST WAY TO PREPARE A HEALTHY MEAL.

ONE LADY SAID, "OUR BODIES NEED SOME FAT." SHE WAS THE OVERWEIGHT ONE. **HA! HAA! HAAA!**

I EXPLAINED TO THEM THE BIBLE'S TEACHINGS REGARDING OUR DIETARY INTAKE AND I QUOTE SCRIPTURES TO THEM. "COOKING OIL IS GOOD FOR YOU, THEY ARE TAKEN FROM THE NATURAL SEED AND NATURE." THE LADY CONTINUES. "THAT IS A GOOD OBSERVATION." I SAID. WHEN **GOD** FIRST MADE ALL THE SEEDS FOR PLANTING, **GOD** SAW THAT IT WAS GOOD.

THE HOLY BIBLE STATES: IN GENESIS CHAPTER 1 VERSE 11 THEN GOD SAID, LET THE EARTH SPROUT VEGETATION, PLANTS YIELDING SEED, AND FRUIT TREES ON THE EARTH BEARING FRUIT AFTER THEIR KIND; AND GOD SAW THAT IT WAS GOOD.

GENESIS CHAPTER 1 VERSE 12: THE EARTH BROUGHT FORTH VEGETATION, PLANTS YIELDING SEED AFTER THEIR KIND AND TREES BEARING FRUIT WITH SEED IN THEM AFTER THEIR KIND; AND GOD SAW THAT IT WAS GOOD.

GOD DIVINELY MADE THE OLIVES, SUNFLOWER SEED AND CORN WITH THE RIGHT AMOUNT OF NUTRIENTS FOR OUR DAILY DIET. AMEN! I WANT TO REMAIN HEALTHY THEREFORE I PREFER TO EAT THE SEED AND THE NATURAL ORGANIC FOOD THAT **JESUS CHRIST CREATED.** BUY SIX CORNS, BOIL THEM AND EAT THEM FRESH, YOUR BODY WILL CONSUME THE RIGHT AMOUNT OF NOURISHMENT **GOD** INTENDED FOR YOU.

TOO MUCH OF OUR FOOD HAS UNHEALTHY INGREDIENTS WHICH CAUSES HEALTH PROBLEMS, DEATHS AND HAS BECOME A **PEST.** BUY CARROT SEEDS, CUCUMBER SEEDS, TOMATO SEEDS AND PLANT YOUR OWN GARDEN. IF YOU DON'T HAVE A BACK YARD PLANT

THE SEEDS IN A LARGE GARDENING POT AND PLACE IT NEAR THE SUNLIGHT IN YOUR APARTMENT AND ENJOY YOUR HARVEST. AMEN!

SELECTING THE RIGHT FOOD CHOICE IS SIMILAR TO SELECTING THE RIGHT MARRIAGE PARTNER. WE MUST CHOOSE THE BEST THAT WILL NEVER HARM US. AMEN!

*ONE OF MY INTENTION IS TO ENCOURAGE WOMEN TO AVOID SELECTING A DETRIMENTAL MARRIAGE PARTNER AND TO ENCOURAGE MEN NOT TO PERPETRATE A CRIME AGAINST A FEMALE DURING A RELATIONSHIP OR WHILE PURSUING A FEMALE. HAVE SELF CONTROL DO NOT LET JEALOUSY DESTROY YOU OR SOMEONE ELSE. **AMEN! REMEMBER JESUS CHRIST LOVES YOU EVEN IF THEY DON'T. AMEN!**

WOMEN BE PATIENT, LOOK AROUND AND PRAY FOR THE RIGHT DIVINE CONNECTION. AFTER I WAS DIVORCED TWICE BEFORE THE AGE OF THIRTY, I STARTED TO WONDER WHAT WAS HAPPENING TO MY LIFE. I NEVER FELT LESS ATTRACTIVE OR ANYTHING LIKE THAT BUT I WAS LONELY AND DISCONNECTED.

MEN OF VARIOUS AGE GROUPS AND DIFFERENT NATIONALITIES ARE ALWAYS ATTRACTED TO ME. I DON'T LIMIT MYSELF TO ONE NATIONALITY BECAUSE I SEEK TRUE LOVE. **GOD IS LOVE. LOVE** HAS NO COLOUR. **GOD IS SPIRIT** AND IS NOT A BLACK MAN OR A WHITE MAN. **I AM** SEEKING A NEW HUSBAND. ONE OF REPUTABLE CHARACTER AND INTEGRITY. I PREFER A **BORN-AGAIN CHRISTIAN HUSBAND.**

I WILL CONSIDER **SINGLE MEN** IN THESE CATEGORIES. IF YOU ARE A **PASTOR, CHRISTIAN MINISTRY FOUNDER,**

CHRISTIAN AUTHOR, ENGLISH PROFESSOR, **A**

CHRISTIAN PUBLISHER, A PRINCE, A KING, A **GOSPEL** SONG WRITER, A **GOSPEL** SINGER, A FILM MAKER, FARMER, ARTIST, AVIATOR, ENGINEER, ENTREPRENEUR, MEDICAL DEVISE DESIGNER, BUILDER, BIOLOGIST, ANATOMY AND PHYSIOLOGY PROFESSOR, A FURNITURE DESIGNER, INVESTOR, <u>CONSTITUTION</u>-AL LAWYER, ASTRONAUT, **A BORN-AGAIN <u>POLITICIAN</u>,** A JUDGE, FASHION DESIGNER, OR A HEART SURGEON I WILL CONSIDER YOU IF THERE IS **TRUE LOVE.**

A MAN WHO TRULY **LOVES** DOES NOT HAVE TO POSSESS A DEGREE. AMEN! **WOO,** MAN! SAYS THE LORD.

I DESIRE THE **GODLY,** THE BEST, THE HUMBLE AND THE RICH. IF YOU PREVIOUSLY HAVE CHILDREN OR HAS ANY FORM OF DISABILITY I WILL CONSIDER YOU IF THERE **IS TRUE LOVE.** CHILDREN NEED POSITIVE EXAMPLES TO IMITATE. I WANT TO ENCOURAGE THEM TO CHOOSE THE BEST WITH WHOLESOME CHARACTER. AMEN!

I **AM** ONLY ATTRACTED TO HETEROSEXUAL MEN. I SEEK THE SECURE EMBRACE OF LOVE FROM A MAN'S HEART TO MY HEART. I BELIEVE IN BEING FRUITFUL, MULTIPLYING AND INCREASING A NATIONS POPULATION. I WANT A LOVING, LASTING MARRIAGE. I DO NOT JUST WANT SEX. THAT WAS WHAT SOME OF THE MEN I MET BEFORE I BECAME **A BORN AGAIN CHRISTIAN** WANTED AND I DID AVOID THEM.

ONE OF THE MEN I MET A FEW YEARS AGO INVITED ME TO HIS HOME. WHEN I GOT THERE THE NECESSITY NEED FOR THE BATHROOM MOVED ME, SO I WALKED BY HIS BEDROOM AND I SAW A FEMALE NIGHTGOWN THROWN ACROSS HIS BED. I GASP! I WAS SHOCKED TO SEE IT SO OPENLY LAID OUT ON HIS BED. I HAD A

SIMILAR NIGHT GOWN AT HOME EXACTLY LIKE IT. I WAS DISAPPOINTED IN HIM. I DID NOT QUESTION HIM.

THAT SCENE ONLY REVEALED TO ME WHO HE REALLY WAS IN CHARACTER. I HAD SINCERELY THOUGHT THAT HE WAS AN UNATTACHED SINGLE MAN, THIS WAS THE REASON WHY I ACCEPTED HIS INVITATION. I WAS SEEKING SOMEONE WHO WANTED TO EMBARK ON A LONG TERM COMMITTED RELATIONSHIP. I WAS VERY GRACIOUS ABOUT THE WHOLE SITUATION I JUST PRETENDED THAT I DID NOT SEE THE OTHER WOMAN'S NIGHTGOWN ON HIS BED.

THAT EVENING WE HAD JUICE AND COFFEE TO DRINK AND SOMETHING LIGHT TO EAT IN THE KITCHEN THEN I ASKED HIM TO DRIVE ME HOME. IN MY HEART I DECIDED THAT I WOULD NEVER ACCEPT ANOTHER INVITATION FROM HIM AGAIN.

THIS QUESTION JUST ENTERED INTO MY THOUGHTS, "WHERE SHOULD A WOMAN GO WITH A MAN WHEN HE INVITES HER OUT ON A DATE FOR THE FIRST TIME?" "REVELATION COMES IN MANY WAYS." SAYS THE LORD. "I WANT A **FAMILY** AGAIN, A NEW **HUSBAND** AND I WANT A CLOSER RELATIONSHIP WITH ALL OF MY FAMILY MEMBERS. AMEN!

IN THE **HOLY BIBLE BOOK OF GENESIS CHAPTER 1 VERSE 1 IT STATES: IN THE BEGINNING GOD CREATED THE HEAVENS AND THE EARTH.**

GENESIS IN THE **HOLY BIBLE** MEANS BEGINNING, ORIGIN, **GOD'S BEGINNING OF CREATION.** THE WORD **OOGENESIS** MEANS THE ORIGIN AND DEVELOPMENT OF THE OVUM. AN **OVUM** IS THE FEMALE REPRODUCTIVE CELL OR **GAMETE** OF ANIMALS, WHICH IS CAPABLE OF

DEVELOPING, USUALLY AFTER FERTILIZATION INTO A NEW INDIVIDUAL.

A **GAMETE** IS A MATURE SEXUAL REPRODUCTIVE CELL, AS A SPERM OR EGG, THAT UNITES WITH ANOTHER CELL TO FORM A NEW ORGANISM.

GOD WANTS MANKIND TO UNITE MATURELY AND HAVE CHILDDREN LIKE **JACOB AND LEAH** IN THE **HOLY BIBLE.** AMEN!

THE HOLY BIBLE STATES IN GENESIS 1 VERSE 28: GOD BLESSED THEM; AND GOD SAID TO THEM, "BE FRUITFUL AND MULTIPLY, AND FILL THE EARTH, AND SUBDUE IT; AND RULE OVER THE FISH OF THE SEA AND OVER THE BIRDS OF THE SKY AND OVER EVERY LIVING THING THAT MOVES ON THE EARTH.

I AM YOUNG LOOKING. IN MY DAILY LIFE I EMPHASIZE BEING CLEAN AND NATURAL, **I AM** A NATURAL BEAUTY. **I AM** NOT A MAKE UP BEAUTY. FOR MANY YEARS I DID NOT THINK THIS WAY ABOUT MYSELF.

MANY PEOPLE WOULD SAY TO ME, "YOU ARE BEAUTIFUL." I WOULD SHRUG MY SHOULDERS AT TIMES OR SHRINK AWAY IN SHYNESS. AT OTHER TIMES I WOULD SHEEPISHLY REPLY WITH, "THANK YOU VERY MUCH." I HAVE LEARNED TO RECEIVE SUCH COMPLIMENT AS SINCERE TRUTH. I WANT AND DESIRE TO BE TREATED BEAUTIFULLY BY OTHERS.

THE HOLY BIBLE STATES: IN ST. LUKE 6 VERSE 31: "TREAT OTHERS THE SAME WAY YOU WANT THEM TO TREAT YOU." AMEN!

I WAS NOT TAUGHT IN MY YOUTH AND YOUNG ADULTHOOD YEARS HOW TO ATTRACT THE "RIGHT MAN-HUSBAND." MANY WOMEN AND MEN TODAY DO

NOT KNOW HOW TO PREPARE THEMSELVES TO ATTRACT THE DESIRED SPOUSE, HUSBAND OR WIFE. THE **HOLY BIBLE** TEACHES US THE RIGHT WAY.

RUTH IN THE HOLY BIBLE WASHED AND ANOINTED HERSELF FIRST BEFORE VISITING **BOAZ** ON THE FIRST NIGHT SHE SPENT WITH HIM.

RUTH CHAPTER 3 VERSE 3 STATES: WASH YOURSELF THEREFORE AND ANOINT YOURSELF AND PUT ON YOUR BEST CLOTHES, AND GO DOWN TO THE THRESHING FLOOR; BUT DO NOT LET YOURSELF KNOWN TO THE MAN UNTIL HE HAS FINISHED EATING AND DRINKING.

"WASH, ANOINT AND PUT ON YOUR BEST CLOTHES." THESE THREE ADVICE THAT NAOMI GAVE TO RUTH HER DAUGHTER IN LAW BROUGHT RUTH SUCCESS. THESE THREE ADVICE HELPED RUTH TO ATTRACT A WEALTHY MAN OF RENOWN IN HIS COMMUNITY. RUTH WAS A FOREIGNER AMONG THEM, A MOABITESS.

RUTH **OBEYED GODLY DIVINE ADVICE** AND ATTRACTED THE WEALTHY MAN **GOD** CHOSE FOR HER AND SHE BECAME HIS WIFE. THE **HOLY BIBLE** DID NOT SAY THAT RUTH WAS EDUCATED, RICH OR FAMOUS. SHE WAS A BARLEY REAPER, A HUMBLE LADY WHO WANTED THE **GOD OF NAOMI.**

THE **GOD OF NAOMI** IS THE SAME **GOD** I SERVE TODAY. AMEN! **JESUS SAID IN HEBREWS 13 VERSE 8, "JESUS CHRIST IS THE SAME YESTERDAY AND TODAY AND FOREVER." AMEN!**

IN THE HOLY BIBLE BOOK OF RUTH CHAPTER 3 VERSE 14 IT STATES: SO SHE LAY AT HIS FEET UNTIL MORNING AND ROSE BEFORE ONE COULD RECOGNIZE

ANOTHER; AND HE SAID, LET IT NOT BE KNOWN THAT THE WOMAN CAME TO THE THRESHING FLOOR."

IN THE **HOLY BIBLE BOOK OF RUTH CHAPTER 4 VERSE 13 IT STATES: SO BOAZ TOOK RUTH AND SHE BECAME HIS WIFE, AND HE WENT IN TO HER AND THE LORD ENABLED HER TO CONCEIVE AND SHE GAVE BIRTH TO A SON.**

RUTH GAINED **BOAZ** BECAUSE SHE TURNED TO THE RIGHT **GOD.** IF RUTH HAD STAYED IN HER NATIVE LAND OF MOAB AFTER HER FIRST HUSBAND DIED SHE WOULD NOT HAVE MET **BOAZ. GOD** ORDAINED THEIR DIVINE CONNECTION AND **RUTH** BECAME THE GREAT GRANDMOTHER OF **KING DAVID.** AMEN!

THE HOLY BIBLE STATES IN ISAIAH 61 VERSE 3: TO GRANT THOSE WHO MOURN IN ZION, GIVING THEM A GARLAND INSTEAD OF ASHES, THE OIL OF GLADNESS FOR MOURNING THE MANTLE OF PRAISE INSTEAD OF A SPIRIT OF FAINTING...

"...THE OIL OF GLADNESS FOR MOURNING..." BE COMFORTED BY THESE WORDS. JESUS LOVES YOU AND ME ETERNALLY. AMEN!

I HAVE ACCEPTED THE FACT THAT I AM BEAUTIFUL. IT IS A TRUE COMPLIMENT TO SELF AND FROM OTHERS. AMEN! I AM NOT PERFECT HOWEVER IN ANYTHING I DO AND NO HUMAN BEING WILL EVER BE PERFECT IN THIS LIFE.

THE FLESH IS SUSCEPTIBLE TO SINNING AT TIMES AND WHEN WE DO WE MUST REPENT TO **JESUS CHRIST. GOD** ALWAYS HELPS ME GO THROUGH EVERY DIFFICULT SITUATION I ENCOUNTER VICTORIOUSLY. ACCEPT THE FACT THAT YOU ARE BEAUTIFUL, YOU ARE LOVED JUST

THE WAY YOU ARE. USE WHATEVER MAKES YOU LOOK EVEN MORE BEAUTIFUL AND HANDSOME. **GOD MADE MANKIND ORIGINALLY BEAUTIFUL. AMEN!**

WOMEN MUST EXUBERATE THE FEMININE ESSENCE AND MEN THE MASCULINE AURA.

AFTER MY TWO DIVORCES, MY HEART WAS SEALED TIGHT FOR SEVERAL YEARS REGARDING MARRYING AGAIN. I HAD DECIDED NEVER TO MARRY AGAIN. I REMAINED CELIBATE FOR OVER TEN YEARS **I AM** STILL CELIBATE. THE NEXT TIME I MARRY IT WILL TRULY BE "UNTIL DEATH DO US PART." MY CHILDREN ARE NOW ADULTS. I MISS THEIR PRESENCE.

I AM SEEKING LASTING FRIENDSHIPS WITHIN THE **BODY OF CHRIST.** I WANT LASTING FRIENDSHIP LIKE MY MOTHER AND HER FRIEND HADASSAH HAS. THEIR FRIENDSHIP WAS BUILD OVER A LIFETIME AND IS SOLID BASED ON TRUST AND **GODLY LOVE.** I WILL PRAY ABOUT IT NOW.

PRAYER.

DEAR LORD JESUS, I REPENT AND CONFESS ALL OF MY SINS. PLEASE BLESS ME WITH LOVING, KIND, SINCERE AND TRUSTWORTHY FRIENDSHIPS. HELP ME LORD TO BE A FRIEND WHO WILL EXUBERATE THE SAME CHARACTERISTICS THAT I SEEK IN OTHERS. IN JESUS NAME I PRAY TO MY HEAVENLY FATHER. AMEN!

I WAS ENCOURAGED TO DESIRE MARRYING AGAIN BECAUSE OF WHAT THE **LORD** SAID TO ME A FEW YEARS AGO. THE **LORD** SAID TO ME, "OPEN YOUR HEART, OPEN YOUR HEART, YOU HAVE CLOSED YOUR HEART; CONSIDER MARRIAGE AGAIN." I KNEW THAT **GOD** KNEW

ME AND LOVES ME, BUT I DID NOT KNOW THAT **GOD WAS MINDFUL OF ME IN THIS WAY.**

MANKIND YOU MUST BELIEVE THAT **JESUS CHRIST ALMIGHTY GOD LOVES YOU AND IS FOR YOU AND NOT AGAINST YOU FIRST. LOVE GOD FIRST. AMEN!**

I THANK MY **ABBA FATHER FOR HIS LOVE AND CARE FOR ME EACH DAY.** I PRAYED AND ASKED **GOD** TO HELP ME OPEN MY HEART TO CONSIDER AND DESIRE MARRYING AGAIN AND HE DID. I BEGAN TO REJECT LONELINESS INSTEAD OF EMBRACING IT. I STARTED TO THINK ABOUT WHERE I WOULD LIKE TO BE MARRIED.

I AM NOW THINKING ABOUT THINGS I WILL DO TO MAKE MY NEW HUSBAND HAPPY AND **I AM** EVEN THINKING ABOUT A WEEKLY FAMILY MEAL MENU.

I ALREADY HAVE PLANS TO DECORATE MY NEW FAMILY HOME. THE THOUGHT OF MARRYING AGAIN GIVES ME JOY IN MY HEART. **I AM** JOYFULLY LOOKING FORWARD TO SPENDING THE REST OF MY LIFE WITH MY NEW FUTURE HUSBAND. AT THIS THOUGHT I SMILE BECAUSE **GOD IS INVOLVE IN THE PLANS FOR MY FUTURE MARRIAGE.** AMEN!

GOD KNEW THE DESIRES OF MY HEART AND HELPED ME TO SEE MY WANTS AGAIN. I WAS ACCUSTOMED TO BEING SURROUNDED BY A LARGE FAMILY. I DON'T DESIRE TO LIVE AS A SINGLE LONELY ADULT FOR THE REST OF MY LIFE.

I WANT THE JOY OF FAMILY DINNERS TOGETHER AGAIN, SHARING, VACATIONING TOGETHER, EMBRACING LOVE AND JOY WITH MY FUTURE HUSBAND, SHOPPING TOGETHER, PLANNING TOGETHER, WORSHIPPING **GOD** TOGETHER AND LIVING FOR **GOD** TOGETHER. AMEN!

IT IS WONDERFUL TO HAVE FAMILY MEMBERS PRESENT. **I AM** ENCOURAGED TO HAVE A LARGE FAMILY OF MY OWN, BY THE GRACE OF **GOD** I WILL BE SUCCESSFUL. MY PREVIOUS RELATIONSHIPS HAD BEEN WITH UNSAVED MEN AND MUSLIM MEN. THE **BORN-AGAIN CHRISTIANS** KNOWS **LOVE, LOVE** DWELLS IN US, WE LIVE BY **LOVE** AND WE EXUBERATE **LOVE. I DESERVE AND DESIRE TRUE LOVE.** I WILL CHOOSE LOVE FOR MYSELF. AMEN!

I DESIRE THESE ATTRIBUTES IN A HUSBAND: CLEANLINESS, HE MUST DESIRE WHAT IS CLEAN AND KEEP HIMSELF CLEAN, SPIRITUALLY ENCOURAGING TO ME AND HAVE A DISCREET MATURE CHARACTER. MY FUTURE HUSBAND MUST **LOVE JESUS CHRIST ALMIGHTY GOD,** HIMSELF AND HIS FAMILY. FAMILY HIERARCHY RELATIONSHIPS MUST TAKE PRIORITY OVER PERSONAL FRIENDSHIPS.

MY FUTURE HUSBAND MUST **LOVE** ME AND MY TWO CHILDREN. I WANT KINDNESS, SHARING, UNITY, RESPECT, COMMITMENT, FAITHFULNESS, SINCERITY, HONESTY AND THE PRESENCE OF A HUSBAND AGAIN IN MY LIFE.

MY HEART IS FULL OF LOVE AGAIN, I WILL LOVE AGAIN; I AM COMMITTED TO LOVE AGAIN! AMEN!

LONELINESS WILL NOT CAUSE ME TO STUMBLE OR MAKE QUICK UNHEALTHY DECISIONS. PAST DISAPPOINTMENTS WILL NOT DISCOURAGE ME FROM HAVING A LOVING, HEALTHY, KIND, SUCCESSFUL AND LASTING MARRIAGE RELATIONSHIP AGAIN. I AM DETERMINED TO BE HAPPY WITH A FAMILY AGAIN. AMEN!

I PRAYED AND SAID TO **GOD OUR FATHER, "ABBA**

FATHER I REPENT AND CONFESS MY SINS. I THANK YOU FOR BLESSING ME WITH A DESIRE FOR A FUTURE MARRIAGE, I THANK YOU FOR GOING WITH ME INTO MARRIAGE THIS TIME. IN JESUS NAME. AMEN!

THEN ONE DAY THE **LORD** SAID TO ME, "SURRENDER YOUR FUTURE HUSBAND TO ME." I PRAYED. "I SURRENDER HIM **LORD.**" **AMEN!**

I DO NOT YET KNOW OR HAVE CONFIRMATION REGARDING WHO WILL BE MY FUTURE HUSBAND BUT THE **LORD GOD** KNOWS AND I TRUST **GOD TO BRING MY LOVING KIND HUSBAND TO ME.** AMEN! WHEN I CONFIRM MY FUTURE HUSBAND BY **DIVINE KNOWLEDGE** I WILL MAKE AN ANNNOUNCEMENT AND MY SEARCH WILL END. AMEN! **HALLELUJAH! EXCITEMENT!**

MEN AND WOMEN THIS IS WHAT WE MUST FIRST DO TO ATTRACT AND MAINTAIN THE RIGHT HUSBAND OR WIFE FOR OURSELVES. FIRST MAKE A DECISION TO KNOW **JESUS CHRIST. I AM** ENCOURAGING YOU TO BECOME A **BORN-AGAIN CHRISTIAN.** GET TO KNOW JESUS CHRIST THE GOD OF THE HOLY BIBLE AS YOUR LORD AND SAVIOUR FIRST.

IN THE HOLY BIBLE BOOK OF REVELATION CHAPTER 22 VERSE 13: JESUS CHRIST SAID, I AM THE ALPHA AND THE OMEGA THE FIRST AND THE LAST THE BEGINNING AND THE END.

THE HOLY BIBLE BOOK OF GENESIS CHAPTER 2 VERSES 24-25 JESUS STATES: FOR THIS REASON A MAN SHALL LEAVE HIS FATHER AND HIS MOTHER AND BE JOINED TO HIS WIFE; AND THEY SHALL BECOME ONE FLESH. (VERSE 25): AND THE MAN AND HIS WIFE WERE BOTH NAKED AND WERE NOT ASHAMED.

GENESIS CHAPTER 12 VERSE 5 STATES: ABRAM TOOK SARAI HIS WIFE AND LOT HIS NEPHEW, AND ALL THEIR POSSESSIONS WHICH THEY HAD ACCUMULATED, AND THE PERSONS WHICH THEY HAD ACQUIRED IN HARAN, AND THEY SET OUT FOR THE LAND OF CANAAN.

ST. MATTHEW CHAPTER 1 VERSES 20, 24 STATES: BUT WHEN HE HAD CONSIDERED THIS BEHOLD AN ANGEL OF THE LORD APPEARED TO HIM IN A DREAM SAYING, "JOSEPH SON OF DAVID DO NOT BE AFRAID TO TAKE MARY AS YOUR WIFE; FOR THE CHILD WHO HAS BEEN CONCEIVED IN HER IS OF THE HOLY SPIRIT. (VERSE 24): AND JOSEPH AWOKE FROM HIS SLEEP AND DID AS THE ANGEL OF THE LORD COMMANDED HIM, AND TOOK MARY AS HIS WIFE. AMEN!

THIS IS HOW **GOD** ENCOURAGES MARRIAGES IN THE HOLY BIBLE. 1ST. CORINTHIANS CHAPTER 7 VERSE 2 JESUS STATES: BUT BECAUSE OF IMMORALITIES, EACH MAN IS TO HAVE HIS OWN WIFE, AND EACH WOMAN IS TO HAVE HER OWN HUSBAND.

THINK ABOUT THE VERSE YOU JUST READ. "WHY DID **GOD SAY, "BECAUSE OF IMMORALITIES...?"** **GOD** WANTS MANKIND TO LIVE FREE FROM SIN. IMMORALITY IS SIN. LIVING TOGETHER WITHOUT A LEGAL, LOVING COMMITMENT BEFORE GOD IS NOT BIBLICAL. LIVING COMMON LAW IS NOT HONOURABLE TO **GOD.**

THE LAWS OF THE LAND CANNOT NEGATE **GOD'S** ETERNAL **HOLY BIBLE** WORDS THAT LEADS US TO ETERNAL LIFE. WE MUST **OBEY GOD'S ETERNAL WORDS.** AMEN!

BODY OF CHRIST, WE ARE **CHRIST** AMBASSADOR, WE MUST IMITATE **JESUS,** HE IS A **KING: KING OF KINGS AND LORD OF LORDS. AMEN!** WE MUST LIVE TOGETHER

ACCORDING TO **GOD'S WORD** TO PLEASE THE **KING.** WE MUST LOOK OUR BEST TO PLEASE **GOD.**

WE MUST NOT RESEMBLE A TATTERDEMALION. THE **LORD** SAID, **"THE SILVER AND THE GOLD IS MINE."** DO A MAKEOVER, BEGIN FROM HEAD TO TOE TO ATTRACT THE EXCELLENT AND HIGHEST QUALITY. WE MUST LOOK GRAND. AMEN!

I START MY DAY BY PRAYING TO **GOD, JESUS CHRIST FIRST.** I ACKNOWLEDGE **GOD** FIRST. **JESUS CHRIST** WOKE ME UP AND BLESSED ME WITH A NEW DAY AND MORE TIME TO SERVE HIM IN THIS LIFE. THEREFORE I THANK HIM . AMEN!

PRAYER.

THIS IS THE DAY THAT THE LORD HAS MADE WE WILL REJOICE AND BE GLAD IN IT. LORD I REPENT AND CONFESS MY SINS. I THANK YOU FOR A BLESSED NEW DAY. GUIDE ME THROUGH THIS DAY SAFELY. PLEASE HELP ME LORD TO MAKE GODLY DECISIONS THROUGHOUT EACH DAY THAT I SEE. I PRAY FOR PROTECTION FROM EVERY ENEMY SPIRITUAL AND NATURAL. BLESS ME THIS DAY LORD AND HELP ME TO HONOUR YOU IN EVERYTHING I DO. IN JESUS NAME I PRAY TO MY HEAVENLY FATHER JEHOVAH. AMEN!

AFTER I SPEND TIME WITH **GOD,** I TAKE A SHOWER AND CHOOSE CLOTHING THAT ARE SUITABLE FOR THE WEATHER AND APPOINTMENTS I MAY HAVE FOR EACH DAY. I LIKE WEARING WARM KNITTED HATS DURING THE COLD WINTER MONTHS FROM NOVEMBER TO THE MIDDLE OF APRIL. MY SKIN TONE IS THE SHADE BETWEEN GINGER AND HONEY. I LOVE ALL COLOURS;

PINK, VANILLA, EGG SHELL WHITE, COFFEE BEAN, MOLASSES, TAR AND SOY SAUCE SHADES. **GOD** MADE US IN HIS IMAGE AND SOVEREIGNLY ORDAINED OUR HUE ON THE COLOUR SPECTRUM. AMEN!

I WASH MY HAIR DURING MY SHOWERS. THE WARM RUNNING WATER MAKES IT EASY FOR MY LARGE TOOTH COMB TO SLIDE THROUGH MY HAIR. MY HAIR TEXTURE IS WOOLY AND RESEMBLES A SPIRAL COIL ESPECIALLY WHEN IT IS WET. I HAVE A LIMITLESS ARRAY OF HAIR STYLE SELECTION TO CHOOSE FROM. WHEN MY HAIR IS DRY IT LIFTS NATURALLY HORIZONTALLY OFF MY SCALP. I ANOINT MY HEAD WITH OIL.

OIL GIVES MY DARK BROWN HAIR A BEAUTIFUL RADIANT SHEEN AND OCCASIONALLY I SEE ONE OR TWO GRAY HAIR. I ENJOY TAKING CARE OF MY HAIR. IF YOU KNOW AN EXCELLENT HAIR DRESSER OR A BARBER FOR MEN UTILIZE THEIR SERVICES AS OFTEN AS YOU NEED TO.

I WANT TO ENCOURAGE PEOPLE OF AFRICAN DESCENT TO LOVE THEIR HAIR JUST AS IT IS NATURALLY. LOVE YOUR HAIR AND LOVE YOURSELF AS YOU WERE CREATED ORIGINALLY. **GOD IS WISE** AND NOT FOOLISH. **GOD** HEARS GRUMBLINGS AND COMPLAINTS EVERYDAY ABOUT HAIR.

I WENT TO A MIDWEEK CHURCH **PRAYER MEETING** IN FRANCE ONE EVENING AT ABOUT 7 O'CLOCK. **WE MUST COMMIT OURSELVES TO PRAYER AT EACH PRAYER MEETING AND NOT BE EASILY DISTRACTED FROM GOD. AMEN!** AT THE PRAYER MEETING HAIR DISCUSSION CAME UP. WHY? BECAUSE THERE WAS A RECENT EXPLORATION AND ANALYSIS REGARDING THE MOST DESIRABLE DIFFERENT HAIR TEXTURES. WELL!

WELL! LISTEN TO ME SPEAK! LET OUR **ORIGINAL** HAIR TEXTURE FIRST BE EMBRACED IN OUR HEARTS. **GOD** MADE YOU AND ME DESIRABLE. AMEN!

EVERY HUMAN BEING IS MADE IN THE IMAGE OF **GOD.** WE ARE LOVED AND WORTHY OF **LOVE.** WE MUST FIRST LOVE **GOD,** THEN TRULY LOVE OURSELVES. AMEN!

ONE OF THE LADIES AT THE **PRAYER MEETING** SAID, "WHEN I THINK ABOUT ALL THE OTHER RACES AND NATIONALITIES THEY ALL NATURALLY HAVE STRAIGHT HAIR, WHY DID **GOD** MAKE BLACK PEOPLE'S HAIR THE WAY IT IS?" AFTER SHE ASKED THE QUESTION A LOUD RUMBLING STARTED IN THE ROOM. I SAID TO MYSELF, "I MUST SPEAK UP! SHE NEEDS **DIVINE WISDOM.**"

I WILL NOT LET HER FEEL INFERIOR. I WAS DETERMINED TO HELP. I HAD TO WAIT MY TURN BECAUSE EVEN THE MALE LEADER HAD A COMMENT AND THERE WERE MANY SUGGESTIONS.

I SAID, "THINK ABOUT THIS AND I MENTIONED **REVELATION CHAPTER 1 VERSE 14 IT STATES: HIS HEAD AND HIS HAIR WERE WHITE LIKE WHITE WOOL, LIKE SNOW; AND HIS EYES WERE LIKE A FLAME OF FIRE.**

I KNOW THAT **GOD IS A SPIRIT** AND DOES NOT HAVE AN AFRO HAIR STYLE. HA! HAA! HAAA!

REMEMBER THAT MY HAIR IS **WOOLY** AND SPIRALLY AND THE **HOLY BIBLE BOOK OF REVELATION CHAPTER 1 VERSE 14 STATES AGAIN: "...HIS HAIR WERE WHITE LIKE WHITE WOOL..."** THIS CONFIRMED TRUTH REAFFIRMS THAT **I AM** MADE IN THE IMAGE OF **GOD.** AMEN!

1ST. CORINTHIANS CHAPTER 11 VERSE 15 STATES STATES: BUT IF A WOMAN HAS LONG HAIR, IT IS A

GLORY TO HER FOR HER HAIR IS GIVEN TO HER FOR A COVERING.

I ALSO SAID TO THE LADY THAT HAD THE HAIR QUESTION. "EVEN THOUGH ALL THE OTHER NATIONALITIES HAVE STRAIGHT HAIR, WE WITH **AFRICAN HAIR ARE THE ONLY RACE WITH OUR QUALITY HAIR.**

INSTEAD OF LOOKING AT THE COMMONALITY OF EVERYONE ELSE HAIR LOOK AT THE UNIQUENESS OF THE BLACK AFRICAN HAIR. THE AFRICAN HAIR STAND OUT EXCEPTIONALLY BEAUTIFUL ALSO **NATURALLY! AMEN!**

THE HOLY BIBLE STATES IN ST. JOHN 4 VERSE 24: GOD IS SPIRIT, AND THOSE WHO WORSHIP HIM MUST WORSHIP IN SPIRIT AND TRUTH. AMEN!

I ENCOURAGE YOU TO **LOVE JESUS CHRIST.** EMBARK ON CREATIVE WAYS TO TAKE CARE OF YOUR HAIR. REMEMBER! NO RACE IS SUPERIOR NO RACE IS INFERIOR IN THE EYES OF **GOD. WE ARE ALL CREATED EQUAL WITH A SOUL, SPIRIT AND A BODY IN THE EYES OF GOD. AMEN!**

CLEANLINESS MUST BE EMPHASIZE WITHIN THE **CHURCH BODY** AND MORE SO EXTERNALLY OUTSIDE THE CHURCH. WE ARE NOT LACKING WATER IN FRANCE. THE TRUE CHILDREN OF **GOD, THE TRUE BORN-AGAIN CHRISTIANS** ARE NOT CONTAMINATED. WE ARE PURE AND **HOLY.**

GOD'S TRUE BORN-AGAIN CHILDREN OBEY EVERY WORD IN THE **HOLY BIBLE,** WE DON'T COMPROMISE **GOD'S WORD** AND SIN AND CAUSE OTHERS TO SIN. WE ARE SET APART. **THE HOLY BIBLE STATES IN ST.**

MATTHEW 7 VERSE 20, SO THEN YOU WILL KNOW THEM BY THEIR FRUITS.

A FRUITFUL VINE BEARS FRUIT AND DOES NOT DIE QUICKLY. AMEN! SIN CAUSES CONTAMINATION AND FILTH IN EVERY ONE! REPENT WHEN YOU SIN AGAINST **GOD** AND YOUR FELLOW HUMAN. AMEN! "THE SPIRITUAL WASHING MUST BE DONE FIRST. HEARTS, MINDS, SOULS AND SPIRIT NEEDS IMMEDIATE CLEANSING TODAY." SAYS THE **LORD. AMEN!**

CLEANSING AND GROOMING GOES TOGETHER LIKE A MARRIAGE, IT IS IMPERATIVE FOR BOTH MEN AND WOMEN TO DEVELOP THE HABIT OF **DAILY HYGIENIC CARE.** I DO NOT NEGLECT THE SMALL HIDDEN PARTS OF MY BODY WHEN I BATHE MYSELF. I WASH INSIDE MY NAVEL AND BEHIND MY EARS THEN USE A Q-TIP TO CLEAN INSIDE MY EARS.

I USE FACIAL SCRUBS THAT ARE SUITABLE FOR MY SKIN NEEDS. I COMB MY THICK BLACK EYEBROW INTO THEIR ARCHED SHAPE EACH MORNING AND CLEAN MY PRESCRIPTION EYEGLASSES DAILY.

I USE A NOSE STRIP THAT IS EFFECTIVE IN CLEANING MY NASAL PORES. I KEEP MY NASAL PASSAGE CLEAN AND I PREFER TO USE BATHROOMS THAT HAS AN OPEN WINDOW THAT ALLOWS FRESH AIR IN. **I AM** DILIGENT WITH MOUTH AND ORAL CARE THIS ENABLES ME TO MAINTAIN FRESH BREATH, HEALTHY TEETH AND GUMS.

THE **LORD** ALWAYS ENCOURAGES ME TO LOOK MY BEST. **I AM** THE PASTORAL LEADER AND FOUNDER OF **A BEAUTIFUL BORN-AGAIN CHRISTIAN MINISTRY** THEREFORE I WILL SET THE BEST EXAMPLE THAT WILL ENCOURAGE A PERSONAL APPROACH. AMEN! I HAVE A QUIET TEMPERAMENT; A NATURAL QUIET DISPOSITION

AND WHENEVER THE DEVIL AND ENEMIES ATTACK ME I CRY OUT, **"ARMAGEDDON"! ARM AGE DON(E),** HAIL STONES AND COALS OF FIRE! THE **FIRE** IS INTIMIDATING! AMEN!

LET ME INVITE YOU INTO MY PERSONAL FRIENDSHIP CIRCLE; FORCING YOUR WAY IN IS AUDACIOUS; RESPECT MY CHOICE.

WHAT ENTERS INTO YOUR MOUTH AND STOMACH WILL INFLUENCE YOUR HEALTH EITHER FOR GOOD OR BAD. I CUT AND CLEAN MY FINGERNAILS AND TOENAILS REGULARLY.

ONE VERY GOOD REASON WHY I DON'T WEAR NAIL POLISH FREQUENTLY IS BECAUSE I LOVE TO COOK AND MAKE DUMPLINGS. ONE DAY I PRAYED AND ASKED GOD TO HELP ME TO ALWAYS COOK FOR MY FUTURE HUSBAND AND FAMILY.

THERE IS A BLESSED **HOLY BIBLE VERSE** FOR EVERY SITUATION THAT MANKIND WILL EVER ENCOUNTER IN THIS LIFE. **DEUTERONOMY CHAPTER 28 VERSE 5 STATES: BLESSED SHALL BE YOUR BASKET AND KNEADING BOWL. AMEN!**

I DEVELOP THE HABIT OF PUBIC WASHING AFTER EACH BATHROOM USE. A FEW YEARS AGO WHEN I WAS MARRIED TO MY FIRST HUSBAND WE WENT TO VISIT SOME OF HIS RELATIVES WHO WERE FROM **SOMALIA.**

I REMEMBER I WENT TO THE BATHROOM AND BEFORE I CLOSED THE DOOR I WAS GIVEN SOMETHING THAT LOOKED LIKE A GARDENING WATER POT THAT HAD A SPOUT.

THE **SOMALI** LADY WHO GAVE ME THE CONTAINER SAID, "YOU MUST RINSE YOURSELF AFTER YOU ARE

FINISH USING THE TOILET, THIS IS OUR PRACTICE IN OUR CULTURE." I HAVE PRACTICALLY APPLIED THAT PRACTICE TO MY HYGIENIC ROUTINE AND CARRYING A SMALL PLASTIC BOTTLE WITH ME OUTSIDE MY HOME FOR THAT CLEANSING REASON HAS BEEN BENEFICIAL. I BELIEVE MANY WILL BENEFIT FROM THIS CLEANSING PROCEDURE TODAY. AMEN!

AFTER MY REFRESHING SHOWER I MOISTURIZE MY SKIN WITH MY CONCOCTED PERSONAL EMULSION OF OIL AND BODY LOTION. I USE DEODORANT. AFTER I AM REGALLY, HUMBLY AND BEAUTIFULLY DRESSED: I REMIND MYSELF OF THE WORDS OF **GOD** THAT STATES IN **PSALM 139 VERSE 14: "I WILL GIVE THANKS TO YOU FOR I AM FEARFULLY AND WONDERFULLY MADE; WONDERFUL ARE YOUR WORKS AND MY SOUL KNOWS IT VERY WELL! AMEN!**

I EXPERIENCED ANOTHER MIRACLE A FEW YEARS AGO IN MY LATE THIRTIES WHEN I SUFFERED A STROKE. I WILL SHARE THE EXPERIENCE OF THAT EVENT AS ANOTHER TESTIMONY.

THE STROKE OCCURRED ON THE LEFT SIDE OF MY BODY AT APPROXIMATELY 7:30 a.m. WHILE I WAS TEMPORARILY LIVING IN A WOMEN'S SHELTER.

THERE WERE THREE OF US WHO OCCUPIED OUR ROOM. ON THIS PARTICULAR MORNING; THE OTHER TWO WOMEN GOT UP UNUSUALLY EARLY AND WENT OUT FOR THE DAY, THEY WERE NOT PRESENT WHEN I EXPERIENCED THE STROKE.

IT WAS BEFORE BREAKFAST AND I WAS SITTING ON MY BED CONTEMPLATING HOW TO PROCEED THROUGHOUT THE DAY. I WAS PRAYING WITHOUT

CEASING, RESISTING THE DEVIL IN THE SPIRIT BECAUSE I WAS ENGAGED IN SPIRITUAL WARFARE.

I WAS SPIRITUALLY ATTACKED BY DEMONS THAT DAY. I SPOKE THE **HOLY BIBLE WORDS** DIRECTLY TO THE DEMONS WITHOUT CEASING. THE **HOLY BIBLE WORDS** ROLLED OFF MY TONGUE NON-STOP. AMEN! MY RESISTANCE TO SATAN WAS VERY POWERFUL; I DISCERNED THAT MY BLOOD PRESSURE HAD RISEN BECAUSE OF HOW I FELT.

AFTER VIGOROUSLY RESISTING THE DEVIL, USING THE **SWORD OF THE SPIRIT, THE WORD OF GOD** I FELT PHYSICALLY WEAKENED IN MY EXTREMITIES. THE **HOLY SPIRIT** SPOKE TO ME AND SAID, "LAY DOWN." **I OBEYED GOD** AND LAY DOWN SLOWLY ON MY BED.

I BECAME WEAKER AS I LAY DOWN ON MY BED AND I BEGAN TO EXPERIENCE SEVERE PAIN IN THE BACK OF MY HEAD. I FELT A SHARP SHOOTING PAIN THAT RADIATED FROM MY HEART AREA TOWARDS MY BACK. I LAY MOTIONLESS ON MY BED AS I ENDURED THE PIERCING PAIN.

I BECAME FEEBLE IN VIGOUR AND MY DISCOMFORT INCREASED. I WAS ALERT AND BEGAN TO WHISPER MY PRAYER TO **JESUS CHRIST** FOR **DIVINE HELP.** PHYSIOLOGICAL CHANGES BEGAN TO MANIFEST QUICKLY IN MY BODY. THERE WAS NOTICEABLE CHANGES IN MY VISION. TEARS RAN DOWN MY FACE. MY LEFT HAND AND FEET BECAME COLD AND LIFELESS.

I LIFTED MY RIGHT HAND AND REACHED OVER TO MY LEFT CHEEK TO FEEL FOR SENSATION AND I HAD NONE.

I HAD EXPERIENCED A LEFT SIDED HEMIPLEGIA. I ATTEMPTED TO REPOSITION MYSELF ONTO MY RIGHT

SIDE BUT I HAD TO REMAIN STATIONARY DUE TO THE INTENSITY OF THE PAIN.

I CONTINUED TO WHISPER MY PRAYER TO **JESUS CHRIST.** I ASKED **GOD** TO HEAL ME AND HELP ME CONTINUE DOING THE WORK OF MY BEAUTIFUL MINISTRY. THE DEVIL WAS ATTEMPTING TO SNAG AND HINDER THE PROGRESS OF MY MINISTRY BUT I WAS DETERMINED TO CLING TO **JESUS CHRIST** AND CARRY ON WITH THE BLESSED WORK WHICH **GOD** CALLED AND ORDAINED ME TO ESTABLISH, LEAD AND GUIDE FOR THE REST OF MY LIFE. **AMEN!**

THERE WAS NO TELEPHONE IN OUR ROOM AT THE WOMEN SHELTER, WE HAD NO CALL BELL FOR EMERGENCIES. THE TELEPHONES FOR THE SHELTER RESIDENTS WERE LOCATED A LENGHTY DISTANCE OUTSIDE OUR ROOMS .

I COULD HEAR THE ANNOUNCEMENTS BEING MADE OVER THE INTERCOM. BREAKFAST AND LUNCH WERE ANNOUNCED AND I COULD NOT GET UP FOR EITHER MEAL. BETWEEN LUNCH AND DINNER TIME I FELT THE NEED TO GO TO THE BATHROOM. THE BATHROOM WAS LOCATED DOWN THE HALL. IT IS A BLESSING TO HAVE NORMAL BODILY FUNCTION THROUGHOUT OUR LIFE. **HALLELUJAH!** THE URGENT NEED TO URINATE BECAME STRONGER AND I WONDERED IF I WOULD BE ABLE TO MAKE IT TO THE BATHROOM BY MYSELF.

I THOUGHT ABOUT THE SHELTER STAFF AT THIS TIME AND I REALIZE HOW UNUSUAL IT WAS THAT THEY DID NOT MAKE THEIR ROUTINE DAILY MORNING ROUNDS AND ROOM CHECKS. MY RIGHT FOOT AND HAND WERE FUNCTIONING NORMALLY I COULD MOVE THEM BOTH. I CONTINUED TO PRAY FOR A MIRACULOUS HEALING.

I WAS ABLE TO MANUEVER MY BODY BY USING MY RIGHT HAND AND RIGHT FOOT UNTIL I WAS ABLE TO SIT UP ON THE SINGLE BED THAT I SLEPT ON. I WAS STILL VERY WEAK, I DID NOT HEAR THE SOUND OF OR SAW THE PRESENCE OF ANOTHER PERSON. NO ONE WAS IN PROXIMITY TO ME. THIS WAS **SUPERNATURAL.**

THE SHELTER WAS A MULTILEVEL BUILDING WITH MANY RESIDENTS AND THERE WAS NO ONE AROUND FOR ME TO CALL OUT TO AT SUCH A CRUTIAL MOMENT. *GOD LET ME UNDERSTOOD A FEW DAYS LATER THE REASONS WHY HE KEPT EVERYONE AWAY FROM ME ON THAT PARTICULAR DAY. AS I OPENED MY BEDROOM DOOR I STILL EXPECTED TO SEE SOMEONE BUT I DID NOT.

I MADE MY WAY TO THE BATHROOM WITH MY LEFT HAND LIMPED ACROSS MY CHEST; MY LEFT FOOT WAS PARALYZED. MIRACULOUS SUPERNATURAL OCCURRENCES TOOK PLACE, I FELT AS IF I WAS **GLIDING AND NOT WALKING,** I FELT LIFTED AND **RAISED UP** OFF THE NATURAL FLOOR BY OUR AWESOME SUPERNATURAL **GOD. GOD** CARRIED ME AND I REACHED THE BATHROOM WITHOUT FALLING. **HALLELUJAH! AMEN! THE GOD I SERVE IS POWERFUL AND AWESOME THERE IS NO GOD LIKE MY JESUS. AMEN!**

TO MY SURPRISE ALL THE BATHROOM STALLS WERE EMPTY, I WAS ALONE AND I DID NOT FALL. **I GLIDED** BACK TO THE BEDROOM BY THE POWER OF **GOD** WITHOUT SEEING ANYONE. MY OWN STRENGTH COULD NOT CARRY ME. I NEEDED AND HAD **GOD'S POWER AND STRENGTH WITH ME THAT DAY. AMEN!**

I THANK **GOD** THAT I STILL HAVE HIS PRESENCE AND POWER TO HELP ME EACH DAY OF MY LIFE. AMEN! WHEN I RETURNED TO THE BEDROOM I LAY DOWN SLOWLY

BECAUSE I WAS FEELING WEAKER THAN BEFORE, I CONTINUED TO PRAY. MY OTHER TWO ROOMMATES WERE STILL ABSENT. IT WAS ALMOST EVENING AND NONE OF THE STAFF MEMBERS VISITED MY ROOM.

JESUS WAS WITH ME, HE IS MORE THAN ENOUGH. JESUS SAID IN ST. JOHN 14 VERSE 18, "I WILL NOT LEAVE YOU AS ORPHANS I WILL COME TO YOU." WHILE I WAS ON THE BED THE PRESENCE OF **GOD** WAS VERY POWERFUL IN MY ROOM. **GOD'S** PRESENCE COMFORTED ME AND I CONTINUED TO PRAY TO **JESUS CHRIST.** AMEN!

IT WAS AFTER 6 p. m. AND IT WAS BECOMING DARK OUTSIDE, IT WAS WINTER TIME, SUPPER WAS ANNOUNCED IN THE SHELTER BUT I WAS UNABLE TO PARTICIPATE. **JESUS CHRIST** SAID IN THE **HOLY BIBLE ST. JOHN 6 VERSE 48, "I AM THE BREAD OF LIFE." THE LORD SUSTAINED ME THROUGHOUT THAT PARTICULAR DAY.**

I DID NOT FEEL A HUNGER FOR PHYSICAL FOOD EITHER, I WANTED **GOD** TO HELP ME, I WANTED THIS SITUATION TO END. I WANTED TO BE HEALED. I WANTED TO BE REASSURED AND WALK NORMALLY AGAIN. I WANTED TO HAVE TACTILE SENSATION ON THE LEFT SIDE OF MY FACE. I CONTINUED TO PRAY FOR DIVINE INTERVENTION.

IT WAS APPROXIMATELY 6:30 p.m. WHEN I SAW **HOLY ANGELS** AROUND MY BEDSIDE. I SAW THEIR FORM. I KNEW THEY WERE **HOLY ANGELS** BECAUSE I HEARD THE **LORD** SPOKE TO THEM AND SAID, "LET HER BE HEALED." JOY THEN FILLED MY HEART.

I HAVE HEARD THE VOICE OF **JESUS CHRIST EACH DAY SINCE I BECAME A BORN-AGAIN CHRISTIAN. GOD'S VOICE REASSURES ME EACH DAY. AMEN!**

PSALM 29 VERSES 4 AND 5 STATES: THE VOICE OF THE LORD IS POWERFUL, THE VOICE OF THE LORD IS MAJESTIC. THE VOICE OF THE LORD BREAKS THE CEDARS; YES, THE LORD BREAKS IN PIECES THE THE CEDARS OF LEBANON.

MANKIND LET ME ADMONISH YOU AGAINST DELAYING YOUR DECISION TO TURN TO **JESUS CHRIST** TODAY. WE ALL NEED **THE LORD** EACH DAY TO GUIDE, SAVE, HELP AND DELIVER US FROM EVIL IN THIS PRESENT WORLD. **JESUS CHRIST** DEFEATED SATAN AND GAVE US ETERNAL VICTORY. AMEN!

***ACCEPT THAT VICTORY NOW** AND AVOID MANY PITFALLS, DISAPPOINTMENTS AND HURTS IN YOUR LIFE. WITHOUT THE HELP OF **JESUS CHRIST** MANKIND IS POWERLESS AGAINST SATAN AND EVIL SPIRITS. **AMEN!**

THE POWER OF **GOD IS WHAT SHIELDS US EACH DAY OF OUR LIVES FROM SATANIC SPIRITS. YOU NEED GOD'S ETERNAL SHIELD OF SALVATION TO LIVE A BLESSED SPIRITUALLY SUCCESSFUL LIFE.**

1ST. CORINTHIAN 15 VERSE 57 STATES: BUT THANKS BE TO GOD WHO GIVES US THE VICTORY THROUGH OUR LORD JESUS CHRIST. AMEN!

EVERY CHILD HAS VICTORY IN **JESUS** WHEN THEY ARE TAUGHT TO TURN TO HIM. A NEW BORN INFANT MUST BE **CHRISTENED AND DEDICATED** SHORTLY AFTER BIRTH TO **JESUS CHRIST ALMIGHTY GOD.** ONCE THE CHILD IS OLD ENOUGH TO SPEAK AND SAY, "I REPENT AND CONFESS MY SINS." THEN THE CHILD CAN BE BAPTIZED BY FULL BODY IMMERSION UNDERNEATH WATER. THE CHILD WILL NOW KNOW **JESUS CHRIST** AS THEIR LORD AND SAVIOUR. **AMEN!**

A FEW YEARS AGO I WAS ASKED BY A **BORN-AGAIN CHRISTIAN** MOTHER IN FRANCE TO BAPTIZE HER SON AND DAUGHTER. THE CHURCH WHERE THEY WERE ATTENDING HAD SCHEDULED A SPECIFIC DATE IN THE FUTURE FOR WATER BAPTISM AND THE MOTHER WANTED HER CHILDREN BAPTISED IMMEDIATELY.

IT WAS THE LITTLE GIRL'S SECOND BIRTHDAY ON THE DAY THAT I PERFORMED THE WATER BAPTISMS FOR HER AND HER BROTHER. **GOD** KNEW THEIR MOTHER'S HEART AND THE **LORD** ORDAINED THE DIVINE CONNECTION AND LET ME MEET THEM AT A BEAUTIFUL PARK WHICH WAS FILLED WITH WHITE BIRCH TREES AND WAS ADJACENT TO A LOCAL COMMUNITY CHURCH.

THEY WERE LIVING APPROXIMATELY TEN MINUTES AWAY FROM THE PARK. I REMEMBER INTRODUCING MYSELF TO THEIR MOTHER FIRST. **"I AM PASTOR CHRISTIAN."** I SAID TO HER. "THE **LORD** SENT ME HERE TODAY, **I AM** PLEASED TO MEET YOU." THEIR MOTHER THEN TOLD ME HER NAME AND EACH CHILD'S NAME.

AFTER A SHORT CONVERSATION AND ACKNOWLEDGING HOW BEAUTIFUL THE SUMMER DAY WAS I TOLD THEIR MOTHER THAT I COULD PERFORM **THE ORDINANCE OF WATER BAPTISM FOR HER TWO CHILDREN.** "CAN YOU DO THE **BAPTISM** TODAY? SHE ASKED ME. **"I AM** ABLE AND WILLING TO DO IT TODAY." I SAID TO HER. "DO YOU HAVE A **BATHTUB** AT HOME? I ASKED HER.

"YES, WE DO." SHE ANSWERED. "I WILL BAPTIZE THEM BOTH IN THE BATHTUB." "COME WITH US, LET US WALK OVER TO MY HOUSE." THEY WERE FRENCH NATIONALS. I LOVED THEM.

WHEN WE GOT TO THE HOUSE, WE SAT IN THE LIVING ROOM AND I PRAYED FOR THE THREE OF THEM. I ASKED **JESUS CHRIST** FOR HIS PRESENCE TO BE WITH US AND TO **BLESS** US.

I REMEMBER ASKING THE TWO YEAR OLD IMMEDIATELY BEFORE I BAPTIZED HER, "DO YOU WANT TO **GO TO HEAVEN?** YES! SHE JOYFULLY ANSWERED. "OKAY SAY, I REPENT." I TOLD THE CHILD. THEN WITH THE LOUDEST VOICE THAT A TWO YEAR OLD CHILD COULD PROJECT THE LITTLE GIRL SAID, **REPENT!**

THEN SHE SMILED AND WE ALL SMILED JOYFULLY WITH HER. HER MOTHER EMBRACED HER, THEN I IMMERSED AND **BAPTIZE** HER IN THE BATHTUB FILLED WITH WATER **IN THE NAME OF THE FATHER, IN THE NAME OF THE SON AND IN THE NAME OF THE HOLY SPIRIT. AMEN!**

SHE WAS NOW A CHILD OF **GOD, BORN OF GOD.** SHE NOW HAD THE **NEW BIRTH,** NOT BEING BORN A SECOND TIME OF HER MOTHER WHO STOOD BY AS A WITNESS; BUT BEING **BORN OF GOD THE FIRST TIME, HAVING THE SPIRIT OF GOD, HER <u>SPIRIT</u> <u>NOW</u> <u>QUICKENED</u>** BY THE HOLY SPIRIT PRESENCE IN HER. HALLELUJAH! I BAPTIZED HER BROTHER IMMEDIATELY AFTER HER. AMEN!

ST. JOHN CHAPTER 3 VERSES 3, 4, 5, 6 STATES: JESUS ANSWERED AND SAID TO HIM, "TRULY, TRULY, I SAY TO YOU UNLESS ONE IS BORN-AGAIN HE CANNOT SEE THE KINGDOM OF GOD." (VERSE 4) NICODEMUS SAID TO HIM, "HOW CAN A MAN BE BORN WHEN HE IS OLD? HE CANNOT ENTER A SECOND TIME INTO HIS MOTHER'S WOMB AND BE BORN, CAN HE?" (VERSE 5) JESUS ANSWERED, "TRULY, TRULY, I SAY TO YOU,

UNLESS ONE IS BORN OF WATER AND THE SPIRIT HE CANNOT ENTER INTO THE KINGDOM OF GOD. (VERSE 6) "THAT WHICH IS BORN OF THE FLESH IS FLESH, AND THAT WHICH IS BORN OF THE SPIRIT IS SPIRIT."

I BELIEVE IN SPONTANEOUS WATER **BAPTISM**. WHEN A SOUL CRIES OUT TO **GOD** FOR SALVATION AND WANTS TO BE SET FREE FROM SATAN AND HIS DEMONS LET NOTHING PREVENT YOU FROM BAPTIZING THEM. USE A BATHTUB, THE LAKE, A JACUZZI, A RIVER, THE OCEAN, THE SWIMMING POOL OR DIG A HOLE IN THE GROUND AND FILL IT WITH WATER AND BAPTIZE THEM. AMEN! SAVING A SOUL MUST BE A TOP PRIORITY FOR THE CHILD OF **GOD. AMEN! GOD** DOES NOT ONLY WANT ORDERLY LITURGY.

REPENT AND CONFESS YOUR SINS TO **JESUS CHRIST** NOW AND GET **BAPTIZE** THE **JOHN THE BAPTIST WAY** BY FULL BODY IMMERSION UNDERNEATH A **BODY** OF WATER **IN THE NAME OF THE FATHER, IN THE NAME OF THE SON AND IN THE NAME OF THE HOLY SPIRIT. AMEN!**

I WAS ALREADY A **BORN-AGAIN CHRISTIAN** PASTOR WHEN I SUFFERED A HEMIPLEGIA STROKE A FEW YEARS AGO. I KNEW **JESUS CHRIST**, I KNEW I SHOULD PRAY WITH WHATEVER STRENGTH I HAD. I NEVER LET GO OF **JESUS CHRIST** THAT DAY AND I WILL NOT LET GO OF **JESUS CHRIST TODAY. AMEN!**

I CRIED, YES, BUT I WAS NEVER DISCOURAGED AWAY FROM **JESUS**. I CLUNG TO **JESUS CHRIST**. I KNEW THAT **JESUS CHRIST** HELD ME TIGHTER IN MY MOTHER'S WOMB BEFORE I WAS BORN. I KNOW AND FEEL THE LOVE OF **GOD** DAILY. AMEN!

PLEASE PRAY FOR ME THAT I WILL ALWAYS OBEY AND CONTINUE TO SERVE **GOD** FOR ALL OF MY

LIFE. I NEED YOUR PRAYERS SO THAT I CAN ENDURE THROUGH TRIALS, TRIBULATION AND PERSECUTIONS UNTIL THE LORD TAKES ME HOME. THANK YOU! **GOD BLESS YOU. AMEN!** REMEMBER **I AM** PRAYING FOR YOU TOO. **AMEN!**

I WILL CONTINUE ON WITH THE EVENTS OF MY STROKE: IMMEDIATELY AFTER I HEARD THE **LORD SPOKE TO THE HOLY ANGEL AND SAID, "LET HER BE HEALED."** I FELT WARMTH RETURNING TO MY LEFT HAND AND FOOT.

I WAS ABLE TO WIGGLE MY LEFT TOES. I LIFTED MY LEFT HAND FROM ACROSS MY CHEST AND SENSATION RETURNED TO THE LEFT SIDE OF MY CHEEK. I EXPERIENCED A **MIRACULOUS DIVINE POWERFUL HEALING** TOUCH OF **GOD** WITHOUT MEDICAL INTERVENTION. I WAS STILL ALONE IN MY ROOM WHEN MY **MIRACLE OCCURRED.** I WAS HEALED APPROXIMATELY TWELVE HOURS AFTER EXPERIENCING MY STROKE. **AMEN!**

ST. LUKE CHAPTER 2 VERSE 14 STATES: GLORY TO GOD IN THE HIGHEST AND ON EARTH PEACE AMONG MEN WITH WHOM HE IS PLEASED. IT WAS THE DIVINE PLAN AND PURPOSE OF **GOD** FOR ME TO BE ALONE THAT FAITHFUL DAY WHEN I EXPERIENCED MY STROKE. BEING ALONE WITH **GOD** INCREASED MY FAITH. **GOD** WAS MY PHYSICIAN THAT DAY.

GOD DID NOT WANT OTHERS AROUND ME THAT DAY BECAUSE HE HAD A PLAN TO HEAL, RESTORE AND GIVE ME A MIRACLE. **GOD** DID NOT WANT A **911 EMERGENCY TELEPHONE CALL** TO INTERFERE WITH THE IMMEDIATE **DIVINE MIRACLE** THAT **JESUS CHRIST** HAD FOR ME. **GOD IS A PERSONAL GOD. AMEN!**

AFTER I REGAINED NORMAL MOBILITY AND FUNCTION TO THE LEFT SIDE OF MY BODY IN MY ROOM AT THE SHELTER WHERE I TEMPORARILY LIVED; THE **HOLY SPIRIT SAID, "I HEALED YOU, BUT NOT ONLY FOR YOU TO BE HEALED BUT FOR YOU TO CONTINUE WITH THE WORK I STARTED IN YOU."** THIS IS WHY **I AM** DETERMINED TO PREACH THE GOSPEL AND DO **GOD'S WORK. AMEN! I AM** REJOICING AGAIN! **AMEN!**

ST. LUKE CHAPTER 4 VERSE 23 STATES: AND HE SAID TO THEM, "NO DOUBT YOU WILL QUOTE THIS PROVERB TO ME, 'PHYSICIAN HEAL YOURSELF! WHATEVER WE HEARD WAS DONE AT CAPERNAUM, DO HERE IN YOUR HOMETOWN AS WELL."

NEVER BE DISCOURAGED FROM CALLING **911** WHEN YOU HAVE AN EMERGENCY AND WHEN IT IS THE DIVINE WILL OF **GOD** FOR YOU TO DO SO. WE CANNOT DO ANYTHING IN THIS LIFE UNLESS **JESUS CHRIST ALMIGHTY GOD** ALLOWS US. **GOD** DIRECTS MANKIND'S DECISION MAKING.

THE **HOLY BIBLE SAYS IN 1ST. THESSALONIANS 3 VERSE 8, "FOR NOW WE REALLY LIVE IF YOU STAND FIRM IN THE LORD."**

THERE ARE MANY **BIBLE VERSES** THAT YOU CAN USE AS PRAYERS FOR THE SICK. I PRAY THAT **JESUS CHRIST** WILL USE HIS POWER TO HELP ME EACH DAY. SPIRITUAL WARFARE IS NOT ALWAYS QUIET. THE **HOLY BIBLE STATES IN JAMES 4 VERSE 7, SUBMIT THEREFORE TO GOD, RESIST THE DEVIL AND HE WILL FLEE FROM YOU."** MANY ENEMIES HAVE BEEN STOPPED AND DEFEATED BY **JESUS CHRIST ALMIGHTY GOD** FOR MY SAKE. AMEN!

NOW REGARDING EMBARKING ON A LASTING RELATIONSHIP, PHYSICAL ATTRACTION DOES CONNECT

MEN AND WOMEN TOGETHER. AS I MATURED WITH AGE AND **DIVINE WISDOM, GOD** INSTILLED IN ME THAT IT IS IMPERATIVE TO KNOW A MAN'S FAMILY, HEART, BACKGROUND, HEALTH STATUS AND CHARACTER BEFORE CONSIDERING HIM FOR MARRIAGE. **GOD** DID NOT SAY, "KNOW HOW MUCH MONEY HE HAS OR EARNED, KNOW WHO HE HAS IN HIS WILL, OR KNOW HIS FRIENDS **FIRST**." **I AM** FAMILY ORIENTED THEREFORE **I AM** VERY PLEASED TO KNOW A MAN AND HIS FAMILY FIRST.

GOD JUST REMINDED ME THAT THE SPIRITUAL FAMILY COMES **FIRST** BUT THE BIOLOGICAL FAMILY IS FIRST IN THE NATURAL. **GOD** REMINDS ME TO BE MORE THOROUGH AND SEEK MORE INFORMATION FROM MY FUTURE HUSBAND. AMEN!

IT IS WONDERFUL TO GAIN THE ATTENTION OF SOMEONE YOU LOVE AND ARE ATTRACTED TO. MEN AND WOMEN ARE ATTRACTED TO DIFFERENT PEOPLE FOR INDIVIDUAL UNIQUE REASONS.

I REMEMBER HOW A YOUNG MAN IN CASTRIES ST. LUCIA DREW, HELD, AND ATTRACTED MY ATTENTION TO HIM A FEW YEARS AGO WHILE I WAS ON VACATION. ONE AFTERNOON AS MY MOTHER KAY AND I WALKED ADJACENT TO THE CROWDED CASTRIES MARKET THE YOUNG MAN WALKED TOWARDS US.

I REMEMBER HIM CLEARLY. HE WORE NO SHIRT; HIS SPOTLESS BROWN SKIN SOAKED UP THE HOT ST. LUCIAN SUNSHINE; A BELT WAS IN HIS PANT. HE WAS GOOD LOOKING, HIS HAIR WAS CUT LOW AND HE HAD BROWN EYES. HE WAS PHYSICALLY LEAN, WELL TONED AND CLEAN.

AS HE HEADED TOWARDS ME IN THE BUSY ENVIRONMENT OUR EYES LOCKED AS HE CAME CLOSER.

HE HELD ONTO MY GAZE THEN PAUSED; AS HE STOOD INCHES AWAY FROM ME. LOOKING DIRECTLY AT ME HE SAID IN A LOUD VOICE, **CHAMPION! CHAMPION!** I SMILED AT HIM BEFORE HE PROCEEDED WITH THE MOVING CROWD. MY MOTHER KEPT WALKING AHEAD, SHE WAS DETERMINED TO COMPLETE HER SHOPPING.

MY PACE WAS LESSENED, THEN I REMEMBERED MY MOTHER AND QUICKENED MY STEPS TO REACH HER. HIS WORDS STIRRED MY EMOTIONS AND LET ME REALLY FEEL LIKE A **CHAMPION.** HE DECLARED **VICTORY** OVER ME WITH HIS BOLD **CHAMPION** DECLARATION.

WHAT A WONDERFUL WAY TO LET A WOMAN KNOW THAT YOU ARE ATTRACTED TO HER. HE WILL NOT HAVE ANY DIFFICULTY ATTRACTING WOMEN TO HIM I REMEMBER THINKING THAT DAY. I WENT HOME WALKING LIKE A **CHAMPION.** SOME MEN ARE BLESSED BECAUSE OF THEIR GRACIOUS WORDS. AMEN!

GOD IS NOW THE CENTRE OF MY LIFE, RELATIONSHIPS AND DECISION MAKINGS. WHEN I BECAME **A BORN-AGAIN CHRIST IAN, GOD** REALLY MADE A DIFFERENCE IN MY LIFE. **GOD** INDWELLS ME AND QUICKENS MY SPIRIT. I DO FEEL THE PRESENCE OF **GOD** IN ME DAILY.

THE BEST WAY TO DESCRIBE THE FEELING OF **GOD'S** PRESENCE; THE **HOLY SPIRIT** INDWELLING IN ME IS COMPARATIVELY TO THIS; "HAVE YOU EVER MADE JELLO? WELL, ONCE THE JELLO IS PLACED IN THE FRIDGE IT BECOMES FORMED AND MOVES, SHAKES AND QUIVER IN THE CONTAINER, IT HAS A GENTLE, **"SOFT MOVE"** IN THE BOWL.

THIS IS THE BEST WAY IN WHICH I CAN EXPLAIN THE **"FEELING"** OF THE PRESENCE OF **GOD DWELLING IN ME. GOD** MOVING IN ME IS LIKE A **"DISTINCT SOFT**

MOVE" THAT I FEEL EVERYDAY. **I AM QUICKENED** BY THE PRESENCE OF THE HOLY SPIRIT. **AMEN!**

THE HOLY SPIRIT CONNECTS TO OUR SPIRIT AS A TESTIMONY THAT WE BELONG TO **JESUS CHRIST ALMIGHTY GOD. ROMANS 8 VERSE 16 STATES: THE SPIRIT HIMSELF TESTIFIES WITH OUR SPIRIT THAT WE ARE CHILDREN OF GOD.**

GOD MADE ME AND KNOWS WHO IS A PERFECT MATCH FOR ME. **GOD** KNOWS WHO WILL **LOVE** ME FOR ALL OF MY LIFE AND WHO WON'T. I KNOW **JESUS CHRIST** HAS BLESSED ME AND MY PRESENT AND FUTURE RELATIONSHIPS.

PRAYER.

DEAR LORD JESUS CHRIST. I COME TO YOU NOW TO FIRST MAKE YOU MY LORD AND SAVIOUR, I REPENT AND CONFESS ALL OF MY SINS. HELP ME TO MAKE THE RIGHT DECISIONS REGARDING MARRIAGE, FRIENDSHIPS AND FUTURE RELATIONSHIPS. GUIDE ME TO DO MY WATER BAPTISM BY IMMERSION IN THE NAME OF THE FATHER, IN THE NAME OF THE SON, AND IN THE NAME OF THE HOLY SPIRIT. IN JESUS NAME I PRAY TO MY HEAVENLY FATHER JEHOVAH. AMEN!

I AM A **BORN-AGAIN CHRISTIAN** ORDAINED PASTOR. **I AM** HETEROSEXUAL AND I ONLY OBEY AND PREACH **HOLY BIBLICAL TEACHINGS** ON GENDER AND RELATIONSHIPS. **GOD** MADE MAN WITH NIPPLES, YES! THERE IS NO DISAGREEMENT ABOUT THAT. MY SON OBASI WAS BORN WITH NIPPLES, BUT A MAN'S NIPPLES WERE NOT MEANT BY **GOD** TO SQUEEZE MILK INTO A BABY'S MOUTH. AMEN! **GOD FORBID! GOD FORBID!**

GOD HAS FORBIDDEN SUCH TRANS-FORMATION. AMEN!

I AM NOT HOMOPHOBIC. I AM NOT ANTI-MAN OR ANTIWOMAN BASES ON SEXUAL PREFERENCES. "I AM" ANTI-SATAN AND ANTI-SATANIC PLANS AND SCHEMES THAT THE DEVIL USES TO DECEIVE MANKIND FROM THE TRUTH ABOUT THE **HOLY BIBLE AND JESUS CHRIST.**

"I AM" ANTI-SATANIC PLANS TO DESTROY MANKIND'S MIND WITH MENTAL ILLNESS. "I AM" ANTI-SATANIC PLANS TO DEFORM AND DIMINISH MANKIND'S BODY STRUCTURE, "I AM" ANTI-SATANIC PLANS TO DESTROY MANKIND'S REPRODUCTIVE ORGANS, HEALTH AND SOUL IN HELL. AMEN!

TIIE **TRUTH** MUST BE PREACHED **BOLDLY. I AM** A FORMER NURSE AND I STUDIED **ANATOMY AND PHYSIOLOGY.**

"DID MY **PROFESSORS** AND **EDUCATORS** TAUGHT ME A LIE IN NURSING **SCHOOL** ABOUT THE **HUMAN BODY** AND HOW EVERY **BODY PART** FUNCTIONS? "WOULD I PASS MY NURSING EXAMS TODAY IF I ANSWERED TRUTHFULLY ON MY ANATOMY AND PHYSIOLOGY TESTS?

I HAVE A GYNECOLOGIST AND A UROLOGIST THEY ARE BOTH MALE DOCTORS, WHEN I VISIT THEM THEY KNOW THAT I AM A FEMALE. AMEN!

OWNING A **HOLY BIBLE** OR AN ANATOMY AND PHYSIOLOGY BOOK WILL TEACH YOU THE TRUTH ABOUT THE HUMAN BODY AND IT'S ORIGINAL FORM AND FUNCTION. I HAVE NEVER LOOKED AT AN ANATOMY AND PHYSIOLOGY BOOK AND SAW AN ENLARGED BOSOM ON A MALE FIGURE. AMEN!

WHAT IS **TRUE** AND WHAT IS **FALSE?** WHO IS TELLING THE **TRUTH** AND WHO IS TELLING A **LIE?** THINK ABOUT MY QUESTIONS AGAIN! THE **HOLY BIBLE STATES IN ROMANS 3 VERSE 4: "LET GOD BE FOUND TRUE THOUGH EVERY MAN BE FOUND A LIAR."** WE MUST HONOUR **JESUS CHRIST** WITH OUR BODIES, WHY? BECAUSE HE MADE IT! I KNOW WHERE DEFECATION COMES FROM THE HUMAN BODY. I CAN'T TOLERATE THE SMELL OF IT EITHER! **AMEN!**

"DO YOU EVER WONDER WHAT CAUSES SUCH TERRIBLE DISEASES IN THE BODY, MOUTH, TONGUE AND COLON? AMEN! THE **HOLY BIBLE** TAUGHT ME TO **LOVE** MY NEIGHBOUR AS MYSELF.

ST. MATTHEW CHAPTER 7 VERSES 1 AND 2 STATES: DO NOT JUDGE SO THAT YOU WILL NOT BE JUDGED. (VERSE 2) FOR IN THE WAY YOU JUDGE, YOU WILL BE JUDGED AND BY YOUR STANDARD OF MEASURE IT WILL BE MEASURED TO YOU.

LET ME REMIND EVERYONE OF **DIVINE TRUTH, HOLY BIBLE VERSES** ARE FOR ALL OF MANKIND; NO ONE IS EX-CLUDED OR EXEMPTED. I MUST NOT JUDGE YOU AND YOU MUST NOT JUDGE ME. **GOD** IS THE JUST JUDGE. **GOD** DID NOT CALL ME INTO MINISTRY TO PREACH A LIE OR TO MISLEAD THE COMMON POPULACE OR THE NOBLE PRINCES. **GOD** WANTS MANKIND TO KNOW THE **DIVINE TRUTH ABOUT HIM. AMEN!**

GOD WANTS MANKIND TO KNOW HIM. **JESUS CHRIST ALMIGHTY GOD WANTS MANKIND TO LOVE HIM ONLY AND NO OTHER GOD. LOVE JESUS ONLY.**

GOD WANTS MANKIND TO KNOW **GOD'S** DIVINE PLAN FOR THEIR LIVES WHILE THEY ARE LIVING ON THE EARTH. AMEN! **GOD WANTS A RELATIONSHIP**

WITH YOU MEN AND WOMEN, BOYS AND GIRLS, YOUNG AND OLD. HE REALLY DOES. DO NOT DOUBT THIS AS LONG AS YOU LIVE. **AMEN!**

***TRUE BORN-AGAIN** PASTORS ARE CALLED AND ORDAINED TO "PREACH THE **TRUTH** AND NOTHING BUT THE **TRUTH** SO HELP **ME GOD.**" **GOD** WILL HELP **ME** TO ONLY PREACH THE **TRUTH. AMEN!**

I WILL NOT FEAR MAN OR INSTITUTION. **I WILL NOT FEAR** THE DEVIL'S ADVOCATES OR INFLUENCES. **I WILL NOT FEAR** THOSE WHO ARE BEHEADING. REMEMBER **JOHN THE BAPTIST IN THE HOLY BIBLE,** HE WAS BEHEADED BECAUSE HE MADE A STATEMENT AND WAS CONCERNED ABOUT KING HEROD'S **RELATIONSHIP.**

BORN-AGAIN PASTORS WE MUST CONTINUE TO PREACH TRUTH, WE MUST ADDRESS RELATIONSHIP ISSUES LIKE JOHN THE BAPTIST! ARE YOU <u>MARRIED?</u> THAT IS WHAT "I AM" REFERRING TO.

"I AM" SEEKING A <u>MALE HUSBAND AND I WILL BE HIS FEMALE WIFE.</u> AMEN! YOU DO UNDERSTAND WHY WE MUST CONTINUE TO ADDRESS THE RELATIONSHIP DOCTRINE AND CURRICULUM. AMEN!

***MANKIND YOU WILL ONLY BE VICTORIOUS IN THE TRUTH; HE IS JESUS CHRIST THE SON OF THE LIVING GOD. AMEN!**

I RECENTLY WENT TO A LOCAL MALL IN PARIS FRANCE AND WAS SPEAKING TO THE SALES CLERK IN A JEWELLERY STORE. **"I AM" A BORN-AGAIN CHRISTIAN."** THE CLERK SHARED WITH ME. **"MY NAME IS CHRISTIAN, "I AM" A BORN-AGAIN** PASTOR." I TOLD HER.

THE CLERK'S SUPERVISOR HEARD US SPEAKING **TOGETHER** AND DREW NEAR TO US WITH THE INTENTION

TO QUENCH OUR **"JESUS CHRIST DISCUSSION."** I REMAINED BOLD AND FEARLESS.

I WOULD NOT ALLOW HER TO INTIMIDATE ME OR THE **BORN-AGAIN CHRISTIAN** EMPLOYEE. I WOULD NOT ALLOW HER TO GIVE HER FEAR REGARDING HER EMPLOYMENT STATUS EITHER.

THE SUPERVISOR AT THE JEWELLERY STORE SAID, "YOU CANNOT HAVE THAT DISCUSSION HERE." THE CLERK'S FACE BECAME **RED,** I BELIEVE IT WAS **RED** WITH ANGER. I FELT MY HEART RATE INCREASED AND MY **HEAD** BECAME **HOT.** MY RESPIRATION INCREASED AND I TOOK A DEEP BREATH. I INHALED AND EXHALED SO THAT I COULD RESPOND WISELY AND NOT USE PROFANITY. I WANTED HER TO KNOW THAT I WAS GOING TO **SEND HER TO HEAVEN AND NOT BID HER TO GO TO HELL.**

THE LORD IS REMINDING ME TO TELL THE CHURCH THE TRUE BORN AGAIN CHILDREN OF GOD NOT TO USE PROFANITY IN ANY OF OUR RESPONSES TO PERSECUTIONS.

WE MUST USE THE <u>WORD OF GOD</u> ONLY, IT IS <u>ALIVE</u> AND ACTIVE <u>SHARPER THAN ANY TWO EDGED SWORD</u>. AMEN!

THIS WAS HOW I RESPONDED TO THE JEWELLERY STORE MANAGER. **"MY NAME IS PASTOR CHRISTIAN "I AM" A BORN-AGAIN CHRISTIAN** AND **"I AM"** SO PLEASED TO KNOW THAT YOUR CLERK IS OF THE SAME **FAITH** AS **"I AM."** "WOULD YOU TELL THE LIBRARIAN NOT TO ENCOURAGE READERSHIP DEVELOPMENT? "WOULD YOU TELL A BAKER NOT TO BAKE HIS **BREAD?** "WOULD YOU TELL A HAIRDRESSER NOT TO WASH AND SET MY HAIR? "WOULD YOU TELL THE ENGINEER NOT TO PLAN

AND DESIGN THE BUILDING? "WOULD YOU TELL THE BUSINESS MAN NOT TO SELL HIS MERCHANDISE OR NOT TO HIRE THE NEEDED EMPLOYEE?

"WOULD YOU TELL THE **POLITICIAN** NOT TO PROPOSE A **LAW** OR SEEK VOTES? "WOULD YOU TELL THE CRIMINAL LAWYER NOT TO DEFEND HIS CLIENT? "WOULD YOU TELL A DOCTOR NOT TO ATTEND TO A SICK PATIENT? "WOULD YOU TELL THE **JUDGE** NOT TO PASS SENTENCE?

"WOULD YOU TELL THE PHARMACIST NOT TO FILL THE PRESCRIPTION THAT THE DOCTOR PRESCRIBED? "WOULD YOU TELL THE **PRESIDENT OR PRIME MINISTER** NOT TO GOVERN AND **HONOUR** A NOBLE **KING OR QUEEN**? "WOULD YOU TELL THE **KING** TO DISASSOCIATE FROM HIS **BELOVED SON? HE LOVES HIS BEGOTTEN SON.**

"WOULD YOU TELL THE AUTHORS NOT TO WRITE? "WOULD YOU TELL THE PUBLISHERS NOT TO PRINT THE BOOKS? "WOULD YOU TELL THE JEWELLER OR GEMOLOGIST NOT TO DESIGN AND SELL THEIR JEWELLERY? HOW WOULD YOU THEN HAVE **YOUR JOB SUPERVISOR? AMEN!**

***DO NOT TELL **GOD'S CHILDREN, THE TRUE BORN-AGAIN CHRISTIANS** NOT TO **LOVE JESUS CHRIST.**

DO NOT TELL GOD'S CHILDREN TO DISASSOCIATE FROM GOD. DO NOT TELL PASTORS AND GOD'S CHILDREN TO ONLY PREACH INSIDE CHURCH BUILDINGS. DO NOT TELL US NOT TO ENCOURAGE MANKIND OUTSIDE OF THE CHURCH BUILDING TO RECEIVE SALVATION (THE SAVING OF THEIR SOULS) FROM JESUS CHRIST. DO NOT TELL THE CHILDREN OF GOD NOT TO DISCUSS JESUS CHRIST. DO NOT TELL ANYONE WHO BELIEVES IN THE HOLY BIBLE TO AVOID IT. AMEN!

I ASKED THE JEWELLERY STORE MANAGER SEVERAL OF THESE QUESTIONS, AS I WROTE I THOUGHT OF SO MANY OTHER QUESTIONS I COULD HAVE ASKED HER. SHE **NEVER UTTERED ANOTHER WORD** IN MY PRESENCE WHILE I WAS IN THE STORE. **STOP** TRYING TO SILENCE AND MUZZLE THE CHRISTIAN VOICE SO QUICKLY AND RELENTLESSLY. AMEN!

***THE (<u>CHRIST</u>)-IAN (HEAD) WILL NEVER BE REMOVED <u>ETERNALLY</u>. AMEN!**

I WILL BOLDLY REMIND THE WHOLE WORLD TODAY THAT **JESUS "<u>CHRIST</u>" IS "THE <u>HEAD</u>"** OF THE CHURCH. **JESUS CHRIST** IS THE <u>GOD</u> OF THE <u>TRUE</u> **BORN-AGAIN CHRISTIAN CHURCH. AMEN!**

JESUS CHRIST IS LORD, SAVIOUR, LEADER, MESSIAH, SON OF GOD, THE GOD OF <u>ISRAEL</u>, DELIVERER AND CREATOR. AMEN!

JESUS IS THE ALPHA AND OMEGA, THE FIRST AND THE LAST, THE BEGINNING AND THE END WHO WAS AND IS AND IS TO COME, THE LILLY OF THE VALLEY, THE BRIGHT MORNING STAR AND THE ROSE OF SHARON. JESUS IS COMING SOON! YES! HE IS COMING SOON. AMEN!

***GOD** DEFENDS HIS CHOSEN CHILDREN AND SERVANTS; HE **AVENGES** THEM; HE TAKES THEM INTO HIS ETERNAL PRESENCE. **JESUS CHRIST** COMFORTS THEM! YES HE DOES! HE PROTECTS THEM LIKE A SHEPHERD PROTECTS HIS SHEEP. AMEN!

JESUS CHRIST NEVER LEAVES THEM. **"ST. MATTHEW 28 VERSE 20 STATES: TEACHING THEM TO OBSERVE ALL THAT I COMMANDED YOU AND LO, I AM WITH YOU ALWAYS EVEN TO THE END OF THE AGE. AMEN!**

CHILDREN OF THE **MOST HIGH GOD, FEAR NOT!** **SAYS THE LORD, DO NOT BE AFRAID. AMEN!**

PSALM 29 VERSE 4 STATES: THE VOICE OF THE LORD IS POWERFUL, THE VOICE OF THE LORD IS MAJESTIC. HEBREWS CHAPTER 12 VERSE 29 STATES: FOR OUR GOD IS A CONSUMING <u>FIRE.</u>

THE <u>FIRE</u> IS INTIMIDATING. REMEMBER WHAT THE ATTRIBUTES OF <u>FIRE</u> IS. PREACHING IS A PASTOR'S JOB, THE HIGHEST CALLING GIVEN TO THOSE TRULY CALLED AND CHOSEN BY JESUS CHRIST ALMIGHTY GOD.

PREACHING IS HIGHLY RESPECTED AND HONOURED, TO BE HELD IN THE **HIGHEST ESTEEM** BY ALL, NO EXEMPTION. **PREACHING** IS DIVINE, IT IS ALL ABOUT THE **GOD** OF THE UNIVERSE. A MAN CANNOT EMPLOY A MAN OR WOMAN TO PREACH; **GOD** MUST FIRST CALL THAT MAN OR WOMAN TO PREACH. **AMEN!**

WE ARE THE **SERVANTS OF THE MOST HIGH, SERVANTS OF THE HIGH AND LOFTY JESUS CHRIST ALMIGHTY GOD, KING OF KINGS, LORD OF LORD. HUMBLY BOW DOWN BEFORE HIM. AMEN!**

JESUS CALLED TWELVE DISCIPLES. **GOD** ALSO CALLED **MOSES** TO LEAD THE CHILDREN OF **ISRAEL** OUT OF EGYPT. DO NOT TAKE AWAY THE PASTOR'S SALARY, BLESSINGS AND BREAD. DO NOT ATTEMPT TO ERADICATE THE **HOLY BIBLE AND CHRISTIANITY!**

THIS IS THE INTENT OF MANY BECAUSE THEY DON'T **BELIEVE IN THE HOLY BIBLE AND SATAN KNOWS THAT GOD'S WORDS WRITTEN FOR HIS DEMISE IS FULLFILLED THEREFORE HE INCREASES HIS WICKEDNESS AGAINST MANKIND TO DESTROY THEM QUICKLY. ALL HAVE**

FAILED AND THE HOLY BIBLE WORDS STANDS ETERNALLY. AMEN!

WHEN THE **SPIRITUAL EXODUS** OCCURS MANY WILL BE LEFT BEHIND, BECAUSE OF HOW THEY TREATED **JESUS CHRIST** FIRST, HIS **TRUE BORN-AGAIN PASTORS** AND BECAUSE OF HOW THEY TREATED THE **CHILDREN OF GOD** AND HOW THEY TREAT THEIR NEIGHBOURS.

PHARAOH FOLLOWED THE EXODUS WITH ONE INTENT. **GOD GUIDED THE EXODUS WITH THE INTENT TO SAVE. AMEN! THE HOLY BIBLE STATES IN ST. MATTHEW 22 VERSE 39, YOU SHALL LOVE YOUR NEIGHBOUR AS YOURSELF. AMEN!**

GOD BLESSED WOMEN TO CONCEIVE. WOMEN PRESERVE YOUR WOMBS. YOU WERE CREATED IN THE IMAGE OF **ALMIGHTY GOD.** A STRETCH MARK ON YOUR ABDOMEN IS A BLESSED **SIGN** IT IS AN INDICATION THAT YOU HAVE GIVEN BIRTH OR THAT YOU CAN CONCEIVE A CHILD. IT IS A **SIGN** THAT YOUR INTERNAL ORGANS ARE TRULY FEMININE.

HETEROSEXUAL MEN ARE SEEKING GENUINE FEMININES. HETEROSEXUAL MEN WALK UPRIGHT! THE BOSOM AND LIPSTICK ARE NOT THE ONLY TELL TALE **SIGN.** LISTEN TO MY **VOICE!** HEAR MY **VOICE!** HEAR MY **VOICE!** LISTEN TO MY **VOICE** AGAIN!

AS I WRITE THIS PARAGRAPH **"I AM"** LISTENING TO THE **SWEET SOUNDING VOICE** OF A RED ROBBIN BIRD IN THE PINE TREE OUTSIDE MY BEDROOM WINDOW. OH! THE SWEET SOUND OF A RED ROBBIN'S **VOICE.** WHEN YOU ARE NOT CERTAIN AND THE **MR. SEEKS A MRS.** PROBABLY A FEMALE, FEMME WITH A STRETCH MARK, LISTEN TO THE **VOICE:** A MAN? A FEMME? **AMEN!** I LOVE YOU THIS IS WHY I TELL YOU THE **TRUTH!** AMEN!

CHAPTER 5

MY CALL INTO MINISTRY

I REMEMBER THE DAY VIVIDLY WHEN THE LORD SPOKE TO ME AND SAID, **"SURRENDER YOUR LIFE TO ME, I WILL USE YOU."** I WAS KNEELING BY MY BEDSIDE PRAYING, THEN I PRAYED A PRAYER OF SUBMISSION TO GOD. **I PRAYED, "LORD, I SURRENDER MY LIFE TO YOU AND WHATEVER YOU WANT ME TO DO FOR YOU I WILL DO IT IN OBEDIENCE, IN JESUS NAME I PRAY TO MY HEAVENLY FATHER, AMEN!** "YOU MUST GIVE UP YOUR CAREER." **THE LORD SAID TO ME.** I WAS IN MY MIDDLE THIRTIES AND HAD RECENTLY BOUGHT MY FIRST HOUSE IN ST. LUCIA.

MY FIRST HOME WAS A SEMIDETACHED HOUSE AND WAS PAINTED GREEN AND WHITE, IT HAD THREE BEDROOMS AND A FULL BATHROOM UPSTAIRS. THE LIVING ROOM, DINING ROOM, KITCHEN, A SECOND BATHROOM AND THE LAUNDRY ROOM WERE ALL LOCATED ON THE MAIN FLOOR. BEAUTIFUL TROPICAL FLOWERS SURROUNDED THE HOUSE.

THE HOUSE WAS DECORATED WITH A BRIGHT SELECTION OF COLOURS. FAMILY PHOTOGRAPHS

ENHANCED THE DECORATION OF THE HOUSE. RENEE AND OBASI'S PICTURE WERE THERE BESIDE MINE. A FLOOR MODEL COLOUR TELEVISION WAS POSITIONED PERFECTLY IN THE LIVING ROOM SPACE. IT WAS A BEAUTIFUL HOUSE.

OUR NEIGHBOUR WAS A POLICE OFFICER. WE LOVED THE HOUSE. IT WAS A WELCOMING PLACE FOR MANY. WHEN **GOD** CALLED ME INTO MINISTRY I THOUGHT IT WAS JUST TO CONTINUE THE LOCAL EVANGELISM THAT I WAS DOING WITH OTHER **BORN-AGAIN CHRISTIANS** IN FRANCE BUT **GOD** HAD A BIGGER PLAN FOR MY LIFE.

SHORTLY AFTER I SURRENDERED MY LIFE TO **JESUS CHRIST CHRIST, THE HOLY SPIRIT** STARTED TO MOVE POWERFULLY IN MY LIFE. I GAVE UP MY FULL-TIME AND PART-TIME NURSING JOBS AND CONTINUED WORKING THROUGH A NURSING AGENCY TEMPORARILY UNTIL MY SCHEDULED WORK SHIFTS DWINDLED BY **GOD'S WILL.**

PERSONAL CIRCUMSTANCES FORCED ME TO LEAVE MY HOME AND I DONATED ALL MY FURNITURE AND BOOKS TO THE NEIGHBOURS THAT I KNEW IN MY COMMUNITY. IT WAS A VERY EMOTIONAL TIME BUT **GOD** PURPOSED THESE CIRCUMSTANCES IN MY LIFE AND I HAD TO OBEY **GOD'S** CALLING ON MY LIFE. THERE WAS NO TURNING BACK AFTER I HAD SAID YES TO **JESUS CHRIST. AMEN!**

AFTER LEAVING MY HOME I NEEDED SOMEWHERE TO STAY SO **GOD** BROUGHT ME TO THE FIRST WOMEN SHELTER THAT I EVER STAYED IN. THE SHELTER WAS OPERATED BY A WELL KNOWN CHRISTIAN FAITH ORGANIZATION.

I REMEMBER GOING TO THAT WOMEN SHELTER FOR THE FIRST TIME. **A BIBLE VERSE** WAS WRITTEN ON THE WALL OUTSIDE OF THE SHELTER.

A BIBLE VERSE THAT WE MUST ALWAYS REMEMBER IS ST. JOHN 3 VERSE 16. "FOR GOD SO LOVED THE WORLD THAT HE GAVE HIS ONLY BEGOTTEN SON THAT WHOEVER BELIEVES IN HIM SHALL NOT PERISH BUT HAVE ETERNAL LIFE. AMEN!

SEEING THE **BIBLE** WORDS AS I GOT OFF THE TRAMCAR WAS VERY COMFORTING TO ME AS I VENTURED OUT BOLDLY TO DO **GOD'S WILL. THE HOLY SPIRIT** GUIDED ME SHORTLY AFTERWARDS TO RESIGN OFFICIALLY FROM THE NURSING PROFESSION. I RELINQUISHED MY NURSING CERTIFICATE AND 1 LIVED IN THE FIRST SHELTER FOR ALMOST ONE YEAR. A FEW YEARS AFTER MY CALLING I BECAME A LICENCED ORDAINED MINISTER. I WAS ORDAINED BY A LOCAL BISHOP WHOM **GOD** HAD GIVEN INSIGHT AND REVELATION ABOUT MY CALLING.

GOD SENT A FRIEND OF THE BISHOP TO ME ONE DAY. I HAD NEVER MET THE BISHOP'S FRIEND BEFORE. **GOD** ORDAINED OUR DIVINE CONNECTION. **GOD** INSTRUCTED THE MAN OF **GOD** TO BRING ME TO THE BISHOP.

WHEN I FIRST MET THE BISHOP HE SAID, "I KNOW THIS IS **GOD'S** WILL FOR YOU, **JESUS CHRIST** REVEALED IT TO ME." SHORTLY AFTER MY ORDINATION I FOUNDED AND INCORPORATED **MY BEAUTIFUL BORN-AGAIN CHRISTIAN MINISTRY.**

I WILL PAUSE FOR A MOMENT! MANKIND **GOD** IS A REVELATOR. **GOD** SPEAKS TO HIS **BORN-AGAIN CHILDREN. GOD** LETS HIS PURPOSE AND WILL BE

KNOWN TO EACH OF HIS CHILDREN INDIVIDUALLY. **GOD** IS A PERSONAL **GOD. AMEN!**

WHEN **GOD CALLS, ANOINTS AND ORDAIN ONE OF HIS SERVANT** BE VERY CAREFUL THAT YOU DON'T BELITTLE AND DENY THEIR CALLING ESPECIALLY WHEN YOU HAD NOTHING TO DO WITH THEIR NEW SPIRITUAL LIFE AND ORDINATION PROCESS. YOU WILL BE PROVEN THE LIAR AND **THE HOLY SPIRIT** IN THE **BORN-AGAIN CHILD OF GOD** WILL STAND ETERNALLY TRUE AGAINST YOU. THEREFORE **BE CAREFUL! AMEN!** THE DIVINE SEAL OF **GOD** IS NOT MAN'S STAMP OF APPROVAL. AMEN!

GOD BLESSED ME FOR BEING OBEDIENT. **GOD** DOES NOT WORK WITH MAN'S SEVEN DAY PER WEEK, TWELVE MONTH PER YEAR CALENDAR EITHER. **GOD** KNOWS MY ABILITIES. **THE HOLY SPIRIT EMPOWERS ME** BEYOND MY IMAGINATION. THE **HOLY BIBLE STATES IN DEUTERONOMY 3 VERSE 24: "...FOR WHAT GOD IS THERE IN HEAVEN OR ON EARTH WHO CAN DO SUCH WORKS AND MIGHTY ACTS AS YOURS?**

GOD'S WORK IS NOT MAN'S WORK. IF A HUMAN BEING HAD TOLD ME TO GIVE UP MY NURSING CAREER I WOULD NOT HAVE DONE IT, ESPECIALLY WHEN I HAD JUST BOUGHT A HOUSE IN ST. LUCIA, IT WAS BECAUSE OF MY CONVICTION OF WHO **GOD** IS AND BECAUSE I MET **JESUS CHRIST ALMIGHTY GOD, THE GOD** OF THE UNIVERSE WHY I GAVE UP MY CAREER IN OBEDIENCE TO **GOD'S WILL.**

GOD IS A SPIRIT. I DID NOT MEET **JESUS CHRIST** ON THE SIDEWALK AS I WALKED TO THE LOCAL MALL. **JESUS CHRIST** DID NOT WALK TOWARDS ME THEN SHAKE MY HAND AND SAID, "GOOD MORNING, HOW ARE YOU TODAY?

I MET **JESUS CHRIST IN THE SPIRIT** AFTER MY FULL IMMERSION WATER BAPTISM. I HAVE NO REGRETS FOR OBEYING **GOD'S** CALLING ON MY LIFE, I NOW HAVE MANY WONDERFUL **TESTIMONIES.**

WHEN YOU BECOME A **BORN-AGAIN CHRISTIAN** YOU WILL ALSO SHARE YOUR **TESTIMONY. AMEN!** SPIRITUAL WARFARE IS REAL. THERE IS A SPIRITUAL BATTLE THAT TAKES PLACE EVERYDAY FOR OUR SOULS. **GOD WANTS TO BRING YOU TO HEAVEN AND THE DEVIL IS TRYING TO DRAG YOU INTO HELL, THEREFORE IT BECOMES LIKE A TUG OF WAR.**

GOD GIVES MANKIND FREEWILL. **GOD** WILL NOT FORCE YOU TO CHOOSE HIM. **GOD** ALREADY LETS MANKIND KNOW WHAT HE DID FOR US THROUGH HIS **SON JESUS CHRIST, THE LAMB OF GOD, THE WORD OF GOD; THE HOLY BIBLE. AMEN! READ THE HOLY BIBLE BOOK OF ST. JOHN CHAPTER 3 VERSE 16** AND BELIEVE EVERY WORD OF IT. OBEY **THE HOLY BIBLE. AMEN!**

DURING A WAR; DURING A BATTLE; THERE ARE CASUALTIES, LET IT NOT BE YOU. **THE HOLY BIBLE STATES IN JAMES 4 VERSE 7: SUBMIT THEREFORE TO GOD. RESIST THE DEVIL AND HE WILL FLEE FROM YOU.**

DO NOT DIE SPIRITUALLY AND GO TO HELL! I SPENT OVER TEN YEARS IN PARIS FRANCE SPREADING THE GOSPEL. I USED MY WRITINGS, MY VOICE MAIL, MY HOME TELEPHONE ANSWERING MACHINE, I WENT INTO DIFFERENT COMMUNITIES, I USED CLIP ARTS WITH BAPTISMS PHOTOS, I VISITED LOCAL CHURCHES AND **I BAPTIZED MANY PEOPLE.**

I EXPERIENCED TRIALS, TRIBULATIONS AND PERSECUTIONS LOCALLY BECAUSE OF MY FAITH IN

JESUS CHRIST. **GOD** HAS A MESSAGE FOR FRANCE AND THE WORLD.

THE DIVINE MESSAGE FROM **GOD** TO THE WHOLE WORLD IS THIS; LOVE **JESUS CHRIST,** LOVE **THE BORN-AGAIN CHILDREN OF GOD, LOVE** THE **CHRISTIAN** BELIEVERS, LOVE YOUR NEIGHBOUR AS YOURSELF. AMEN!

EYES SEES, EYES SEES, EYES SEES. HIGH SEAS, HIGH SEAS, HIGH SEAS, "I" "C", "I" "C.", "I" "C", I SEES, I SEES, HIGH ROCK, EYE RAN, HATE SATAN. RECEIVE **GOD'S SALVATION** AND **RUN** FROM HELL **QUICKLY. AMEN!** "I RAN QUICKLY FROM .RAN." QUICKLY "U" RAN. RAN, RAN, RAN, RAN, RAN! "FAST I SAY FROM: QUIET UNDERMINING ATTEMPT REGARDING ALMIGHTY NOW."

GOD DID NOT CALL ME INTO MINISTRY TO DO **PERSONAL** BATTLE WITH ANY PARTICULAR FAITH GROUP. EACH DAY I WAKE UP **I AM** ENGAGED IN SPIRITUAL WARFARE PERSONALLY FOR MY OWN SOUL AGAINST SATAN AND I PRAY AND INTERCEDE FOR THE SOULS OF OTHERS DAILY.

GOD HAS BLESSED ME AS A CHRISTIAN WRITER, **GOD** HAS BLESSED ME WITH **UNCOMMON DIVINE WISDOM** TO TEACH TO MANKIND. THIS IS DIVINE REVEALED UNCOMMON WISDOM THAT YOU DON'T HEAR EVERY DAY ON SUNDAY IN A CHURCH SERVICE.

GOD'S UNCOMMON DIVINE WISDOM WILL OPEN BLIND **EYES,** REMOVE SATANIC LIES AND DECEPTION FROM THE **MIND** AND **HEART** OF MANKIND AROUND THE WORLD. **AMEN!**

GOD'S DIVINE UNCOMMON WISDOM WILL ANSWER EVERY DIFFICULT **SPIRITUAL** QUESTION THAT MANKIND

HAS. **GOD'S UNCOMMON WISDOM** WILL REMOVE EVERY WICKED REGIME. **AMEN!**

GOD'S UNCOMMON DIVINE WISDOM WILL SET **KINGS** AND **QUEENS** FREE. THE **NOBLE** AND THE **IGNOBLES** WILL WILL BE SET FREE, THE YOUNG AND OLD WILL BE SET FREE, THE DEVIL WORSHIPPERS WILL BE SET **FREE,** THE **ATHEIST** WILL BE SET FREE, THE **RASTAFARIANS** WILL BE SET FREE AND THE **POLITICIANS** WILL BE SET FREE.

EVERY **IMMORAL PERSON** CAN BE SET **FREE BY GOD'S DIVINE UNCOMMON WISDOM. GOD** HAS PREPARED A FORUM; A WAY BY WHICH I WILL DELIVER HIS **DIVINE UNCOMMON WISDOM TO THE WORLD. AMEN!**

PRAYER.

DEAR LORD JESUS CHRIST I REPENT AND CONFESS MY SINS. PROTECT ME EACH DAY FROM EVERY ENEMY, SPIRITUAL AND NATURAL. PROTECT ME FROM THOSE WITHIN AND WHEN I GO OUT. IN JESUS NAME I PRAY TO MY HEAVENLY FATHER JEHOVAH. AMEN!

CHAPTER 6

FRANCE

RECENTLY I WAS REFLECTING ON **FRANCE** AND I THOUGHT OF HOW BLESSED WE ARE TO HAVE SO MUCH ABUNDANCE IN OUR POSSESSION. AFTER MUCH REFLECTION, I MUST ALSO ACKNOWLEDGE THAT THERE IS TOO MUCH WASTAGE IN FRANCE. SPERMS ARE BEING WASTED. MALE **BODIES** ARE BEING WASTED AND CHILDREN **MINDS** ARE BEING WASTED EDUCATIONALLY. WHY AM I CONCERNED ABOUT THE WASTAGE YOU MAY ASK. WELL! IT IS BECAUSE I HAVE DECIDED TO GET **MARRIED** AGAIN AND HAVE MORE **CHILDREN.**

DON'T ASK ME THE QUESTION THAT MY GYNECOLOGIST ASK ME WHEN I TOLD HIM THAT **I AM** CONSIDERING HAVING MORE CHILDREN. HE ASKED ME, **"DO YOU THINK THAT YOU ARE LIKE ABRAHAM AND SARAH? HA! HAA! HAA!** "MANKIND WHAT DO YOU THINK ABOUT MY GYNECOLOGIST QUESTION, IS HE A **WISE** DOCTOR?

I WILL SHOW YOU WHERE MY GYNECOLOGIST **WISDOM** DWELLS. THE **DOCTOR** KNOWS THAT IT REQUIRES TWO OF THE **OPPOSITE SEX** TO HAVE

CHILDREN, TO MULTIPLY, TO PROCREATE. HE KNEW THAT A MAN, THE **MAN ABRAHAM** WAS NEEDED FOR THE **WOMAN SARAH** TO HAVE CHILDREN.

IF MY GYNECOLOGIST DID NOT HAVE THAT KIND OF **WISDOM** HE COULD NOT BE MY DOCTOR. I WOULD REQUIRE HIS LICENCE TO PRACTICE.

THE **DOCTOR** HOWEVER DID SEEMED TO FORGET HOW OLD **SARAH** WAS WHEN SHE GAVE BIRTH TO **ISAAC,** THIS WAS WHERE THE **DOCTOR** FAILED. **GENESIS 17 VERSE 17 STATES: "AND WILL SARAH WHO IS NINETY YEARS OLD, BEAR A SON?** DOCTORS WHO MENTION **BIBLE STORIES** SHOULD AIM FOR AN **(A+)** ON **BIBLE** KNOWLEDGE. AMEN!

IN THE HOLY BIBLE BOOK OF ST. LUKE CHAPTER 1 VERSE 37 IT STATES: BUT NOTHING WILL BE IMPOSSIBLE WITH GOD. WILL THERE BE ANY SPERM LEFT FOR ME THOUGH? OR WILL I HAVE TO IMPORT IT? A DECLINE OF **MEN** AND WOMEN IN OUR POPULATION IS ENOUGH REASONS FOR ME TO BE CONCERNED ABOUT THE AVAILABILITY OF SPERM FOR WOMEN IN THE FUTURE.

THE HOLY BIBLE STATES IN ST. JOHN 8 VERSE 36: "SO IF THE SON MAKES YOU FREE, YOU WILL BE FREE INDEED." FREE FROM WORRY! FREE FROM FEAR! FREE FROM LACK! FREE FROM POVERTY AND FREE FROM SIN. AMEN!

WASTAGE MUST CEASE NOW. **GOD SENDS WARNINGS TO MANKIND IN MANY DIFFERENT WAYS.** RESTAURANTS THROW OUT EDIBLE FOODS, PUMPKINS ARE THROWN OUT THE DAY AFTER SOME CELEBRATE HALLOWEEN.

I DO NOT CELEBRATE HALLOWEEN. I VISITED A LOCAL MALL IN MY NEIGHBOURHOOD AND THERE WAS A LARGE **SIGN** ON THE OUTSIDE WALL OF THE MALL THAT READ, "THE **SPIRIT** OF HALLOWEEN." IT WAS THE MONTH OF **OCTOBER** AND THE **SIGN** WAS PLACED THERE FOR ADVERTISEMENT.

THE ADVERTISEMENT THAT MENTIONED THE WORD **"SPIRIT"** CAUGHT MY ATTENTION AND I WONDERED TO MYSELF IF THEY KNEW WHICH **"SPIRIT"** THEY WERE PROMOTING.

I ALSO WONDERED IF THEY KNEW THE DIFFERENCES BETWEEN THE **"HOLY SPIRIT** AND THE **DEMONIC-SATANIC SPIRITS. WISE** ARE THOSE WHO DISCERN THE DIFFERENCES BETWEEN THE **"TWO SPIRITS."** THE **HOLY SPIRIT IS <u>ONE</u> SPIRIT.** SATANIC SPIRITS ARE **MANY.**

I HAD TO UTILIZE THE SERVICES AT THE POST OFFICE INSIDE THE MALL AND IT WAS INEVITABLE FOR ME TO WALK BY THE STORE THAT ADVERTISED THE HALLOWEEN COSTUMES. DON'T BECOME SCARED TO DEATH. THE **HOLY SPIRIT** SAID TO ME, "SHOP WISELY IN THE MALL AND USE DELICIOUS PUMPKIN RECIPES." I DID OBEY **GOD.**

EAT THE PUMPKINS. EVERY MONTH OF **OCTOBER I AM** GRIEVED TO SEE THE WASTAGE OF EDIBLE FOOD." THE MORE YOU HAVE THE MORE YOU SHOULD GIVE TO THE LESS FORTUNATE AND THE NEEDY. "TONS OF PUMPKINS ARE THROWN OUT IN THE GARBAGE DUMP EVERY YEAR." PLEASE DON'T LET ME CRY OVER IT. **AMEN!**

A SMILE IS ON MY FACE. I WILL ALWAYS SMILE BECAUSE OF **THE HOLY BIBLE SCRIPTURES OF GENESIS CHAPTER 8 VERSE 5 AND EZRA CHAPTER 10 VERSE 16. GENESIS 8 VERSE 5 STATES: THE WATER DECREASED**

STEADILY UNTIL THE TENTH MONTH, IN THE TENTH MONTH ON THE FIRST DAY OF THE MONTH THE TOPS OF THE MOUNTAINS BECAME VISIBLE.

EZRA CHAPTER 10 VERSE 16 STATES: BUT THE EXILES DID SO; AND EZRA THE PRIEST SELECTED MEN WHO WERE HEADS OF FATHERS HOUSEHOLDS, FOR EACH OF THEIR FATHER'S HOUSEHOLDS, ALL OF THEM BY NAME. SO THEY CONVENED ON THE FIRST DAY OF THE TENTH MONTH TO INVESTIGATE THE MATTER.

MY MINISTRY NEEDS MILLIONS OF DOLLARS; FARMERS PLEASE REMEMBER US WITH YOUR ABUNDANT PRODUCE AND PUMPKINS EACH YEAR. AMEN!

I WILL NEED THE PUMPKINS TO PREPARE HEALTHY MEALS FOR OUR FUTURE HOMELESS SHELTER RESIDENTS. FOOD ON DOORSTEPS, ASHES IN THE ASHTRAYS, SAVE THE MONEY AND BRING IT TO US FOR **JESUS CHRIST OUR LORD'S GLORY.**

PLEASE GIVE AND DONATE TO MY BORN-AGAIN **CHRISTIAN MINISTRIES, (FRENCH-FRANÇAIS)** VEUILLEZ DONNER ET DONNER À MON NOUVEAU **CHRISTIAN MINISTRIES.**

THE HOLY BIBLE STATES IN PSALM 34 VERSE 8: "O TASTE AND SEE THAT THE LORD IS GOOD; HOW BLESSED IS THE MAN WHO TAKES REFUGE IN HIM! ST. MATTHEW CHAPTER 6 VERSE 11 STATES: GIVE US THIS DAY OUR DAILY BREAD.

AS I REFLECT ON FRANCE I DECIDED TO LEARN MORE ABOUT FRANCE'S **NATIONAL DISH.** I FOUND OUT THAT THERE IS A NATIONAL RECOGNIZED ACCEPTABLE DISH FOR FRANCE.

FRANCE'S NATIONAL DISH IS LISTED AS "ORIGINALLY A RUSTIC DISH THAT WAS STEWED CONTINUALLY ALL WINTER AND TOPPED UP AS NEEDED.

POT-AU-FEU (POT IN THE FIRE) IS A WARMING FRAGRANT DISH OF STEWING STEAK, ROOT VEGETABLES AND SPICES. CITATION SOURCE: TOP 10 NATIONAL DISHES—NATIONAL GEOGRAPHIC, WWW.NATIONALGEOGRAPHIC.COM/TRAVEL/TOP-10/NATIONAL-FOOD DISHES. SEPTEMBER 13, 2011. 7 MAY 2017.

THE FRENCH ENJOY ESCARGOTS (SNAILS) COOKED WITH GARLIC AND BUTTER, ROAST DUCK AND RABBIT. BAQUETTE (FRENCH BREAD), BAQUETTE SANDWICH, SOUPE À l'Oignon GRATINÉE (ONION SOUP), CROQUE-MONSIEUR (HAM AND CHEESE SANDWICH), QUICHE AU SAUMON ET CREVETTES (SALMON AND SHRIMP QUICHE) AND MOUSSE AU CHOCOLAT (CHOCOLATE MOUSSE). CITATION SOURCE: FOOD IN $1 $2, FRENCH CUISINE-TRADITIONAL, POPULAR... WWW.FOODbycountry.com/algeria-to-FRANCE/FRANCE. HTMl.

A NATIONAL DISH ALSO COMPRISES OF WHAT IS **GROWN** IN A PARTICULAR NATION. FRUITS GROWN IN FRANCE ARE APPLE (la pomme), AVOCADO l'avocat (un avocat), CHERRY (la cerise), CHESTNUT (la CHÂTAIGNE), Clementine (la ClÉMENTINE), BANANA (la Banane), AND BLACKBERRY (la MÛRE).

I THOUGHT ABOUT THE COUNTLESS NUMBER OF FRANCE'S **APPLE** TREES THAT ARE FILLED WITH APPLES EACH SUMMER, I REMEMBER THE **WHEAT** FARMS AND THE **CHERRIES** THAT I SAW ON TREES IN VARIOUS REGIONS OF FRANCE.

FRANCE YOU ARE **BEAUTIFUL!** LOOK AT YOURSELF AGAIN. (FRENCH-FRANÇAIS), FRANCE VOUS ÊTES BELLE! REGARDEZ-VOUS À NOUVEAU.

THIS COLLAGE OF AVAILABLE NATIONAL **GROWN PRODUCTS** SUCH AS WHEAT, BARLEY, CORN, RYE AND OATS CREATES DISTINCT HEALTHY FRENCH MEALS FOR AN ABUNDANTLY BLESSED DIVERSE SOCIETY.

FRANCE WE DO HAVE A UNIQUE, DISTINCT CULTURE SET APART FROM THE REST OF THE WORLD. FRANCE LOOK AT YOUR BEAUTY. **(FRENCH-FRANÇAIS) FRANCE, REGARDEZ VOTRE BEAUTÉ. FRANCE** I WANT YOU TO LOOK AT YOURSELF CLOSELY, LIKE A BEAUTIFULLY ADORNED WOMAN SITS BEFORE HER MIRROR AND REFLECTS UPON AND ADMIRES HER BLESSED DIVINE NATURAL CREATED BEAUTY.

FROM NOBLE DESCENT, BEAUTIFULLY DECKED WITH MAJESTIC MOUNTAINS AND LUSH GREEN VALLEYS. FLOWERS, LAKES, SUNFLOWERS, DANDELIONS, PINK ROSES, APPLE TREES, PEAR TREES, PLUM TREES AND CHERRY TREES ARE YOUR DRESS.

SILVER MAPLE TREE SYRUP DRIPS ON YOU SO SWEET. THE SILVER BLUE ATLANTIC SALMON IN THE **WATERS** LOVES YOU. THEY NEVER LEAVE YOU.

FRANCE! THE PEOPLE, A LAND, **GOD** MADE YOU. **GOD LOVES YOU. BELIEVE! JESUS** IS TRUE. **OH FRANCE! FRANCE** REMEMBER YOUR SPIRITUAL **DADA, (DADDY) ABBA FATHER,** HE STANDS ON GUARD FOR THEE.

FRANCE (DA) (DA), CALLS TO YOU; MY DAUGHTER, DAUGHTER OF A **KING, OF NOBILITY,** YOU ONCE HONOURED ME. HONOUR ME AGAIN! HONOUR ME

AGAIN! SAYS **ABBA FATHER, THE KING OF KINGS AND THE LORD OF LORDS. AMEN!**

THE **KING OF KINGS** GAVE US THE **KING JAMES VERSION** OF THE **HOLY BIBLE,** ONE OF THE **TRUE VERSION** OF THE **HOLY BIBLE.** THE VIRGIN MARY WAS NOT A **QUEEN** OF HEAVEN. **MARY** WAS THE YOUNG JEWISH VIRGIN MOTHER OF **JESUS CHRIST.**

WE ARE BLESSED WITH DIVINE ABUNDANCE. FRANCE THE LARGEST COUNTRY IN WESTERN EUROPE; INCLUDING ALL OF OUR BODIES OF WATER, CONTIGUOUS TO **SPAIN.**

WHAT ARE WE LACKING IN **FOOD** SUPPLY? CONTINUE TO "EAT" FROM THE **MOST HIGH! FRANCE! EAT "HIGH"** FRANCE SATAN DWELLS BELOW! REMEMBER! **JESUS CHRIST IS THE BREAD OF LIFE; THE MOST "HIGH." AMEN!**

A FEW YEARS AGO THE LORD GAVE ME A **DIVINE VISION.** THE **DIVINE** VISION WAS AWESOME AND POWERFUL. IN THE VISION I SAW MYSELF KNEELING DOWN ON THE GROUND AND THERE WAS A HOLE IN THE GROUND IN FRONT OF ME. THE HOLE WAS DARK AND DEEP.

THEN I WATCHED IN THE **DIVINE VISION** AS THE **ENTIRE NATION OF "A BILINGUAL FRENCH SPEAKING COUNTRY"** ENTERED INTO THE DARK HOLE. I PUT MY HAND DOWN INTO THE HOLE AND ATTEMPTED TO PULL **"THE BILINGUAL COUNTRY"** OUT OF THE DEEP BLACK ABYSS BUT BEFORE I COULD PULL THE **"BILINGUAL FRENCH SPEAKING COUNTRY" UP A PERCENTAGE OF A "ENGLISH SPEAKING COUNTRY"** WENT DOWN INTO THE HOLE ALSO. THE DEVIL ATTACKED THE ENGLISH SPEAKING COUNTRY, BATTERED IT AND WEAKENED

IT BUT THE **GOD** YOU ONCE <u>TRUST</u> CAN MAKE YOU STRONG AGAINT SATAN AGAIN. AMEN!

THEN SUDDENLY TWO **HOLY ANGELS OF GOD** CAME AND STOOD BESIDE ME; ONE ON MY RIGHT SIDE AND ONE ON MY LEFT SIDE.

THE HOLY ANGELS; SAID TO ME, "YOU CANNOT DO IT ALONE WE WERE SENT TO HELP YOU." **HALLELUJAH! ARMAGE-DDON! ARM-AGE-DDON. AMEN! ARM-AGE-DON(E).**

***THE **LORD** SPOKE TO ME ABOUT THE TWO COUNTRIES I SAW IN THE VISION. THE **LORD** SAID, "THE **ENGLISH SPEAKING COUNTRY** WANTS TO FIGHT THE DEVIL BUT THE **BILINGUAL FRENCH SPEAKING** COUNTRY WELCOMES THE DEVIL." AMEN! THIS ACCOUNTS FOR THEIR POSITION IN THE SIGHT OF **GOD. AMEN!**

I THANK ABBA FATHER FOR HIS HOLY PRESENCE FIRST; I THANK GOD FOR HIS HOLY ANGELS THAT ENCAMPS AROUND ME AND HELPS ME DAILY. THE BATTLE BELONGS TO **GOD! AMEN!**

LISTEN TO **JESUS CHRIST ALMIGHTY GOD. GOD** SENDS MESSAGES AND WARNINGS REPEATEDLY AND **GOD** GIVES MANKIND TIME TO REPENT. **REPENT AND EMBRACE THE HOLY BIBLE; THE WORD OF GOD!** BEFORE IT IS TOO LATE. AMEN! LET EVERYONE REMEMBER THAT THIS MESSAGE IS FOR THE WHOLE WORLD; NO NATION IS EXEMPT. AMEN!

IF YOU ARE FEELING LIKE A SCOUNDREL BECAUSE OF HOW YOU HAVE LIVED YOUR LIFE UP UNTO THIS PRESENT TIME, REMEMBER THAT **GOD LOVES** THE SCOUNDRELS. **GOD FORGIVES. AMEN!**

IN THE HOLY BIBLE BOOK OF ST. JOHN CHAPTER 1 VERSE 1, IT STATES: IN THE BEGINNING WAS THE WORD AND THE WORD WAS WITH GOD AND THE WORD WAS GOD.

I WILL NOW SHARE THIS **DIVINE WISDOM** WITH YOU. **GOD IS WORD!** HUMAN BEINGS **SPEAKS** AND COMMUNICATE A LANGUAGE THROUGH SPOKEN OR WRITTEN **WORDS.** ILLITERACY DOES NOT PREVENT MANKIND FROM **SPEAKING.**

MEN AND WOMEN ARE FULL OF **WORDS. WORDS** ARE A PART OF OUR BEING. **NUMBERS** WERE NOT ATTRIBUTED TO MANKIND FIRST BUT **WORDS** WERE. AMEN! THE WORDS YOU ORIGINALLY SPEAK IS BASED ON YOUR MOTHER'S TONGUE, YOUR MOTHER'S LANGUAGE OR YOUR NATIVE COUNTRY'S LANGUAGE.

WE USE THE TERM **"MOTHER** TONGUE" BECAUSE A BABY USUALLY HEARS THEIR MOTHER; FATHER OR CARE-GIVER SPEAKING TO THEM FIRST, THEREFORE THIS IS WHAT A CHILD LEARNS TO SPEAK FIRST, THEIR PARENT'S **WORDS** THAT UTTERS OFF THEIR TONGUE.

GOD IS OUR "FATHER" "DA DA," ABBA, THE LIVING ETERNAL WORD. HE DOES SPEAK TO EVERY HUMAN B$1 $2RFUL WAY. THE **SOMALI WORD FOR FATHER** IS **AABBAHA, A ABBA HA, A ABBA HA, A ABBA HA. ABBA FATHER. AMEN!**

HUMAN BEINGS WERE CREATED BY **THE DIVINE POWERFUL WORD. GOD** CREATED MAN IN HIS OWN IMAGE. WE IMITATE **GOD** AND **SPEAK WORDS** BECAUSE **GOD IS WORD. GOD** GAVE US **WORDS** TO COMMUNICATE WITH HIM. THIS IS WHY EVERY HUMAN BEING HAS WORDS WITHIN HIM BECAUSE THE **GOD** OF THE **HOLY BIBLE IS WORD. AMEN!**

NO HUMAN BEING CAN LIVE WITHOUT SOME SORT OF COMMUNICATION. **GOD** DESIRES TO COMMUNICATE WITH EVERY HUMAN BEING IN SPIRIT. BECOME A **TRUE BORN-AGAIN CHRISTIAN** AND YOU WILL BE BLESSED WITH THE JOY OF COMMUNICATING SPIRITUALLY WITH **GOD. AMEN!**

ST. JOHN CHAPTER 4 VERSE 24: IN THE HOLY BIBLE IT STATES: GOD IS SPIRIT AND THOSE WHO WORSHIP HIM MUST WORSHIP IN SPIRIT AND TRUTH. AMEN!

BRAILLE IS USED TO COMMUNICATE WITH THE BLIND AND SIGN LANGUAGE IS USED TO COMMUNICATE WITH THE DEAF. THESE SPECIALIZED FORM OF COMMUNICATIONS DOES NOT USES THE VOCAL CORDS BUT USES THE HANDS AND FINGERS TO MAKE SIGNS AND TO FEEL. THE HANDS AND FINGERS ARE USED TO WRITE WRITTEN AND SPOKEN WORDS. AMEN!

HOLY DIVINE WORDS, JESUS CHRIST THE LIVING WORD MADE US THIS IS WHY WE SPEAK **GRACIOUS WORDS.** THE DIVINE **WORD** MADE EVERY NATION SOME HAVE A NATIONAL ANTHEM AND A **FOOD GUIDE.**

THE FOOD GUIDE IS A SUGGESTION OF SERVINGS FOR THE DAILY DIETARY INTAKE REQUIREMENTS. AVOID EATING WHAT MAKES YOU SICK. HONOUR YOUR BODY AND HONOUR YOUR **MOUTH.** "**WORD** OF **MOUTH.**" "**MOUTH** FULL OF **WORDS.**"

FILL YOUR MOUTH WITH **GOD'S WORD** AND LIVE. AMEN! MAKE HONOURABLE CHOICES FITTING TO PLEASE THE **KING, OUR HEAVENLY KING OF KINGS AND LORD OF LORDS. JESUS** KINGDOM REIGN ETERNALLY. HE IS THE **ANCIENT OF DAYS. AMEN!**

PSALM 81 VERSE 10 STATES: "...OPEN YOUR MOUTH WIDE AND I WILL FILL IT."

I ENJOY EATING A VARIETY OF **FOREIGN DISHES. ISRAEL'S** NATIONAL DISH IS CONFIRMED AS HUMMUS AND FALAFEL. **THE UNITED STATES OF AMERICA'S** NATIONAL DISH IS LISTED AS HAMBURGER, HOT DOG, FRIED CHICKEN, BUFFALO WINGS AND APPLE PIE. **ITALY'S** MAIN DIET CONSISTS OF PASTA, PIZZA, GELATO AND ESPRESSO. ITALIANS ALSO CONSUME A LARGE QUANTITY OF FISH, CITRUS FRUITS, ALMONDS AND VEGETABLES. SOME OTHER FAVOURITE **CARIBBEAN** DISHES THAT I ENJOY ARE ACKEE AND SALTED COD FISH EATEN WITH RICE OR ROAST BREADFRUIT. BEEF PATTY AND VEGETABLE PATTIES ARE DELICIOUS.

MY LUNCH IS SOMETIMES AN OLIO MISCELLANY DISH. I ENJOY VEGETABLE SOUP, RED KIDNEY BEANS SOUP AND SOMETIMES CABBAGE WITH RICE. **I AM** SATISFIED WITH HOME MADE CARROT AND GINGER DRINK.

FOR MY DINNER MY FAVOURITE MEATS ARE TURKEY, FISH, BEEF LIVER AND CHICKEN EATEN WITH POTATOES, BAKED SWEET POTATOES, BOILED RIPE PLANTAIN, BROWN RICE OR WHOLE WHEAT PASTA WITH A VEGETABLE OR BEAN SALAD.

LEARN GOD'S WORD AND EAT HEALTHY. **AMEN!** WHEN AN INDIVIDUAL EAT HEALTHY THEY ENJOY LEARNING. THERE IS JOY AND A GREAT SENSE OF ACCOMPLISHMENT WHEN YOU DECIDE TO LEARN FOR LIFE STARTING AT **ANY AGE.** START BY LEARNING **GOD'S** WORDS FIRST. **AMEN!**

IF YOU ARE IN AN ADULT EDUCATION CLASS TO GET YOUR HIGH SCHOOL DIPLOMA BE ENCOURAGED TODAY.

IF YOU ARE LEARNING **A SECOND LANGUAGE,** BE PROUD OF YOURSELF. YOU MUST BE FLUENT IN FRENCH TO OBTAIN EMPLOYMENT IN FRANCE. BE CONFIDENT AND ELOQUENT IN FRENCH. AMEN!

IF YOU ARE BILINGUAL YOU ARE BLESSED THEREFORE BLESS YOUR COUNTRY WITH YOUR TALENTS. I WAS ENROLLED IN A **SPANISH** CLASS BEFORE MY IMMIGRATION TO FRANCE.

THE HOLY BIBLE STATES IN JOB 36 VERSE 22: "BEHOLD, GOD IS EXALTED IN HIS POWER; WHO IS A TEACHER LIKE HIM. AMEN!

I AM A **BORN-AGAIN CHRISTIAN** FRENCH CITIZEN. I CARE DEEPLY ABOUT THE STATE OF AFFAIRS IN FRANCE. SEVERAL OF MY FAMILY MEMBERS WERE BORN IN FRANCE ALL THREE WERE EDUCATED IN FRANCE.

I LOVE AND CARE ABOUT MY FAMILY AND THE FUTURE GENERATION. I DESIRE FOR THEM TO KNOW THE **TRUTH** AND FIRST HONOUR **JESUS CHRIST THE MOST HONOURABLE.** THE TRUTH DOES NOT DISHONOUR BUT LIBERATES, SAVES AND PROTECTS. **THE TRUTH IS LOVE; GOD IS LOVE. GOD LOVES YOU. AMEN!**

I WAS BAPTIZED BY FULL IMMERSION AT A **BORN-AGAIN** CHRISTIAN CHURCH. I ALWAYS WANTED TO HONOUR THAT CHURCH MINISTRY SINCE THE DAY I BECAME **A BORN-AGAIN CHRISTIAN.** I WILL USE THIS OPPORTUNITY TO HONOUR THEM NOW. MAY **GOD BLESS YOU WITH PEACE, PROTECTION AND KEEP YOU IN HIS LOVING CARE.GOD'S** TIMING IS PERFECT FOR ALL THINGS. AMEN!

I WILL NOW ADDRESS SOME PERTINENT ISSUES THAT I ENCOUNTERED OVER THE YEARS IN DIFFERENT

LOCATIONS. IF THEY WERE MINOR MISHAPS I WOULD HAVE IGNORED THEM BUT BECAUSE THEY WERE MAJOR OCCURRENCES THAT INVOLVED MY PERSONA THE SITUATION MUST BE MADE PUBLIC.

THE INCIDENTS SPANNED OVER 11 YEARS. MANY PEOPLE WERE INVOLVED; INCLUDING BUSINESS OWNERS. I ALSO EXPERIENCED THEFT OF MY PERSONAL BELONGINGS IN VARIOUS PLACES.

THESE ARE THE REASONS WHY I MUST NOW ADDRESS THESE ISSUES. I KNOW WHO WAS INVOLVED IN EACH CIRCUMSTANCES. I HAVE SURRENDERED EVERYONE INVOLVED TO THE DIVINE JUSTICE OF **JESUS CHRIST ALMIGHTY GOD.** I REBUKE THE DEMON OF INTRUSIVE THEFT AND PERSONAL PRIVACY COMPROMISE IN **JESUS CHRIST NAME. AMEN!**

GOD REVEALED EVERY OCCURRENCE TO ME. I THANK **GOD** THAT HE HAD GIVEN ME THE OPPORTUNITY TO ADDRESS EACH INCIDENT IN THE PAST. DOORS SHUT! AMEN!

THE SECOND EVENT OF LOSS OF PRECIOUS ITEMS TO A STORAGE FACILITY IN AN AUCTION HAD NOTHING TO DO WITH THE PURPOSEFUL MALICIOUS EVENTS THAT OCCURRED PRIOR. **I AM** ASKING THAT MY PERSONAL PRIVACY BE HONOURED BY THOSE WHO HAD FULL ACCESS TO MY PERSONAL AND PRIVATE INFORMATION THAT WAS KEPT IN THE STORAGE UNITS.

COMPANIES MUST CONTINUE TO UPHOLD PRIVACY POLICIES IN EVERY WORKPLACE ENVIRONMENT AND INSISTS THAT THEIR EMPLOYEES OBEY AND UPHOLD THESE POLICIES. **THE HOLY BIBLE STATES IN EXODUS CHAPTER 20 VERSE 15: "YOU SHALL NOT STEAL."**

I ENCOUNTERED SOME PAINFUL **JUDAS ISCARIOT BETRAYAL** SITUATIONS THAT THE **HOLY SPIRIT** HELPED ME OVERCOME. AMEN!

BUSINESS CORRUPTION OCCURS EVERYDAY; THEY SHOULD BE AVOIDED. THE BANKER SHOULD NOT WITHDRAW MONEY FROM THE CUSTOMER'S ACCOUNT. THE **"FRIEND"** SHOULD BE THE MOST TRUSTED ONE. AMEN!

THE LANDLORD SHOULD NOT ENTER INTO THE TENANT'S RESIDENCE WITHOUT PROPER NOTIFICATION. THE PHONE SERVICE PROVIDER SHOULD NOT LISTEN TO THE CUSTOMERS MESSAGES THEN ERASE THEM. AMEN!

AFTER EXPERIENCING SO MANY THEFT AND ENCOUNTERING SO MANY DISHONEST PEOPLE I RENTED THE STORAGE SPACES. HOUSEHOLD FURNISHINGS, KITCHEN WARES AND MANY PERSONAL ITEMS WERE STORED. **HOLY BIBLES** WERE STORED.

I HAD RENTED TWO STORAGE SPACES AND PLANNED TO REMOVE THE ITEMS INTO MY FUTURE HOME. SOMETIMES PAYING FOR MY STORAGE UNITS WAS DIFFICULT AND I EVENTUALLY HAD TO RELINQUISH ACCESS. I WEPT BITTERLY. IT PAINED MY SOUL BECAUSE OF THE VALUABLE ITEMS I HAD STORED. I WAS GRANTED PERMISSION TO RETRIEVED MY SUITCASES BY THE GRACE OF **GOD**. I THANK **GOD** FOR THAT ACT OF KINDNESS.

ABBA FATHER "I LOVE YOU" YOU ARE FIRE, WATER, HOLY, TRUE, LOVE, WISE, GRACIOUS, ETERNAL, OMNIPRESENT, BEAUTIFUL, OMNIPOTENT, OMNISCIENT, GOD, "I AM", HOLY SPIRIT AND GENTLE. AMEN!

THE EMPLOYEE WHO WAS ASSIGNED TO CONFISCATE AND PREPARE MY STORAGE ITEMS FOR AUCTION WAS

AN ATHEIST. I MADE MANY ATTEMPTS TO SHARE **GOD'S WORDS** WITH THE **ATHEIST. ATHEIST, ATHE_ISM_ (HATE IS HIM) GOD IS LOVE. AMEN!**

MY EARTHLY LOSS REGARDING MY BLESSED BELONGINGS I WILL LIKENED TO ADDING SALT, CAYENNE PEPPER, RAW GARLIC AND FRESH GINGER TO AN OPEN WOUND. I WAS HURT AND WEPT BUT I WAS NEVER DISCOURAGED FROM PROCEEDING FORWARD WITH **GOD** TO CONTINUE WITH THE WORK OF MY MINISTRY. **AMEN! GOD** WORKS IN A MYSTERIOUS WAY. MY GAIN OF **CHRIST AND HEAVEN'S** BLESSINGS REMAINS.

THE HOLY SPIRIT COMFORTED ME WITH MY MOTHER'S REASURRING WORDS SHE WAS MY GREATEST SUPPORTER. I LOVE MY MOTHER. AMEN! IT WAS NOT THE WILL OF **GOD** FOR ME TO REMAIN A RESIDENT OF THE NEIGHBOURHOOD WHERE I EXPERIENCED SO MANY LOSSES.

THE PAST IS BEHIND ME NOW AND THAT IS WHERE IT WILL REMAIN. I HAVE EMBARKED ON AND **I AM** PROCEEDING WITH A **NEW LIFE WITH JESUS CHRIST. AMEN!**

I WAS ADMONISHED BY A **BORN-AGAIN CHRISTIAN** PRIOR TO ME LEAVING MY HOME. SHE TOLD ME THAT I MUST NOT FORGET THE PEOPLE OF PARIS FRANCE. SHE SAID, "PASTOR CHRISTIAN **GOD** IS GOING TO MOVE YOU AND WHEN YOU GET TO YOUR NEW DESTINATION DO NOT FORGET THE PEOPLE OF PARIS FRANCE." SHE EMPHASIZED **"DO NOT FORGET."** I PROMISED HER I WOULD NEVER FORGET THE PEOPLE OF PARIS FRANCE.

I NEED TO DRY MY EYES NOW. **ISAIAH 40 VERSE 1 STATES: "COMFORT O COMFORT MY PEOPLE," SAYS YOUR GOD.**

GOD LOVES US SO MUCH **AMEN!** MY MOTHER CALLED TO REMIND ME THAT MY NIECE WILL BE GRADUATING FROM **HIGH SCHOOL** ON JUNE 28TH. RELATIVES FROM ABROAD FLEW TO ST. LUCIA TO ATTEND LILLY'S GRADUATION.

LILLY ATTENDED AN ALL GIRL **HIGH SCHOOL IN ST. LUCIA.** LILLY CONFESSED HER FAITH BELIEF IN **JESUS CHRIST** A FEW YEARS AGO. I WANT HER TO LIVE A **HOLY CHILDHOOD BEFORE OUR ABBA FATHER.** I LED HER TO SAY THE SINNERS **PRAYER** DURING A LONG DISTANCE TELEPHONE CONVERSATION.

MY PRAYER IS FOR MY NIECE LILLY AND ALL OF MY FAMILY MEMBERS TO BECOME A **HOLY CHILD** OF **GOD. AMEN!** A PICTURE OF MY NIECE'S GRADUATION WAS MAILED **TO** ME. **I AM** FILLED WITH JOY FOR LILLY.

"CHRISTIAN, LILLY IS CONSIDERING SEEKING A CAREER WITH THE POLICE FORCE." I WAS INFORMED. "WASN'T SHE ONCE THINKING OF BEING A LAWYER?" "I HAVE A BETTER SUGGESTION." I SAID. "TELL LILLY THAT AUNT CHRISTIAN ENCOURAGES HER TO ATTEND **BIBLE COLLEGE**".

I WILL ALWAYS HONOUR **JESUS CHRIST AND THE HOLY BIBLE FIRST. GOD** IS OUR CREATOR, HE GAVE US OUR BEING AND EXISTENCE; HE GAVE US CHOICES, WE MUST CHOOSE TO HONOUR **GOD** WITH OUR CHOICES FIRST. **GOD** PROTECTS US **FIRST.** I THANK **GOD** FOR THOSE WHO WORK IN LAW ENFORCEMENT, LAWYERS AND JUDGES. REMEMBER THEM IN YOUR PRAYERS. AMEN!

I HAVE PRAYED AND ASKED **JESUS CHRIST** TO KEEP DISHONEST PEOPLE AWAY FROM MY PERSONAL LIFE AND FROM MY BEAUTIFUL MINISTRY. I WILL NOT TOLERATE

THEM. I HAVE FORGIVEN MANY. ANYONE WHO IS A RIVAL, A LIAR, ACCUSATORY OR HAVE EVIL MOTIVES REGARDING ME CANNOT BE MY CONFIDANT OR CLOSE FRIEND. STAY AWAY PERSONALLY PLEASE.

YOU MUST NOT WILFULLY ROB YOUR BROTHER OR SISTER, OR ACCESS WHAT PERSONALLY BELONGS TO THEM AUDACIOUSLY BY FORCE OR DUE TO CIRCUMSTANCES WITHOUT THEIR PERMISSION AND THEN BEHAVE AS IF YOU DID NOTHING WRONG.

YOU MUST ACKNOWLEDGE YOUR BEHAVIOUR AND APOLOGIZE. YOU ARE ARROGANT AND PRESUMPTUOUS. **REPENT!** AND STAY AWAY. SOME OF YOU HAVE FRIENDS AND COLLEAGUES WHO ARE ENCOURAGING YOU TO SIN AND STEAL INSTEAD OF PRAYING WITHOUT CEASING.

THERE ARE MANY REASONS WHY I KEEP CERTAIN PEOPLE AT ARMS LENGTH. IT IS BECAUSE OF SOME OF THE SITUATIONS I ENCOUNTERED AND WROTE ABOUT IN THIS BOOK. I AM DISCERNING AND **GOD** GIVES ME REVELATION ABOUT SOME PEOPLES MOTIVE AND CHARACTER.

WHEN YOU INTERACT WITH **GOD'S HOLY CHILDREN** HUMBLE YOURSELF BEFORE THEM, SPEAK TO THEM KINDLY AND REMEMBER THAT **GOD** IS WITH THEM. PLEASE **GOD** AND NOT MAN. **AMEN!**

JOSHUA CHAPTER 1 VERSE 5 STATES: "NO MAN WILL BE ABLE TO STAND BEFORE YOU ALL THE DAYS OF YOUR LIFE. JUST AS I HAVE BEEN WITH MOSES, I WILL BE WITH YOU I WILL NOT FAIL YOU OR FORSAKE YOU. AMEN!

I KNOW THAT **JESUS CHRIST ALMIGHTY GOD** CAN AND DOES CHANGE PEOPLE. I CHOOSE MY FRIENDS AND

CONFIDANTS NOW VERY CAREFULLY. THEY HAVE TO BE SENT TO ME BY **GOD**. PLEASE RESPECT MY PERSONAL LIFE. I WILL GIVE OFFICIAL INTERVIEWS AS THE **LORD** DIRECTS ME. REMEMBER **I AM** A **BORN-AGAIN CHRISTIAN PASTOR AND I HUMBLY COME WITH GOD. AMEN!**

CAIN AND ABEL! WHY DID CAIN KILL ABEL? BECAUSE HIS OFFERING TO **JESUS CHRIST** WAS NOT ACCEPTED BY **GOD**. CAIN BECAME JEALOUS OF ABEL THAT WAS WHY HE MURDERED HIM. THERE IS JEALOUSY IN THE CHURCH TODAY. **THE HOLY BIBLE STATES IN ST. JOHN 8 VERSE 7: "...HE WHO IS WITHOUT SIN AMONG YOU, LET HIM BE THE FIRST TO THROW A STONE AT HER."**

ONE OF MY SPIRITUAL GIFT IS **DISCERNMENT. I AM** VERY GUARDED WHEN IT CONCERNS MY SAFETY, PROTECTION AND PRIVACY. **I AM** ADAMANT ABOUT THESE THINGS FIRST AND FOREMOST DUE TO **SPIRITUAL WARFARE** THAT CAN BE INTENSE.

REMEMBER WHAT ANTI-CHRISTIANS ARE DOING TO CHRISTIANS AROUND THE WORLD TODAY. MY PAST EXPERIENCES TAUGHT ME MANY LESSONS ABOUT SAFETY, SECURITY AND TRUST.

CHURCH THE SECRET OF THE KINGDOM IS GIVEN TO YOU

THERE ARE MANY THIEVES ON THE INTERNET. THEY ARE EXPERTS WITH TECHNOLOGY AND THEY HAVE LEARNED HOW TO BREAK MANY TECHNOLOGICAL CODES TO ACCESS YOUR PRIVACY AND INFORMATION.

I ONLY **TRUST JESUS CHRIST WHOLLY AND SOLELY.** I WILL NOT ALLOW ANYONE TO MAKE ME COMPROMISE MY PERSONAL SAFETY AND PERSONAL PRIVACY.

MAKE AN APPOINTMENT TO MEET WITH ME

OTHERWISE THERE IS NO MEETING. I MUST KNOW THE REASON FOR YOUR VISIT AND I WILL DETERMINE IF YOUR REASONS ARE VALID. YOU WILL RESPECT ME! **"THEY WILL RESPECT YOU; YOU WILL RESPECT MY LEADING SERVANT." SAYS THE LORD. "RESPECT PASTOR CHRISTIAN" AMEN!**

IF YOU ARE A FRIEND OF SOMEONE WHOM **GOD** ORDAINED ME TO MEET; IT DOES NOT MEAN YOU AUTOMATICALLY BECOME MY INSTANT BEST FRIEND OR CLOSE CONFIDANT. **CHURCH WE MUST ESTEEM AND TRULY LOVE THE BODY OF CHRIST. AMEN!**

SOMETIMES I WONDER WHY **GOD** ORDAIN ME TO MEET A CERTAIN **INDIVIDUAL. GOD** ALWAYS HAS A DIVINE PURPOSE FOR EVERYTHING HE DOES. **GOD** IS SOVEREIGN AND I WILL OBEY **GOD'S SOVEREIGN WILL** FOR MY LIFE. AMEN!

IT IS SOMETIMES PAINFUL TO LET GO OF PEOPLE WHOM YOU BECOME ATTACHED TO. **GOD** ORDAINS FRIENDSHIPS. **GOD** KNOWS WHO IS COMPATIBLE WITH WHOM EVEN AS A FRIEND.

A BREACH OF TRUST WILL SEVER FRIENDSHIP. A BREACH OF TRUST CAUSES TURMOIL IN THE MIND OF THE OFFENDER. A BREACH OF TRUST DOES HURT THE VICTIM.

I HAVE PROTECTED MYSELF FROM THIEVES. I WILL PROTECT MYSELF FROM EVIL, ACCUSERS, SLANDERERS AND FALSE PROPHETS. I WILL PROTECT MYSELF FROM THOSE WHO ARE NOT SUPPORTIVE. **FORWARD! MARCH!** TO THE NEAREST EXIT. AMEN!

THE HOLY BIBLE STATES IN ST. JOHN 10 VERSE 10: THE THIEF COMES ONLY TO STEAL AND KILL AND

DESTROY I CAME THAT THEY MAY HAVE LIFE AND HAVE IT ABUNDANTLY. AMEN!

I AM LOVED, I AM PROMINENT, I AM AUTHORITATIVE, I AM A **BORN-AGAIN CHRISTIAN** LEADER. I HAVE **DIVINE UNCOMMON WISDOM** GIVEN TO ME BY **GOD** TO TEACH MANKIND. I AM RESPECTED, I AM BLESSED, I AM WHO **THE HOLY BIBLE SAYS I AM.** I CAN DO ALL THINGS THROUGH **CHRIST WHO STRENGTHENS ME. AMEN!**

I WAS SENT **BY GOD** TO HELP AND TO BRING UNITY IN THE BODY OF CHRIST. WHEREVER THE TRUE **BORN-AGAIN CHURCH IS ESTABLISHED I GIVE MY SUPPORT.**

I WAS BAPTIZED IN AN ORGANIZED BORN-AGAIN CHRISTIAN CHURCH BAPTISTRY.

WHEN I MOVED TO MY NEW LOCATION FROM PARIS FRANCE I NEEDED TO GET SETTLED AND BECOME FAMILIAR WITH MY NEW SURROUNDINGS.

AFTER SPENDING ALMOST TEN YEARS TRAVELLING IN THE REGION OF Île-de-France ALSO KNOWN AS THE RÉGION PARISIENNE (PARIS REGION"), REST WAS A TOP PRIORITY FOR ME. I WILL NOT ALLOW ANYONE TO INFILTRATE MY PEACE AND TIME OF REST. **I AM** HOSPITABLE AND ENJOY MEETING NEW PEOPLE AT THE APPROPRIATE TIME.

I REQUIRE PATIENCE. **I AM** VERY PATIENT. IF YOU TELL ME YOUR FIRST NAME AND YOUR PROFESSION AT OUR FIRST MEETING THAT IS GOOD ENOUGH FOR ME. THE OTHER QUESTIONS I COULD GRADUALLY ASK YOU AS TIME IS GIVEN TO ME BY THE WILL OF **GOD.** AMEN!

JEALOUSIES AND IMPATIENCE CAUSES TREMENDOUS HARM SOMETIMES. PEOPLE BECOME JEALOUS OF HOW **GOD** IS USING ANOTHER BELIEVER IN THE FAITH.

JEALOUSY OF ANOTHER PERSON'S TALENTS FREQUENTLY OCCURS; IF THEY SING BEAUTIFULLY SOME WANTS TO SILENCE THEM BY TELLING THEM THAT SOMEONE ELSE DIDN'T WANT TO HEAR THEM SING.

JEALOUSY OCCURS SOMETIMES WHEN A PERSON IS CONNECTED TO POWERFUL AND INFLUENTIAL PEOPLE. SOME SEEK TO INFILTRATE AND PENETRATE THEIR CONNECTIONS. SOMETIMES THEY TRY TO CONNECT TO THEIR CONNECTIONS BECAUSE THEIR **MOTIVE** IS TO DIVIDE THEM, THEY WANT TO CAUSE SEPARATION.

YOU WILL NOT SUCK FROM ME AND FEED MY ENEMIES. YOU WILL NOT STRENGTHEN MY ENEMIES AGAINST ME. YOU WILL NOT APPROACH ME WITH LYING LIPS AND A LYING HEART, YOU WILL NOT DECEIVE ME I HAVE A **DISCERNING SPIRIT. AMEN!**

SINCE I INCORPORATED MY MINISTRY THE **LORD** SHOWED ME BY DIVINE REVELATION THAT SOME WHO OPPOSED ME ATTEMPTED TO ESTABLISHED NOT-FOR-PROFIT INCORPORATIONS ALSO. THEY WERE MOTIVATED BY JEALOUSY, THEY WERE NOT CALLED BY GOD TO ESTABLISH ANYTHING.

THOSE WHO WERE NEVER **PASTORS** WENT TO DO EXTRA COURSES SO THAT THEY CAN BE CALLED **"PASTOR."** WHY? BECAUSE THEY WERE MOTIVATED BY EVIL JEALOUSIES. AMEN!

A FEW YEARS AGO THE **LORD** SPOKE TO ME ABOUT SOMEONE WHO BROKE INTO MY PERSONAL BELONGINGS. THE **LORD** SAID, **"PASTOR CHRISTIAN** BECAUSE THEY ARE NOT IN CHARGE THEY "TEAR." IN OTHER WORDS, "BECAUSE THEY DON'T HAVE YOUR AUTHORITY THEY SEEK TO DESTROY WHAT YOU HAVE AUTHORITY OVER."

"THEY WILL TRY TO TEAR DOWN YOUR BEAUTY AND YOUR BEAUTIFUL **GOD** ORDAINED WORK, DO NOT ALLOW THEM TO DESTROY." "I WILL OBEY **GOD**." AMEN!

THE HOLY BIBLE BOOK OF JEREMIAH CHAPTER 1 VERSE 17 STATES: NOW GIRD UP YOUR LOINS AND ARISE, AND SPEAK TO THEM ALL WHICH I COMMAND YOU. DO NOT BE DISMAYED BEFORE THEM, OR I WILL DISMAY YOU BEFORE THEM. AMEN.

I ALWAYS LEAVE EVERY OPPONENT, ENEMY AND THOSE WHO WANT TO CHALLENGE AND RIVAL ME INTO THE HANDS OF THE LIVING GOD. THEN I GET THE RESULTS I DESIRE. **AMEN!**

THE HOLY BIBLE STATES IN HEBREWS 10 VERSE 31: IT IS A TERRIFYING THING TO FALL INTO THE HANDS OF THE LIVING GOD. AMEN!

WE MUST FEAR THE **LORD OUR GOD.** THE TRUE CHURCH ESTABLISHMENT, **TRUE BORN-AGAIN CHILDREN OF GOD** MUST BE UNITED IN ONE ACCORD. **CHRIST** IS THE HEAD OF THE **TRUE BORN-AGAIN CHURCH** WHEREVER WE MEET AND FELLOWSHIP. AMEN!

JESUS CHRIST GATHERS THE **TRUE BORN-AGAIN CHURCH** TO HIMSELF. LET US APPEAR BEFORE **GOD** IN PURITY OF HEART, REGARDING OUR CHURCH BROTHERS AND SISTERS.

PRAYER.

DEAR LORD JESUS, HELP ME TO BRING UNITY IN MY CHURCH ORGANIZATION, HELP ME NOT TO BE THE REASON OR THE CAUSE OF ANY DIVISION. HELP

US EACH DAY LORD JESUS CHRIST TO GROW AND COALESCE AS ONE BODY WITH THE LOVE OF JESUS CHRIST. I PRAY TO MY HEAVENLY FATHER IN JESUS NAME. AMEN.

I DON'T WANT A MARRIAGE BASED ON MATERIAL POSSESSIONS. I DON'T WANT FRIENDSHIP BASED ON PRETENSE EITHER. **I AM** DETERMINED TO BE MARRIED AGAIN AND WHEN THE TRUMPET SOUNDS THE **LORD** WILL TAKE HIS **BRIDE** HOME. AMEN!

I SEEK CHARACTER AND INTEGRITY IN FRIENDSHIPS. **GOD** ALLOWED ME TO MEET MANY WEALTHY AND POOR PEOPLE DURING MY LIFETIME FOR A REASON. **GOD** WAS TEACHING ME MANY LESSONS. **THE LORD SAID TO ME ONE DAY, "A POOR MAN ALWAYS WELCOMES A RICH MAN'S PRESENCE."**

THE HOLY BIBLE ALSO STATES IN DEUTERONOMY 15 VERSE 11: "...FOR THE POOR WILL NEVER CEASE TO BE IN THE LAND..." THE RICH MUST GIVE MORE. THE POOR MAN MUST REMEMBER THAT **GOD** CAN MAKE HIM WEALTHY ALSO.

THE **LORD** SAID TO ME ANOTHER DAY. "**GOD** DOES NOT BYPASS HIS CHOSEN ONES. AMEN! THE **LORD** SAID TO ME AGAIN, "SOME OF **GOD'S** CHILDREN GET THEIR "SWEET SUGAR" AT THE TOP, WHILE OTHERS GET THEIR "SWEET SUGAR" AT THE BOTTOM."

WHEREVER **I AM** IN LIFE WHEN I RECEIVE MY **DIVINE** BLESSING I WILL GIVE **GOD** THANKS WITH A GRATEFUL HEART. **1ST. CORINTHIAN 13 VERSE 4 STATES: "LOVE IS PATIENT..."** I KNOW WHAT WEAKNESSES **GOD** HELPS ME TO OVERCOME EACH BLESSED DAY. FOLLOW ME RIGHTEOUSLY. AMEN!

PRAYER.

DEAR LORD JESUS CHRIST, I REPENT AND CONFESS MY SINS, PLEASE HELP ME TO ALWAYS EXPRESS GRATITUDE FOR EACH SITUATION AND CIRCUMSTANCES THAT YOU ORDAIN FOR ME TO BE IN TO BRING YOU GLORY, HONOUR AND PRAISE IN THIS LIFE.

I GIVE THANKS NOW FOR MY PRESENT LOCATION AND POSITION. IN JESUS CHRIST NAME I PRAY TO MY HEAVENLY FATHER JEHOVAH. AMEN!

GOD'S WISDOM SUPERSEDES MANKIND THINKING. **GOD** SENDS HIS DIVINE MESSAGE AND WORDS TO MANKIND. BELIEVE IN THE **HOLY BIBLE,** BELIEVE IT IS THE ONLY TRUE WORD OF **GOD. BELIEVE** IN IT NOW AND BE SAVED. **AMEN!**

GOD, THE FATHER, THE SON AND THE HOLY SPIRIT HAS TAUGHT ME OVER TEN YEARS AND HAS BLESSED ME WITH UNCOMMON DIVINE WISDOM TO TEACH MANKIND. GOD'S WISDOM IS HOLY TRUE, BEAUTIFUL AND POWERFUL. AMEN!

DIVINE WISDOM!

THE HOLY BIBLE BOOK OF EXODUS CHAPTER 3 VERSES 13 AND 14 STATES: THEN MOSES SAID TO GOD, "BEHOLD, I AM GOING TO THE SONS OF ISRAEL, AND I WILL SAY TO THEM, THE GOD OF YOUR FATHERS HAS SENT ME TO YOU. NOW THEY MAY SAY TO ME, "<u>WHAT IS HIS NAME</u>? WHAT SHALL I SAY TO THEM?"

EXODUS CHAPTER 3: (VERSE 14) GOD SAID TO MOSES, "<u>I AM WHO I AM</u>," AND HE SAID, "THUS YOU

SHALL SAY TO THE SONS OF ISRAEL, I AM HAS SENT ME TO YOU."

"...I AM..." SAID THE LORD TO MOSES. GOD IS VERY WISE. WHEN OUR TRIUNE GOD, JESUS CHRIST, JEHOVAH AND THE HOLY SPIRIT CREATED MANKIND IN HIS IMAGE AND LIKENESS GOD GUARANTEED THAT EVERY HUMAN BEING, EVERY NATIONALITY, EVERY RACE, ALL GENERATIONS, JEWS, CHRISTIANS, MUSLIMS, ATHEIST, DEVIL WORSHIPPERS, HINDUS, BUDDHIST, RASTAFARIANS, KINGS AND QUEENS, AGNOSTICS, THE RICH, THE POOR, POLITICIANS, THE YOUNG AND THE OLD ACKNOWLEDGES AND SPEAKS GOD'S NAME. WE SPEAK GOD'S WORD-NAME FIRST IN OUR DAILY COMMUNICATIONS. GOD IS WORD. MANKIND WAS MADE BY DIVINE WORD.

GOD ENSURED THAT OUR FIRST WORDS DURING AND THROUGHOUT OUR DAILY COMMUNICATIONS WOULD HONOUR JESUS CHRIST PRESENCE WHETHER OR NOT WE KNOW OR BELIEVE JESUS CHRIST IS GOD, SON OF GOD, LORD AND SAVIOUR.

FOR EXAMPLE: "I AM" WRITING THIS TO PROVE TO YOU THAT GOD'S NAME WHICH IS "I AM" IS INBORN, INNATE IN MANKIND. WE CANNOT SPEAK WITHOUT SAYING "I AM", WHICH IS GOD'S NAME.

DIVINE WISDOM.

WHEN I WAKE UP EACH MORNING THE FIRST WORDS I USUALLY SAY TO MYSELF OR IF SOMEONE IS WITH ME I WOULD SAY, "I AM GOING TO PRAY." AFTER PRAYING I SAY, "I AM GOING TO TAKE MY SHOWER." AFTER THAT I SAY, "I AM GOING TO BRUSH MY TEETH." "I AM GOING

TO PREPARE BREAKFAST." "**I AM** GOING TO GET DRESS FOR WORK." "**I AM** GOING TO WEAR MY GREEN AND BLUE COLOURED DRESS TO THE MEETING."

ON MY WAY TO THE MEETING IF I MEET A STRANGER I WOULD INTRODUCE MYSELF AND **THE HOLY SPIRIT** WOULD LET ME DISCERN IF THEY ARE A CHILD OF **GOD** OR UNSAVED. IF THE PERSON IS UNSAVED I WOULD ASK THEM "DO YOU BELIEVE IN **GOD?** DO YOU BELIEVE IN **THE HOLY BIBLE AS THE WORD OF GOD?** THE RESPONSE I RECEIVE SOMETIMES IS THIS, "**I AM** A... I BELIEVE **GOD** IS ONE."

THROUGHOUT THE DAY I OR SOMEONE ELSE MAY SAY, "**I AM** GOING TO CALL THE DENTIST TO MAKE AN APPOINTMENT FOR NEXT WEEK MONDAY." "**I AM** GOING TO HAVE LUNCH WITH SOME OF MY COLLEAGUES THIS AFTERNOON." "**I AM** GOING TO SEND MY MOTHER A TEXT MESSAGE." "**I AM** GOING TO SEND AN EMAIL TO MY DAUGHTER TO REMIND HER TO COME TO OUR HOME FOR DINNER."

"**I AM** GOING TO DRIVE THE SPEED LIMIT TO AVOID GETTING A SPEEDING TICKET TODAY." "**I AM** GOING TO STOP AT THE GROCERY STORE TO BUY SOME INGREDIENTS FOR MY CARROT MUFFIN."

AN ENGLISH TEACHER WOULD SAY, "**I AM** GOING TO EXPLAIN THE DIFFERENCE BETWEEN A NOUN AND A PRONOUN TO MY STUDENTS TODAY," OR "**I AM** GOING TO THE PRINCIPAL'S OFFICE FOR A BRIEF MEETING BEFORE LUNCHTIME."

THE SINGLE BACHELOR WOULD SAY, "**I AM** SEEKING A BEAUTIFUL **BORN-AGAIN** CHRISTIAN BRIDE, A WOMAN WHO LOVES **JESUS CHRIST**." THE **POLITICIAN** WOULD SAY, "**I AM** RUNNING FOR OFFICE AND I EXPECT TO WIN

THE UPCOMING ELECTION." THE HOMELESS PERSON WOULD SAY, "I AM GOING TO THE NEAREST SHELTER TO GET OUT OF THE COLD FOR THE NIGHT."

THE PUBLISHER WOULD SAY, "I AM HAPPY TO PUBLISH THAT CHRISTIAN BOOK." AMEN! THE REAL ESTATE AGENT WOULD SAY, "I AM GOING TO SHOW YOU THE NEWLY BUILT NEIGHBOURHOOD."

THE SCHOOL ENGLISH **TEACHER** WOULD EXPOUND THE LETTER "**I**" AND THE **WORD** "**AM**" EXPLAINING THAT "**I**" IS A VOWEL USED BY A WRITER OR **SPEAKER** WHEN REFERRING TO **HIMSELF** OR HERSELF. "**AM**" IS **FIRST PERSON, A <u>PRESENCE</u>** INDICATION.

***MANKIND ONLY SAY, "I AM..." BECAUSE WE ARE <u>PRESENT</u> BUT THERE IS A TIME WHEN MANKIND DON'T SPEAK." WE IMITATE **GOD** IN **LIFE** IN **SPEECH**. AMEN!

"**I AM** THINKING OF GOING ON A VACATION BECAUSE I HAVE NOT HAD ONE FOR A VERY LONG TIME." "**I AM** GOING TO TRY TO BE HOME BY 6 p.m. TO MAKE DINNER." SOMEONE MAY SAY, "**I AM** GOING TO PRAY FOR **PASTOR CHRISTIAN** BEFORE I GO TO BED TONIGHT." "**I AM** GOING TO ENSURE THAT I AM IN BED NO LATER THAN 10:00 p.m. TONIGHT." AMEN!

WE ACKNOWLEDGE **GOD** WHOM IS "**I AM**" DAILY AND THROUGHOUT EACH DAY WITH THE **FIRST WORDS** WE SPEAK AND WITH THE **BEGINNING** OF EACH SENTENCE WHETHER OR NOT WE KNOW **THE TRUE HOLY GOD OF THE BIBLE. THIS IS TRULY DIVINE WISDOM. AMEN!**

GOD DOES NOT FORCE MAN TO COME TO HIM; BUT **GOD** SOVEREIGNLY CREATED MAN TO FIRST ACKNOWLEDGE HIM IN THOUGHTS, SPEECH AND COMMUNICATIONS BECAUSE **GOD IS WORD. WORD**

COMMUNICATES, BELIEVE THE TRUE HOLY BIBLE WORDS. AMEN!

***BELIEVE AND TRUST IN THE **HOLY BIBLE** AS THE WORD OF GOD. THE **HOLY BIBLE** IS THE WORD OF GOD. "<u>I AM</u>" EMPHASIZING THIS DIVINE TRUTH AGAIN THE **HOLY BIBLE** IS THE ONLY TRUE WORDS OF GOD. AMEN!

"**I AM** GOING TO BUY, READ AND OBEY MY **HOLY BIBLE WORDS** EVERYDAY." AMEN!

THERE HAD TO BE A <u>**COMMONALITY**</u> THAT UNITES MANKIND TO THE **TRUTH** OF THE **HOLY BIBLE** AND THE DIVINE PERSON WORD COMMUNICATOR COMMONALITY IS HE, "I AM." AMEN!

ISAIAH CHAPTER 42 VERSE 8 STATES: IN THE NEW AMERICAN STANDARD BIBLE. <u>I AM THE LORD THAT IS MY NAME;</u> I WILL NOT GIVE MY GLORY TO ANOTHER NOR MY PRAISE TO GRAVEN IMAGES. AMEN!

1ST. CORINTHIANS CHAPTER 13 VERSE 11 STATES. WHEN I WAS A CHILD, I USED TO SPEAK LIKE A CHILD, THINK LIKE A CHILD, REASON LIKE A CHILD; WHEN I BECAME A MAN I DID AWAY WITH CHILDISH THINGS. AMEN!

PRAYER.

ABBA FATHER, IN JESUS HOLY NAME I COME, OUR FATHER I REPENT AND CONFESS MY SINS. ABBA FATHER YOU ARE MERCIFUL, POWERFUL, GRACIOUS, LOVING AND KIND. YOU FORGAVE MOSES AFTER HE MURDERED AN EGYPTIAN. FATHER YOU FORGAVE SAUL WHOM PERSECUTED THE CHURCH. SAUL LATER BECAME APOSTLE PAUL A SERVANT OF GOD. I PRAY

NOW FOR THE INHABITANTS OF EVERY NATION LORD. ABBA FATHER IN JESUS NAME BLESS WITH MERCY, SALVATION, SPIRITUAL DELIVERANCE FROM SATAN. SET FREE LORD. INTERVENE POWERFULLY AND MERCIFULLY LORD. IN JESUS NAME I PRAY. AMEN!

THE HOLY BIBLE BOOK OF REVELATION CHAPTER 22 VERSE 13 STATES: I AM THE ALPHA AND OMEGA, THE FIRST AND THE LAST, THE BEGINNING AND THE END. "I LOVE YOU MANKIND." SAYS THE LORD. I PASTOR CHRISTIAN LOVES YOU TOO. SHALOM! PEACE! AMEN!